In *Wisdom-Based Business*, Stolze brilliantly connects winning business practices to biblical truths. She leverages academic research and thoughtfully curated business cases to prove that business leaders can simultaneously pursue—and achieve—both profit and purpose. A must-read for all business leaders who strive to honor God in their calling.

—**KRISTIN COLBER-BAKER,** global head,
talent development, Mars, Inc.

More than ever, this generation of business students and experienced professionals want to connect their work with the deeper purpose of human and societal flourishing. Where is wisdom found that can provide such elemental guidance? This ground-breaking book from Professor Hannah Stolze, anchored in her thorough grasp of management research and coupled with her deep dive into Old Testament wisdom literature, provides just such new and exciting possibilities for business and business professionals. As you follow the author's intriguing story of discovery, *Wisdom-Based Business* reveals to the reader a business model grounded in evidence-based business research yet revealed clearly in an ancient Old Testament poem. This is the book that, if followed, has the potential of influencing and guiding Christians in business for decades to come.

—**GARY LINDBLAD,** dean, Crowell School
of Business, Biola University

In *Wisdom-Based Business*, Hannah Stolze takes the integration of Christian faith and business to an unprecedented level of depth and precision. With impeccable exegetical rigor, she mines the wealth of practical business wisdom in the Bible, overlooked and overspiritualized since the dawn of the industrial revolution. She begins by recognizing, correctly, that the business woman of Proverbs 31 is actually a business woman, not a metaphor for wifely domesticity, and then proceeds to uncover passage after passage about business, hidden in plain sight. But what does this abundance of biblical wisdom mean in a world of data-driven management? As a professor of logistics, Stolze's knows this world cold, and she demonstrates how the biblical material undergirds, enriches, and, at times, challenges twenty-first century empirical management science and practice. A lot in contemporary business is not godly, but it could be. Business can—and should—be a preeminent mission for people of faith seeking to make the world a make better place. *Wisdom-Based Business* shows how.

—**WILL MESSENGER,** chief editor,
Theology of Work

In *Wisdom-Based Business*, Dr. Hannah Stolze first takes us to Proverbs and specifically Proverbs 31 with particular emphasis on verses 10–31 (the Noble Woman), which "captures a woman who is leading a global company in ancient Israel to the benefit of everyone with whom she interacts." In a scholarly way, she takes us into other passages of Old Testament scriptures to support the premise that "all work can be a form of worship to God and service to others."

Stolze then takes us through eleven "case studies" that solidify biblical teachings on how we should, as God's people, conduct business. In each case study, we better understand how we can take our faith into the workplace. Each case study introduces companies and their leaders who have exemplified one or more tenants of our Christian faith. Each chapter concludes with questions to help reinforce the lesson taught and to be learned.

Wisdom-Based Business holds together well in its entirety, but each chapter also stands alone. I particularly enjoyed and found beneficial chapters on the "Virtue of Profit," the "Foundation of Servant Leadership," "Supply Chain Orientation," and "Comparative Advantage." *Wisdom-Based Business* is a challenging read, but Stolze's writing style quickly absorbs the reader into each chapter.

—**PHILIP M. PFEFFER,** president and CEO of Treemont Capital, Inc., retired president of Random House, Inc.

Dr. Hannah Stolze serves as codirector of Wheaton's Center for Faith and Innovation—a place for top Christian executives to strengthen their marketplace leadership by examining best practices, reflect on biblical principles, and enjoy cutting-edge research. This rare combination of Christian conviction, business acumen, and academic rigor is on full display in Stolze's new book, *Wisdom-Based Business*. Readers will profit by gaining a more biblical and more practical understanding of what it means to do business for the glory of God.

—**PHILLIP RYKEN,** president, Wheaton College

Wisdom-Based Business is a needed invitation and illustration of the adventure for followers of Jesus to shatter the daylight between faith and vocation, sacred and secular, and to experience the wisdom of God prevail across all domains of life, including the heart of industry. Hannah Stolze's passionate curiosity of the intersection of faith and industry—particularly heavy industry, rigorous supply-chain-intensive enterprises—is a needed advancement of the discussion about faith and work from the academy to the boardroom. I pray readers will be moved to pursue great business, greater purpose, and integrated faithfulness from the spurring of this book!

—**MIKE SHARROW,** CEO, C12 Group

WISDOM-BASED BUSINESS

WISDOM-BASED BUSINESS

APPLYING **BIBLICAL PRINCIPLES** AND **EVIDENCE-BASED** RESEARCH FOR A **PURPOSEFUL** AND **PROFITABLE** BUSINESS

HANNAH J. STOLZE

ZONDERVAN ACADEMIC

Wisdom-Based Business
Copyright © 2021 by Hannah J. Stolze

Requests for information should be addressed to:
Zondervan, *3900 Sparks Dr. SE, Grand Rapids, Michigan 49546*

Zondervan titles may be purchased in bulk for educational, business, fundraising, or sales promotional use. For information, please email SpecialMarkets@Zondervan.com.

ISBN 978-0-310-10728-6 (hardcover)

ISBN 978-0-310-10733-0 (audio)

ISBN 978-0-310-10729-3 (ebook)

Cover Design: Brand Navigation
Cover Image: © Sashatigar; Tiwat K. / Shutterstock
Interior Design: Kait Lamphere

Printed in the United States of America

21 22 23 24 25 26 27 28 29 30 31 /TRM/ 15 14 13 12 11 10 9 8 7 6 5 4 3 2 1

CONTENTS

FOREWORD

In *Wisdom-Based Business*, Hannah J. Stolze suggests that the doing of business should be both purposeful and profitable. There is virtue in providing a product or delivering a service that is both profitable and meets the needs of the recipient. As one learns to serve as they lead others, they can embrace the wisdom and importance of a value system. Those of us who have accepted Jesus Christ as our Savior should view our work in business as a vehicle to live and share our faith. Thus, the doing of business can have an eternal value for the people you work with and the people you serve.

I discovered this reality when I joined the ServiceMaster team in 1977. ServiceMaster was a company that was led by Christians who focused on being masters of service as they sought to serve the Master. Its objectives were to honor God in all we do, to help people develop, to pursue excellence, and to grow profitably. The first two objectives were end goals, and the second two were means goals.

The business was founded by Marion Wade in 1929 as a moth-proofing business. As it grew, it provided cleaning services, and by 1947 it was generating $125,000 in revenue. As the company grew in providing these services, it also developed a franchise system to expand its growth. Wade recruited a young pastor, Ken Hansen, to join him in the business. Hansen grew in his knowledge of business and his desire to care for the people who worked in the business. He also was instrumental in recruiting another key person for the business, and that was Ken Wessner. Both Kens were Wheaton College graduates.

As the business grew and reached $1 million in revenue, Wade became chairman of the board and Hansen became CEO and served in that capacity for seventeen years as the business grew to over $80 million in revenue. Hansen then stepped back from the CEO position, and Ken Wessner was elected to be president of the company. Wessner continued to lead in the growth of the business and in developing a new service for hospitals. Over the next eleven years revenue grew to $700 million with net profit at $25 million.

It was during Ken Hansen's tenure that the business became a public company, with a clear focus on serving customers, generating profit, developing its people, and honoring God—all as part of its original objectives.

I joined the ServiceMaster team in 1977. Prior to that time I had practiced law for ten years and then served as a senior officer at Wheaton College for five years.

I had never conceived of a business that could have an eternal impact as part of being successful, but that is what ServiceMaster was doing. The two Kens had recruited me to join with them in continuing to develop and grow the business.

The reality of the initial vision of Marion Wade, developed and made practical by Ken Hansen and Ken Wessner, reflected their combined desire to have their work in the market place reflect Colossians 3:17: "Whatever you do, in word or deed, do everything in the name of the Lord Jesus, giving thanks to God the Father through him."

In January of 1983, after five years of serving as a senior officer of the company, I was elected to become the next CEO of ServiceMaster, with Ken Wessner serving as chairman and Ken Hansen being available to advise and support us.

Ken Wessner and his team had done a great job growing the business, including providing services to hospitals across the United States. However, as part of a focus on continued growth, it was time to consider expanding the business internationally and also to make acquisitions of other companies that could fit our objectives and desire to serve others.

For the acquisitions, we created a new division that we called ServiceMaster Consumer Services. One of the first companies to be considered was Terminix, and that acquisition was completed by the end of 1986. Other acquisitions that would follow included Merry Maids (1988), American Home Shield (1989), TruGreen (1991), and ChemLawn (1992).

By 1993, revenue generated from our Consumer Services division grew to $940 million with net income of $70.6 million. During this period, the Management Services division grew in revenue to $1.8 billion with profit of $61 million.

In 1994, Carlos Cantu, the president of Terminix, became the next CEO of ServiceMaster, and I was elected as chairman. At the end of the year in 1998, Carlos had to step back because of a serious diagnosis he received of having cancer, and I was asked by the board to come back and serve as CEO until a new CEO could be appointed. I agreed to do so. The board then formed a committee to search and select the next CEO. The committee decided to search outside the company for the next CEO. Jon Ward was selected and assumed the position of CEO in 2001.

Soon Ward began making major changes with an intent of improving profitability. I did not agree with the changes he was making and decided to retire from ServiceMaster. Although many significant changes were made, Ward's attempt at improving profitability failed, and financial results stagnated. In May of 2006, Jon Ward was asked to resign, and board member J. Patrick Spainhour was appointed interim chairman of the board and CEO of the company. In 2007, ServiceMaster was sold to a New York-based private equity firm.

The story of ServiceMaster reflects the importance of this book written by Hannah Stolze. The market place is a *mission field*. During my time at ServiceMaster, there were many opportunities to both *live* and *share* my faith. Every time I presented the business on Wall Street, I would review our four corporate objectives. After the meetings, I would often get cornered and questioned about integrating religion with our work which gave me the opportunity to share my faith. For us, the market place was more than the doing of business. It was also a mission field with the business being a vehicle for sharing the reality of God and his gift of salvation. Yes, the doing of business can have an *eternal* value.

C. William Pollard

CHAPTER 1

WHY WISDOM?
WHY BUSINESS?

[Solomon] composed three thousand proverbs, and his songs numbered a thousand and five. . . . People came from all the nations to hear the wisdom of Solomon; they came from all the kings of the earth who had heard of his wisdom.

—1 Kings 4:32–34

Nothing compares to wisdom. Those who find it gain understanding and value far more profitable than silver and gold, more precious than rubies.[1] Where can wisdom be found? As I have pursued wisdom over the past decades, I have found it in expected and unexpected places: among friends and family as I navigated changing career and seasons of life as well as in the marketplace and in the day-to-day transactions of business.

Throughout my business career, I have served as a US Army soldier, a global supply chain manager, and a supply chain professor. In each role, I sought wisdom. I found wisdom in the advice of commanding officers as I started out in psychological operations (PSYOPS). When I moved from PSYOPS to ordnance (Army explosives supply), wisdom was there in the help of a sergeant first class. I ultimately landed in public affairs as a broadcast journalist with a full scholarship to pursue my MBA. I found wisdom in the counsel of many as I shifted to civilian work as an operations manager overseeing the global supply chain of polypropylene (plastic) packaging for a packaging importer. With wisdom as my friend, I engaged people all over the world. My network grew to span Guatemala, India, and China with manufacturing customers including PepsiCo and ADM in the US. After the completion of my MBA,

---

1. Job 28:12; Proverbs 3:13–15; 8:10–11.

I spent a few restless years working in packaging imports before I shifted my focus to higher education.

Amidst the splendor of fall, my family uprooted from our home in the Chicago suburbs and moved to the beautiful mountains of Tennessee. With the aim to gain skills, business knowledge, and wisdom, I began my PhD in business at the University of Tennessee specializing in logistics and marketing. My husband transitioned his career to Knoxville, Tennessee, and my two children, at that time ten months and four years old, quickly adjusted to being southerners.

In the PhD program, I immediately found myself working on contract research for the Department of Defense and partnering with Fortune 500 companies to discover the best practices for sustainable supply chain management. Not previously an environmentalist or particularly knowledgeable about social and environmental practices, I was on the fast lane to learning all I could about the profitable applications of sustainable management. I learned quickly that this involved the flow of products from raw material to the end customer while reducing pollution, empowering people from farm to retail, and pursuing a net positive impact for profitability, people, and the planet. I sat with business leaders as they discussed the importance of environmental initiatives for corporate cost savings and to meet customer requirements. Across these conversations, I glimpsed care for the customer, employee, and supplier (people), and care for the environment (creation).

We explored how these leading companies were navigating cutting-edge lean strategies in partnership with environmental initiatives. Initially, the Toyota production system employed lean strategies to increase efficiency and reduce waste. Toyota created a leaner supply chain while creating better employee engagement, more selective supplier networks, and an environment of continuous improvement. Lean strategies implemented by Toyota uniquely empowered employees to create solutions on the assembly line and to highlight bottlenecks immediately (this was *not* a standard practice in the assembly lines of Ford, GM, and Chrysler).

To add to the green and lean strategies, all of these organizations were operating in a global economy with suppliers and customers all over the world. We talked with dozens of manufacturing, retail, and logistics companies, including global giants like John Deere, Walmart, and FedEx. Many of these companies globalized their supply chains in search of low-cost sourcing. Low-cost, global sources prove to be a challenge to many companies as they pursue high-quality products and leaner, lower inventory levels with long supply chains.

The cutting-edge strategies[2] we identified through this work reflected concepts I comfortably categorized as biblical stewardship. It struck me that it was wise to produce quality products with an awareness of the resources necessary to move those products to market, from raw material to finished good. Both natural resources and people are necessary to sustain the creation and growth of a profitable product in the marketplace. I spent the next year working closely with one of the largest railroad providers in North America as I collected and analyzed data to complete my first-year research project. I found many of the same themes. These were all "secular" organizations. I didn't have any evidence that the founders were Christian or that the current leaders had any kind of religious inclination. However, the principles of honoring people and caring for creation rang as biblical to me.

It was at this time in my PhD research that I turned to Christian books and teaching, but I couldn't find a framework that reflected a biblical model of conducting business. Pastors seemed to focus on virtue: be a good person, preach the gospel, invite people to church, and tithe. After all, successful business leaders can use their resources to sow into the church through tithes and offerings or develop kingdom-related, nonprofit enterprises. But there was no model for how to conduct business. I found loads of virtue ethics (who you should be) but no consequence ethics (how to weigh the results of your actions). How does Scripture influence our decisions beyond personal piety? I had learned through the green, lean, and global study that most decisions in business have an impact on someone, somewhere. There are consequences to our actions every day in work, not just in our acts of service in the church. As I reflected on the science—science that indicates that treating people well and taking care of God's creation boosts profitability—a specific passage of Scripture persisted in my study throughout the entire first year of my PhD program.

A few months before embarking on my PhD journey, on a winter Saturday in the Chicago suburbs, I had a *gestalt*: a moment in which all the moving pieces in a great mystery I had been pondering started to come together, a moment that guided my thinking for years to follow. That day, my pastor in Chicago hosted a Bible study. The speaker was an international guest, the wife of a gentleman who ran a church ministry training program in the UK. The topic of study for the day was "the Proverbs 31 wife."

---

2. D. A. Mollenkopf, H. J. Stolze, W. Tate, and M. Ueltschy, "Green, Lean, and Global Supply Chains," *International Journal of Physical Distribution and Logistics Management* 40, no. 1–2 (2010): 14–41.

We all sipped coffee as the guest speaker began, admitting that she struggled with this passage. She never felt like she added up to this elusive exemplar of a woman. Ladies jumped in with stories of husbands' expectations, marriage, child raising, and household chaos. Some talked about how they aspired to live up to this incredible woman's example. As I sat and listened, I started to feel dissatisfied with the conversation and the reading itself. The majority of the ladies in the room didn't grow flax, weren't making clothing, didn't have households full of servants, and their husbands didn't have citywide reputations because of their actions. The passage says nothing of traditional duties of an American housewife. The Proverbs 31 woman isn't cleaning or cooking (although she is providing meals), and the passage says nothing about her interaction with her children aside from their praise. The passage is an acrostic from A to Z (in the Hebrew alphabet). These twenty-one verses capture a woman who is leading a global company in ancient Israel to the benefit of everyone with whom she interacts.

PROVERBS 31:10–31

Aleph	10	A capable wife[3] who can find? She is far more precious than jewels.
Beth	11	The heart of her husband trusts in her, and he will have no lack of gain.
Gimel	12	She does him good, and not harm, all the days of her life.
Daleth	13	She seeks wool and flax and works with willing hands.
Hey	14	She is like the ships of the merchant; she brings her food from far away.
Waw	15	She rises while it is still night and provides food for her household and tasks for her servant-girls.
Zayin	16	She considers a field and buys it; with the fruit of her hands she plants a vineyard.
Heth	17	She girds herself with strength and makes her arms strong.
Teth	18	She perceives that her merchandise is profitable. Her lamp does not go out at night.
Yod	19	She puts her hands to the distaff, and her hands hold the spindle.
Kaph	20	She opens her hand to the poor and reaches out her hands to the needy.

3. American Standard Version: a worthy woman; King James Version: a virtuous woman; New International Version; a wife of noble character; Septuagint Bible (Greek Translation to English): a virtuous woman; Orthodox Jewish Bible: a woman of valor.

Lamed	21	She is not afraid for her household when it snows, for all her household are clothed in crimson.
Mem	22	She makes herself coverings; her clothing is fine linen and purple.
Nun	23	Her husband is known in the city gates, taking his seat among the elders of the land.
Samek	24	She makes linen garments and sells them; she supplies the merchant with sashes.
Ayin	25	Strength and dignity are her clothing, and she laughs at the time to come.
Pey	26	She opens her mouth with wisdom, and the teaching of kindness is on her tongue.
Tsade	27	She looks well to the ways of her household, and does not eat the bread of idleness.
Koph	28	Her children rise up and call her happy; her husband too, and he praises her:
Resh	29	"Many women have done excellently, but you surpass them all."
Sin, Shin	30	Charm is deceitful, and beauty is vain, but a woman who fears the Lord is to be praised.
Taw	31	Give her a share in the fruit of her hands, and let her works praise her in the city gates.

Could this passage written 3,000 years ago really be promoting the Western ideal of a stay-at-home mom, a concept that has only existed since the industrial revolution? Her children are only mentioned once, her husband three times, and the entirety of the other verses are dedicated to her virtue and actions in industry. It seemed impossible that the Bible would actually talk about a woman engaged in business. Just in case, I informed my husband that I was more than happy to adopt all practices of the Proverbs 31:10–31 businesswoman—just as soon as I had servants and the capital to launch my textile company. In the meantime, I continued to study those verses to understand implications for the Christian life beyond household duties.

In 2012, I finished my PhD at the University of Tennessee and took a faculty position at Florida State University in Tallahassee. I continued my ten-year journey with this capable wife who fears the Lord, first exploring the passage as an analogy that applies to all believers, all seekers of wisdom. The next leg of my journey with the Proverbs 31 woman was about to unfold.

Into the World of Faith and Business Integration

In 2015, I transitioned to Wheaton College, a unique and providential place for me to land. As a Christian institution, its mission is to do all things for Christ and his kingdom—including business. For the first time, I found myself in an environment that didn't shy away from the integration of faith and business. In the business schools where I learned to think critically and do research, faith was viewed as subjective and unscientific. In the churches I had grown up in and served in over the years, the most positive view of business was that it was an opportunity to generate wealth to support kingdom work, primarily for those in "full-time ministry" like missions and pastoral work. However, business was viewed as a means to an end (to provide money *for* kingdom work) but not an end in and of itself (business *as* kingdom work). Wheaton offered me the opportunity to explore the practicality of integrating biblical understanding with business research. Actually, the school required it. To apply for tenure and promotion, each faculty member must write an integrative paper discussing the intersection of the Christian faith and their disciplinary field.

I felt confident in my ability to synthesize and discuss business research, theories, and ideas. I felt less confident in my knowledge of theological and biblical history as it pertained to business. It's a good thing I love studying the Bible! One year into my time at Wheaton, I began a master's program in biblical studies with some of the most amazing Bible and theology faculty I have ever encountered. My first year in the program covered the Old Testament, which, of course, includes the book of Proverbs. By that time, I had spent years studying Wisdom Literature and Proverbs, and this was my opportunity to test my ideas and learn, to glean new perspectives about wisdom. During that first year in the program, each time I was required to write an essay or paper, I tried to shoehorn an analysis of Proverbs 31 into the assignment. I learned that Proverbs was part of a larger body of literature—the biblical books of wisdom and the ancient Near East wisdom/court literature. I had approached the passage of Proverbs 31:10–31 naively in the past without enough historical and cultural context for the genre of literature it represents. This book captures what I learned.

Biblical Case for Wisdom

Rewind 3,000 years. Solomon was on the throne of Israel in the wake of losing his father. Responsible for the spiritual, social, and economic welfare of the kingdom, he embarked on a mission to build international relations and secure Israel's borders by marrying the daughter of Pharaoh, King of Egypt. Solomon loved the Lord, but was also influenced by the cultures of the great nations around him. He appeared to adopt the worship and ruling practices of neighboring nations—Egypt, Assyria, Philistine, and Babylon—by allowing the establishment of local temples and pursuing intellectual treasuries through establishing a tradition of court literature. However, Solomon's pursuit of court literature did not emerge merely out of international exposure; it was born out of divine inspiration.

Solomon had secured the throne and liaised with the great nations of his day. As he lay asleep one night, God appeared to him in a dream.[4]

> God said, "What do you want? Ask, and I will give it to you!"
>
> Solomon replied, "You showed great and faithful love to your servant my father, David, because he was honest and true and faithful to you. And you have continued to show this great and faithful love to him today by giving him a son to sit on his throne.
>
> "Now, O Lord my God, you have made me king instead of my father, David, but I am like a little child who doesn't know his way around. And here I am in the midst of your own chosen people, a nation so great and numerous they cannot be counted! Give me an understanding heart so that I can govern your people well and know the difference between right and wrong. For who by himself is able to govern this great people of yours?"
>
> The Lord was pleased that Solomon had asked for wisdom. So God replied, "Because you have asked for wisdom in governing my people with justice and have not asked for a long life or wealth or the death of your enemies—I will give you what you asked for! I will give you a wise and understanding heart such as no one else has had or ever will have! And I will also give you what you did not ask for—riches and fame! No other king in all the world will be compared to you for the rest of your life! And if you follow me and obey my decrees and my commands as your father, David, did, I will give you a long life."

Solomon brought unity and prosperity to the nation of Israel. He created great wealth for Israel while also pursuing knowledge and speaking

---

4. 1 Kings 3:5–14 paraphrased from the New Living Translation.

authoritatively about many topics, both social[5] and environmental.[6] Kings from every nation sent their ambassadors to listen to the wisdom of Solomon. During his reign, King Solomon composed 3,000 proverbs, according to 1 Kings 4:32. The repository of court literature created under the influence of Solomon has come to be known as the biblical books of wisdom, including Proverbs, Ecclesiastes, and Job, as well as Song of Songs and parts of Psalms. Of these five books of wisdom, Proverbs is one of the most complete manuscripts that emerged from an international, pan-oriental broader court literature[7] genre called Wisdom Literature. Proverbs captured the poetic traditions of the broader body of Wisdom Literature found in ancient Egypt, ancient Mesopotamia, old Babylonian kingdoms, and Neo-Sumerian traditions. The Egyptian literature, especially the "Teachings of Amenemope,"[8] most closely parallel the Hebrew wisdom texts.[9]

The biblical wisdom books provide a guide for proper stewardship of wealth, society, and the natural environment with which we have been entrusted. Proverbs 1:1–7 outlines the book's manifold purpose:

The proverbs of Solomon son of David, king of Israel:

> For learning about wisdom and instruction,
>   for understanding words of insight,
> for gaining instruction in wise dealing,
>   righteousness, justice, and equity;
> to teach shrewdness to the simple,
>   knowledge and prudence to the young—
> let the wise also hear and gain in learning,
>   and the discerning acquire skill,
> to understand a proverb and a figure,
>   the words of the wise and their riddles.

> The fear of the LORD is the beginning of knowledge;
>   fools despise wisdom and instruction.

---

5. 1 Kings 3:16–28: the trial of the two prostitutes.

6. 1 Kings 4:20–34: wealth and knowledge of plants, animals, birds, smalls creatures, and fish.

7. Bruce K. Waltke, "The Book of Proverbs and Ancient Wisdom Literature," *Bibliotheca Sacra* 136 (July–September 1979): 211–38.

8. William Kelly Simpson, ed., *The Literature of Ancient Egypt: An Anthology of Stories, Instructions, Stelae, Autobiographies, and Poetry* (New Haven, CT: Yale University Press, 2003), 223–43.

9. Andrew E. Hill and John H. Walton, *A Survey of the Old Testament* (Grand Rapids: Zondervan, 2000), 380.

Practical wisdom, understanding, and knowledge are all the result of instruction and counsel. Divine wisdom, understanding (revelation), and knowledge are gifts rooted in the fear of the Lord. These three concepts are central to the biblical wisdom books.

Knowledge consists of the facts and information acquired through instruction. Proverbs 18:15 states that "an intelligent mind acquires knowledge, and the ear of the wise seeks knowledge." For instance, my father is a craftsman and a carpenter—growing up, he taught me a lot about carpentry, and I know all of the tools and materials necessary to repair or build a cabinet.

Understanding is the ability to process knowledge and find meaning and application. If the Word of God provides knowledge, it takes understanding to find meaning in it. Psalm 119:130 says that "the unfolding of your words gives light; it imparts understanding to the simple." Continuing with my carpentry example, I understand the process of gathering all of the materials and measuring twice and cutting once in order to have the right sizes of wood to nail together into the intended shape.

Wisdom is the ability to decide or discern the best course of action. Wisdom builds on understanding and knowledge, leading to right action. I have learned the wisest course of action in all carpentry projects I take on is to not build anything myself—I prefer to call my father.

Solomon's Wisdom Literature did not just inform virtue. The biblical books of wisdom provide instruction for insight and knowledge; prudent behavior; and doing what is right, just, and fair. The concepts and lessons in the biblical books of wisdom cover topics from spirituality to social interactions to treatment of the environment to proper behavior in business. Not only did it tell Israelites how to be godly; it also informed them what skills to attain in their pursuit of peace, harmony, and prosperity in service to God and others.

Lady Wisdom and the Noble Woman

Wisdom Literature was a well-developed literary tradition in the ancient Near East.[10] In ancient history, the concept of wisdom was frequently personified as a woman. In Assyria, Ishtar was the goddess of love and war. In Greece, Sophia was the goddess of wisdom. This is true of the biblical wisdom books as well. When the concept of wisdom is first introduced in Proverbs, wisdom is personified as an elusive woman of immeasurable worth. Proverbs 1–9 contrast

---

10. Hill and Walton, *A Survey of the Old Testament*, 377.

Lady Wisdom with Lady Folly, both personified as female characters. These chapters provide a prologue to chapters 10–31:9, which provide principles for wise living. The Noble Woman in Proverbs 31:10–31 appears as the capstone to what comes before, the personification of wise living in the summary passage of Proverbs and perhaps all of the Wisdom Literature.

In this light, Lady Wisdom in Proverbs 1–9 and the Noble Woman in Proverbs 31:10–31 form a chiasm in the book of Proverbs. Chiasms function as brackets in Hebrew writing in which a passage begins and ends with the same premise with explanatory material in the middle. When Proverbs was written, people didn't have multiple Bibles lying around their homes. Most Hebrew people would only hear the Bible read from scrolls in the temple or repeated orally from memory. The chiasm method of writing reiterated important truths to make them more memorable as they were taught and passed on by word of mouth. If Proverbs is indeed a chiasm, Lady Wisdom and the Noble Woman form the brackets as personifications of the same thing: wisdom.

Table 1.1, "Wisdom and Lady Wisdom Compared to the Noble Woman," is by no means an exhaustive comparison of Proverbs 31:10–31 with the rest of biblical Wisdom Literature. However, it lends some evidence that I have collected throughout my biblical studies to the summative nature of the passage for all the wisdom genre in the Bible.

Wisdom and Lady Wisdom	The Noble Woman
Proverbs 1:7; Psalm 111:10	*Proverbs 31:30*
• Proverbs 1:7 The fear of the LORD is the beginning of knowledge; fools despise wisdom and instruction. • Psalm 111:10 The fear of the LORD is the beginning of wisdom.	Charm is deceitful, and beauty is vain, but a woman who fears the LORD is to be praised.
Proverbs 3:13–15; 8:10–11 NIV	*Proverbs 31:10, 29 NIV*
• Proverbs 3:13–15 Blessed are those who find wisdom, those who gain understanding, for she is far more profitable than silver and yields better returns than gold. She is more precious than rubies; nothing you desire can compare with her. • Proverbs 8:10–11 Choose my instruction instead of silver, knowledge rather than choice gold, for wisdom is more precious than rubies, and nothing you desire can compare to her.	A capable wife who can find? She is far more precious than jewels. Many women do noble things, but you surpass them all.

Proverbs 9:1–3; Psalm 111:5	Proverbs 31:14–15
• Proverbs 9:1–3 Wisdom has built her house, she has hewn her seven pillars. She has slaughtered her animals, she has mixed her wine, she has also set her table. She has sent out her servant girls, she calls from the highest places in the town. • Psalm 111:5 He provides food for those who fear him; he is ever mindful of his covenant.	She is like the ships of the merchant; she brings her food from far away. She rises while it is still night and provides food for her household and tasks for her servant girls.
Proverbs 3:16–17, 19:17 NIV; Psalm 112:9 NIV	**Proverbs 31:18–20 NIV**
• Proverbs 3:16–17 Long life is in her right hand; in her left hand are riches and honor. Her ways are pleasant ways, and all her paths are peace. • Proverbs 19:17 Whoever is kind to the poor lends to the LORD, and he will reward them for what they have done. • Psalm 112:9 They have freely scattered their gifts to the poor, their righteousness endures forever: their horn will be lifted high in honor.	She sees that her trading is profitable, and her lamp does not go out at night. In her hand she holds the distaff and grasps the spindle with her fingers. She opens her arms to the poor and extends her hands to the needy.
Psalm 112:6–7 NIV	**Proverbs 31:21**
• Psalm 112:6–7 Surely the righteous will never be shaken; they will be remembered forever. They will have no fear of bad news; their hearts are steadfast, trusting in the LORD.	She is not afraid for her household when it snows, for all her household are clothed in crimson.

TABLE 1.1—Wisdom and Lady Wisdom
Compared to the Noble Woman

The Noble Woman from Proverbs 31:10–31 is not often taught as comparable to Lady Wisdom from Proverbs 1–9. Instead, it is usually translated as a direct instruction to women. It follows the instruction of King Lemuel's mother regarding the selection of a wife (Proverbs 31:1–9). While these two passages are in the same chapter in the Christian Bible, the Masoretic text (the Hebrew Bible) locates these two passages in separate places in Proverbs.[11] Scholars believe that Proverbs 31:10–31 was likely written by a different author

---

11. Tremper Longman III, *Proverbs*, in *Baker Commentary on the Old Testament Wisdom and Psalms*, ed. Tremper Longman III (Grand Rapids: Baker, 2006), 539.

from the first nine verses.[12] Scholars agree that the two texts in Proverbs 31 were not originally meant to be linked.[13]

Proverbs 31:10–31 describes a woman who is valiant, noble, and excellent (*chayil*) in all that she does. The title of the passage doesn't necessarily translate to "noble wife." *The Theology of Work Bible Commentary* suggests that some translators use "wife" instead of "woman" because the woman's husband and children are mentioned.[14] The Hebrew word *ēšet* can be translated into wife or woman.

The ode to the Noble Woman (*ēšet chayil*) begins similarly to Proverbs 3:13–15, highlighting the elusiveness of her existence: "an *ēšet chayil*, who can find?" The term *chayil* (חַיִל)—translated here as "noble"—has a rich history in the Hebrew literature associated with strength, might, military force, efficiency, wealth, and competition. Because of the *chayil* terminology, scholars believe Proverbs 31:10–31 carries warrior imagery.[15] Further, the *chayil* terminology is highlighted to reflect profits from trade and economic worth.[16] In two short lines, the opening verse of Proverbs 31:10–31 conveys valor, wealth, righteousness, and competitiveness reflecting Lady Wisdom from earlier in Proverbs. Thus, we can conclude that Proverbs 31:10–31 is a personification of Lady Wisdom in action in the public square, succeeding in business and in the marketplace.

Integrating Wisdom and Business

Within the Jewish and Christian traditions, followers of God have been called to be a blessing to the nations and to make disciples of the nations (Gen. 12:2–3; Matt. 28:19). Historically, the focus within the Christian church on achieving this mandate has primarily empowered church ministries and missions.[17] However, people were not created to worship God only through ministry in the local church. All work can be a form of worship to God and service to others. I had always viewed work as a result of the fall, a Genesis 3 version of

---

12. Longman, *Proverbs*, 538; Richard L. Schultz, "Proverbs," in *The Baker Illustrated Bible Commentary*, ed. Gary M. Burge and Andrew E. Hill (Grand Rapids: Baker, 2016), 557.

13. Longman, *Proverbs*, 539.

14. Theology of Work Project, Inc., *Theology of Work Bible Commentary*, "The Valiant Woman" (Proverbs 31:10–31), Bruce Waltke and Alice Mathews, contributors, accessed online at https://www.theologyofwork.org/old-testament/proverbs/what-do-the-proverbs-have-to-do-with-work/the-valiant-woman-proverbs-3110-31.

15. Al Wolters, "Proverbs xxxi 10–31 as Heroic Hymn: A Form Critical Analysis," *Vetus Testamentum* 38 (1988): 446–57.

16. Proverbs 1:28; Proverbs 8:17.

17. Mats Tunehag, Wayne McGee, and Josie Plummer, "Business as Mission," *Lausanne Occasional Paper* 59 (South Hamilton, MA: Lausanne Committee for World Evangelism, 2005).

work as pain, sweat, and general toil. I hadn't recognized the discussion of work in Genesis 2:15 ESV, which says, "The Lord God took the man and put him in the Garden of Eden to work (*abad*) it and keep (*shamar*) it." God finishes his work in verse 2 and then puts Adam in the garden to work (*abad*, to worship and serve God) and keep it (*shamar*, to guard, care for, and serve others). All of this occurs before the fall. God designed people for work, which was meant to be a blessing, not a curse.

Meanwhile, businesses are changing standards of living, industrializing nations, and shaping the behavior of consumers without most of the world understanding the impact. Over the last decade, the global church has increasingly become aware the impact of business and has engaged in increased dialogue around faith and work.[18] A conversation has emerged about business as mission, recognizing the role of business in reaching nations with the gospel.[19] While the concept of business as mission focuses on business as a means to promoting the gospel, the growing social movement around integrating faith and work sheds light on the bigger picture of business as a redeemable design of God.[20]

One challenge to viewing business as a redeemable design lies in the lack of integration between emerging Christian business scholarship and practice.[21] As of 2008, Christian scholarship had only begun to "touch on business disciplines."[22] The emerging literature at the intersection of Christian scholarship and business highlights two things:

- The Christian virtues and ethics,[23] how Christian managers should behave (brotherly love, submission, obedience, non-worldliness)[24]
- The meaning of good work[25] and philosophies underlying faithful business[26]

---

18. David Miller, *God at Work: The History and Promise of the Faith at Work Movement* (New York: Oxford University Press, 2007).

19. Tunehag et al., "Business as Mission," 4.

20. Tunehag et al., "Business as Mission," i.

21. Kenman Wong and R. Martinez, "Introduction to the Theme Issue: The Iron Cage Unchained: Christian Perspectives on Business in the Post-Modern Age," *Christian Scholar's Review* 38, no. 1 (2008): 11.

22. Wong and Martinez, "Introduction to the Theme Issue," 11.

23. Scott Waalkes, "Money or Business? A Case Study of Christian Virtue Ethics in Corporate Work," *Christian Scholars Review* 38, no. 1 (2008): 15.

24. Bruno Dyke et al., "Unchaining Weber's Iron Cage: A Look at What Managers Can Do, *Christian Scholars Review* 38, no. 1 (2008): 50.

25. Margaret Diddams and Denise Daniels, "Good Work with Toil: A Paradigm for Redeemed Work," *Christian Scholars Review* 38, no. 1 (2008): 62.

26. Stephen N. Bretsen, "The Creation, the Kingdom of God, and a Theory of the Faithful Corporation," *Christian Scholars Review* 38, no. 1 (2008): 153.

However, the emerging literature lacks an integrated scriptural base and business framework that guides how businesses can be managed for kingdom impact.[27] My goal is to integrate a biblical foundation for best practices by integrating Scripture and business research to create a framework for wise business and supply chain management (SCM) today.

The Wisdom-Based Business Model

Echoing Proverbs 3:13, Proverbs 31:10–31 opens with wisdom's immeasurable value. Her husband sits at the city gates and trusts confidently in all the works of his industrious wife. Proverbs 3:18 (NIV) says of wisdom, "She is a tree of life to those who take hold of her; those who hold her fast will be blessed." In Proverbs 31, the Noble Woman is empowered to build an industrious global supply chain.[28] In this example, she seeks supplies from merchants who came from afar, buys flax and wool in the marketplace, transforms the flax and wool, and sells them to merchants. Her business is not domestic; it has scale[29] in the marketplace as it spans multiple companies and nations. Women in early Israel worked alongside their husbands in rural areas, however, their work tended toward domestic work,[30] setting the Noble Woman apart in her engagement in the marketplace. In a similar vein, the Noble Woman seeks out suppliers of wool, manufactures fabrics, and sells finished goods to merchants who come from all over to buy her goods (reflecting the modern-day definition of global supply chain management).

Proverbs not only indicates the characteristics, skills, and practices of a godly business venture, but also the expected outcomes. Echoing Ecclesiastes, Proverbs reveals that wealth, possession, and the ability to enjoy them and be happy in work are gifts from God.[31] Passages throughout the biblical wisdom books reflect on the wealth and blessing that follow wisdom. God rewarded King Solomon with wisdom *and* wealth and honor. When the Noble Woman established her reputation, foreign traders knew her in a time when trade did not include container vessels, cargo planes, or well-built transportation

---

27. Hannah Stolze, Diane Mollenkopf, and Dan Flint, "What is the Right Supply Chain for Your Shopper: Exploring a Shopper Service Ecosystem," *Journal of Business Logistics* 37, no. 2 (2015): 185–97.

28. A global supply chain is three or more companies that work together to transform and move a product from raw material to the end customer.

29. Scale, or market scale, can be defined as proportional growth in production or profit, or as doing things more efficiently with increasing size.

30. Carol Meyers, "The Family in Early Israel," in *Families in Ancient Israel*, ed. Leo G. Perdue (Louisville: Westminster John Knox, 1997), 25.

31. Ecclesiastes 5:19.

infrastructures. Current business research indicates that reputation is a strong driver of profit.[32] With her reputation, she increased her profits to grow her business (with the excess she purchased land). Finally, economic capital, reputation, and relationships are all business resources that are hard to imitate,[33] providing the Noble Woman with a comparative advantage in the marketplace.

These business outcomes, built on biblical tenets, not only affect the short-term outcomes of the business but also impact employees, suppliers, customers, and the community that are ministered to with excess profit or wealth. These are some of the ways a business can change the cultures in which employees operate and have kingdom impact (an impact for unforeseeable generations that honors God and others). That is the end goal: an eternal outcome that honors God and makes disciples of cultures (disciples of nations) with the love of God and neighbor as the primary motivation.

What drives these outcomes from a biblical perspective? It starts with leadership and then flows into the orientations of the business. Solomon, Lady Wisdom, and the Noble Woman all acted for the benefit of others. It's others who have no lack of gain (Prov. 31:11) and who are known at the city gates (Prov. 31:23). Servant leadership doesn't self-promote; it promotes others. Business research has tested the impact of servant leadership and found that it positively impacts operational performance and the overall profitability of companies.[34]

Research shows that leadership is pivotal to the culture of a business and to the adoption of firm orientations (main interests, qualities, or goals).[35] Therefore, building on a foundation of servant leadership, the biblical wisdom books highlight five main orientations of a faith-based organization that also are recognized as contemporary best practices in business: a sustainability orientation, a quality orientation, a stakeholder orientation, a supply chain orientation, and a long-term orientation.

A sustainability orientation is defined as the business goal of making a profit while preserving the planet (resources for the future) and people (having

32. Gregorio Martin De Castro, Jose Emilio Navas Lopez, and Pedro Lopez Saez, "Business and Social Reputation: Exploring the Concept and Main Dimensions of Corporate Reputation," *Journal of Business Ethics* 63 (2006): 361–70; P. W. Roberts and G. R. Dowling, "Corporate Reputation and Sustained Superior Financial Performance," *Strategic Management Journal* 23 (2002): 1077–93.

33. Shelby Hunt and Donna F. Davis, "Grounding Supply Chain Management in Resource-Advantage Theory: In Defense of a Resource-Based View of the Firm," *Journal of Supply Chain Management* 48, no. 2 (2012): 15–20.

34. Cliff C. Defee, Theodore P. Stank, Terry L. Esper, and John T. Mentzer, "The Role of Followers in Supply Chains," *Journal of Business Logistics* 30, no. 2 (2009): 65–84; Robert E. Overstreet et al., "Bridging the Gap Between Strategy and Performance: Using Leadership Style to Enable Structural Elements," *Journal of Business Logistics* 35, no. 2 (2014): 136–49.

35. Jeremy D. Meuser et al., "A Network Analysis of Leadership Theory: The Infancy of Integration," *Journal of Management* 42, no. 5 (2016): 1374–1403.

a positive impact on society).[36] When the Proverbs 31 Noble Woman buys fields and considers the development of vineyards, as a godly woman, she's environmentally friendly (environmental law in Deuteronomy prescribes environmental management and stewardship of those fields).[37]

A stakeholder orientation can be defined as the business goal of treating stakeholders as ends *as well as* means while creating "value" (social as well as economic) for all stakeholders (any individual impacted by a firm, including employees, customers, suppliers, investors, and community)—not just shareholders (investors) alone.[38] The Proverbs 31 woman uses the surplus of her profits to feed the poor and provide for the needy. By doing so, she takes not only a stakeholder orientation but also a socially sustainable orientation. Members of her household, presumably including servants (employees), are all taken care of, are well clothed, and have no fear about the future.

The Amplified Version of Proverbs 11:18 states, "The wicked man earns deceptive wages, but he who sows righteousness *and* lives his life with integrity will have a true reward [that is both permanent and satisfying]." Integrity in business lends itself to quality, creating value for the seller and the customer. A quality orientation is defined as the business goal of ensuring the customer will be satisfied with the product in every respect.[39] All the products the Proverbs 31 woman sells are of fine quality, even fit for royalty.

A supply chain orientation can be defined as "the recognition by an organization of the systemic, strategic implications of the tactical activities involved in managing the various flows in the supply chain."[40] Both Solomon and the Proverbs 31 Noble Woman bought products from foreign merchants. Their customers also came from far away to buy quality goods, implying that they understood the processes and activities necessary to integrate foreign supply with local demand (supply chain orientation).

---

36. A. Kuckertz and M. Wagner, "The Influence of Sustainability Orientation on Entrepreneurial Intentions—Investigating the Role of Business Experience," *Journal of Business Venturing* 25, no. 5 (2010): 524–39.

37. Sandra Richter, "Environmental Law in Deuteronomy: One Lens on a Biblical Theology of Creation Care" *Bulletin for Biblical Research* 20, no. 3 (2010): 355–76.

38. O. C. Ferrell, T. L. Gonzalez-Padron, G. T. M. Hult, and I. Maignan, "From Market Orientation to Stakeholder Orientation," *Journal of Public Policy & Marketing* 29, no. 1 (2010): 93–96.

39. John L. Warne, "Developing a Quality Orientation," *Target* (Summer 1987), https://www.ame .org/sites/default/files/target_articles/87Q2A2.pdf.

40. S. Min, J. T. Mentzer, and R.T. Ladd, "Market Orientation in Supply Chain Management," *Journal of the Academy of Marketing Science* 35 no. 4 (2007), 509; J. T. Mentzer, W. DeWitt, S. Min, N. W. Nix, C. D. Smith, and Z. G. Zacharia, "Defining Supply Chain Management," *Journal of Business Logistics* 22, no. 2 (2001): 1–25.

Finally, a long-term orientation can be defined as the business goal of not operating for short-term gains, but for kingdom (even eternal) impact. Wisdom herself demonstrates such an orientation when she rejoices over the future. Wisdom exemplifies a long-term orientation as she cares for others and teaches with words of kindness. The following chapters in this book explore how these concepts fit into the framework of wisdom for sustainable business impact.

By integrating recently published business research with biblical wisdom books, including Proverbs 31:10–31, the best business practices for a wise and righteous business leader in ancient Israel can be merged with current leading business research and literature to create a general framework of wisdom for business and supply chain management today. The business themes that emerge in Proverbs 31:10–31 include servant leadership, quality orientation, stakeholder orientation, supply chain orientation, sustainability orientation, long-term orientation, reputation, comparative advantage, and kingdom impact.

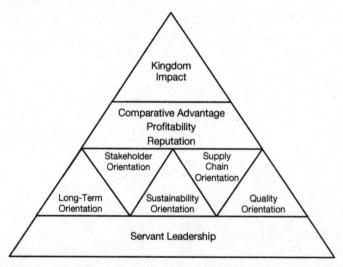

FIGURE 1.1: Proverbs 31:10–31 Means-End Hierarchy

The following chapters review each of these themes in light of the Proverbs 31:10–31 business framework illustrated in Figure 1.1. The framework represents a means-end hierarchy. If the purpose of a company is to glorify and honor God, there must be means to achieve that goal. The goal of the biblical Wisdom Literature is to demonstrate the behavior and skills that are featured in people who are in awe of God (often translated "fear of God") and want to honor and love God and others in all they do. There are many ways to achieve this goal that are highlighted throughout the Wisdom Literature and summarized in Proverbs 31:10–31. The means-end hierarchy represented in Figure 1.1 demonstrates the themes in Wisdom Literature that seem to lead to the goal of eternal impact and honor of God and man.

Reflection Questions

1. What do you think the purpose of Wisdom Literature was? What is the purpose of Wisdom Literature for today?
2. Why is it important to think about biblical ways to do business? What is the impact of not just acting like a Christian but also conducting business as a Christian?
3. Read Proverbs 1–9 and then 31:10–31 for yourself. How would you describe the business activities conducted in these passages?
4. Why do you think many Christian business leaders have viewed business as a means to an end (to provide money *for* kingdom work) but not an end in and of itself (business *as* kingdom work)?

CHAPTER 2

THE VIRTUE OF
PROFIT AS THE MEANS
TO AN ETERNAL END

She perceives that her merchandise is profitable. . . .
She opens her hand to the poor
and reaches out her hands to the needy.
—Proverbs 31:18, 20 (NASB)

"What does it profit a man if he gains the whole world and loses
his own soul?"
—Mark 8:36 (NASB)

Profit is a tool for accomplishing our end goals of honoring God
and developing people. As we manage with economy and care
for those producing the profit, we recognize profit as a virtue of
accountability, not a vice of self-aggrandizement.
—C. William Pollard[1]

Marion E. Wade lay in a hospital bed.[2] After months spent in the
Northwestern University science lab, Wade had created an aerosol
cleaning substance unlike any other product on the market. Not only did it
kill adult moths, but it also had the power to penetrate and kill moth eggs
and larva. Unfortunately, it also had the potential to explode. One morning
in 1944, the Fumakill substance blew up in Wade's face, landing him in the

---

1. Pollard, C. William, "Outline for Talk to Delta One Group" (2015), *C. William Pollard Papers*
149, https://digitalcommons.spu.edu/pollard_papers/149.
2. Marion E. Wade, *The Lord Is My Counsel* (Englewood Cliffs, NJ: Prentice Hall, 1966), 65–84.

hospital. As he lay in his hospital bed recovering his sight and his health, he had the opportunity to reflect.

He had lived to work, but his work had almost cost him his life. As he began to regain his eyesight, he was allowed a minimal amount of reading. He chose to read his Bible. Wade began to read from the book of Joshua: "Keep this Book of the Law always on your lips; meditate on it day and night, so that you may be careful to do everything written in it. Then you will be prosperous and successful" (Josh. 1:8 NIV). He was struck by the words. It seemed to indicate that by meditating on and living out the Word of God, a person could achieve success beyond profitability, and it could include work that honors God. He then read from the book of Samuel: "Those who honor me I will honor" (1 Sam. 2:30). His near-death experience and time of reflection began to shape his long-term aim to honor God.

He had worked with Christian men and prayed regularly with them about personal and individual matters, but never for their company as a moral community that could enact and live out the Scriptures. He wondered what God could do with a company that was entirely his, a company in which every employee did his job for the honor and glory of God.[3] As he continued to read, he arrived in Joshua 24:15. There he read, "Then choose for yourselves this day whom you will serve . . . as for me and my house, we will serve the LORD" (NIV). Wade took hold of this passage and began to apply it based on his definition of *serve*. Serving the Lord meant working for the Lord, which encompassed his business. That day, Wade lay in his hospital bed, closed his eyes in prayer, and dedicated his company and himself to God completely.

Wade had interacted with Christian businesspeople who felt guided by God in their businesses, but he also watched and perceived that as soon as they left their companies, things changed. He endeavored to build a company that didn't just have moral leadership; he wanted to build a company that offered a moral community for the development of human character and behavior. He viewed profit not as the end goal, but as a means to attain his goals of honoring God and developing people. In this way, his business became more than a job; it became a calling and ministry through which God could be glorified.[4] He committed to obey God and apply the Bible to all he did.

What began in 1929 as a moth-proofing company became ServiceMaster, a franchise service company that provides service brands such as ServiceMaster Clean, ServiceMaster Restore, Merry Maids, Terminix, Furniture Medic, AmeriSpec, and American Home Shield. Built on the foundation of honoring God, ServiceMaster grew to generate billions of dollars in revenue and was named

---

3. Wade, *The Lord Is My Counsel*, 82.
4. Wade, *The Lord Is My Counsel*, 85–104.

the number-one service company in America by *Fortune* in 1989 and has been listed as one of the world's most admired companies multiple times (1998, 2016).[5]

ServiceMaster had a longstanding commitment to hiring leadership capable of developing a servant's heart and putting the goals of serving people and God ahead of profitability.[6] For many years, an eleven-foot statue of Jesus washing the feet of the disciples stood outside the headquarters in Downers Grove, Illinois. Marion Wade's primary mission for the company was reflected in the corporate mission statement to "honor God in all we do."[7] He viewed himself and his Christian colleagues as servants of the Master. The leadership at ServiceMaster focused on developing long-term relationships with employees with the goal of developing people and honoring God.

Ken Hansen, CEO of ServiceMaster from 1957 to 1983, established a long-term leadership development strategy he called "shingles on the roof."[8] Shingles on a roof need to be ordered and overlap for the roof not to leak. In the same way, firms that place people in areas of strength to complement the weaknesses of others will create overlap of skills and talents that strengthens the firm.[9] With this strategy, the leadership team developed a long-term on-boarding process. Outgoing leaders overlapped and built relationships with incoming leaders rather than simply handing over the reins and exiting as many corporate leaders do.

This long-term commitment to relationship was exemplified in the way the fourth CEO of ServiceMaster, Bill Pollard, continued relationships with former CEOs Ken Hansen and Ken Wessner throughout his term as CEO and chairman. Wessner, then CEO, and Hansen, then chairman of the board, together hired Pollard in 1977. Pollard recounts in his book *Serving Two Masters* the importance Hansen placed on contribution and service to the employees and people impacted by ServiceMaster. Pollard quotes Hansen's words from his interview process:

> Bill, if you want to come to ServiceMaster to contribute and serve, you will have a great future. But if your coming is dependent on a title or position, including the CEO position, then you will be disappointed. To be successful at ServiceMaster you will have to learn to put the interest of others ahead of your own.[10]

---

5. David Barboze, "In This Company's Struggle, God Has Many Proxies," *New York Times*, November 21, 2001, C.1; and "World's Most Admired Companies 2016," *Fortune*, https://fortune.com/worlds-most-admired-companies/2016/servicemaster-global-holdings/.

6. William Pollard, *Serving Two Masters* (New York: Harper Collins, 2006).

7. Albert M. Erisman. *The ServiceMaster Story* (Peabody, MA: Hendrickson, 2020), 5.

8. William Pollard, *The Soul of the Firm* (Grand Rapids: Zondervan, 1996), 23.

9. Pollard, *The Soul of the Firm*, 139.

10. Pollard, *Serving Two Masters*, 85.

This concept of viewing profit as a means to a greater end and putting others first was exemplified by ServiceMaster. In 1996, Bill Pollard, the fourth Christian CEO of ServiceMaster, stood before an audience in Nairobi, Kenya. In the previous twenty-five years, ServiceMaster had doubled in size every three-and-a-half years, with revenues in excess of $4.5 billion from customers in the US, Canada, and twenty-seven countries around the world. However, ServiceMaster experienced this growth without profit maximization as the primary objective of the firm. Pollard and the CEOs who preceded him worked together to carry on the vision of Wade to create a moral community in the marketplace with the primary goal of honoring God and developing people. In his talk in Nairobi, Pollard stated,

> I believe the firm can do more than maximize profits or provide paychecks because the firm has a soul. The track record of my firm, ServiceMaster, confirms that it does happen and yes, when it does happen, there is also potential for profits, growth in market value, and extraordinary service to the customer.... But the measure of our success cannot be limited to the calculation of a total return value of our shares or the profit we produce. The answer must come from the more than 200,000 people who are making it happen every day as they serve others.[11]

At another talk some years later at Wheaton College, Pollard spoke on the virtue of profit. Pollard understood the necessity of profit: "As a business leader, I wanted to excel at generating a profitable bottom line and creating value for shareholders. If I didn't want to play by the rules, I didn't belong in the ball game."[12] However, Mr. Pollard didn't view profit as the end goal. It was merely a means goal, a measure of effectiveness and accountability, to achieve the end goal of honoring God and honoring people who were created in the image and likeness of God.

Pollard worked closely with Peter Drucker, NYU and later Claremont Graduate University professor and father of modern management. While sitting in a lecture by economist John Maynard Keynes at Cambridge University, Drucker realized that economists were interested in the behavior of commodities while he was interested in the behavior of people. His interest in ServiceMaster and partnership with Bill Pollard seemed like a natural fit with

---

11. C. William Pollard, "The Soul of the Firm (Nairobi, Kenya)" (1996), *C. William Pollard Papers* 49, https://digitalcommons.spu.edu/pollard_papers/49.
12. C. William Pollard, "The Virtue of Profit (Wheaton College)" (2009), *C. William Pollard Papers* 243, 4, https://digitalcommons.spu.edu/pollard_papers/243.

ServiceMaster's goal of honoring God and developing people. As early as 1974, Drucker argued that what determines whether a business will prosper or not is the firm's capability to provide what customers value.[13] The prosperity and success of a firm is then dependent on its ability to serve people and provide value. According to Pollard, Drucker disliked popular leadership books unless they recognized that leaders had an obligation to the people who followed them. He believed the essence of leadership was about achieving meaningful results. For Drucker, leadership was another means to the end goals of the firm.[14]

Means-End Hierarchy and Theories of the Firm

The dominant economic theory of the firm was conceptualized by Milton Friedman to state that the firm exists to maximize shareholder returns (through profit) and that this provides a sufficient motivation for firms to make the best decisions to serve the customer.[15] Drucker and Pollard questioned the ability of profit as an end goal to provide adequate motivation for people to serve their customers and provide what customers value. Further, Pollard believed you couldn't deliver service without people. Thus developing people and honoring God were the end goals for the ServiceMaster organization. Profitability and excellence were the means to achieve these goals.

While means-end reasoning has been applied in marketing most directly to customer value and understanding how the attributes of a product provide value consequences that enable a customer to achieve their end goals in life, means-end reasoning can be extended into other areas of social life. Means-end chain models were popularized in the 1980s and 1990s as a method for understanding how people perceive value. Providing value to the customer was central to Drucker's view of the firm. However, means goals and end goals can also be applied to the value of a corporation. As such, means are objects (for ServiceMaster: products or profits) or activities in which people engage (for ServiceMaster: leading, serving, etc.). Ends, then, are valued states of being, such as happiness, security, or accomplishment (for ServiceMaster: developing people and honoring God).[16]

---

13. Peter Drucker, *Management: Tasks, Responsibilities, Practices* (New York: Harper & Row, 1974).

14. C. William Pollard, *The Tides of Life* (Wheaton, IL: Crossway: 2014), 126–27.

15. C. William Pollard, "The Soul of the Firm (Phoenix)," (1995), *C. William Pollard Papers* 78, 1, https://digitalcommons.spu.edu/pollard_papers/78.

16. Jonathon Gutman, "A Means-End Chain Model Based on the Customer Categorization Process," *Journal of Marketing*, 46, no. 2 (1982): 60–72.

One of the early pioneers of means-end reasoning and analysis, Jonathan Gutman, based his means-end chain on psychologist Milton Rokeach's value surveys.[17] Rokeach divided values into terminal values (end states) and instrumental values (means). The Rokeach and Gutman models of understanding value can be adapted beyond the customer to encompass organizational goals and values as well. For instance, the leadership of the ServiceMaster firm was the means to achieve another means: profitability. Profitability, then, was a means toward the end goal of building a moral community, a purpose that extended beyond creating wealth for shareholders. Means ladder toward the end goals—first, servant leadership, then profit, then developing people, and finally honoring God (see Figure 2.1 below).

The ServiceMaster way of doing business recognized leadership as the foundation of their instrumental means. For Pollard and Drucker, the goal of leadership involved the people who followed, the direction they were headed, and who they were becoming as they fulfilled the mission and purpose of the organization being led.[18] In Pollard's view, the role of the leader was to determine the mission and purpose of the organization, the end goals. Thus ServiceMaster's means-end hierarchy was built on a foundation of servant leadership.

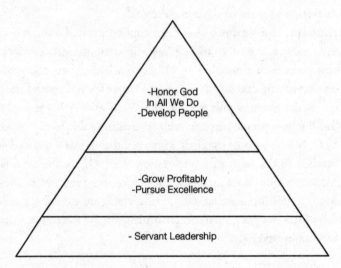

-Honor God
In All We Do
-Develop People

-Grow Profitably
-Pursue Excellence

- Servant Leadership

FIGURE 2.1: ServiceMaster Means-End Hierarchy

17. M. J. Rokeach, *Beliefs, Attitudes and Values* (San Francisco: Jossey Bass, 1968); and Rokeach, *The Nature of Human Values* (New York: Free Press, 1973).

18. Pollard, *The Tides of Life* (Wheaton, IL: Crossway. 2014), 127.

With an end goal of serving people beyond the shareholders of ServiceMaster, the ServiceMaster business model moved from a traditional economic theory of the firm, a theory in which Milton Friedman described the end goal of the firm to maximize shareholder returns, to a stakeholder theory of the firm. Stakeholder theory states that a manager's duty is to balance the shareholders' financial interests against the interests of other stakeholders, such as employees, customers, and the local community, even if it reduces shareholder returns. In the shareholder view of the firm, non-shareholders (such as employees) are viewed as a means to the end goal of maximizing shareholder value (profitability).[19] However, Pollard conceptualized people as the soul of the firm, and companies that didn't value people as soulless organizations.[20] In a talk at the Drucker Education Seminar in Claremont, California, Pollard highlighted the importance of recognizing and leading people to achieve the goals of a firm:

> But with all this change, choice, and diversity, there is, I believe, a constant element, an essential ingredient of the growth and development of any economy, of any business unit, of any educational institution. It is simply, people. People. Whether they be in second grade, ninth grade, twelfth grade, juniors in college, graduate students, young managers, executives, or retirees. People who want to learn, who are creative and can identify opportunities, who want to serve, who need to be nurtured, encouraged, trained, developed, and motivated. People who have individual dignity and worth regardless of rank, task, or assignment. People with the potential to be creative and adaptable. People who are more effective when they work for a cause, not just a living. People who, with more information and choice, will want greater participation and flexibility in their school or work place. People who have the potential to improve and who have varying gifts and talents. People who learn to accept and apply a value system as they relate to others in their work environment. People who exercise judgments within a framework of those values and who have the capacity to both love and hate, to care and to hurt, to detract and to contribute. People who respond to recognition for a job well done. People who grow in their self-esteem and well-being as they learn to serve and contribute to others. People who are looking for a mission and purpose in their school work, in their jobs, and their training and development.[21]

---

19. H. Jeff Smith, "The Shareholders vs. Stakeholders Debate," *MIT Sloan Management Review* 44, no. 4 (2003): 85.

20. C. William Pollard, "Faith in the Workplace" (2008), *C. William Pollard Papers* 73, 9, https://digitalcommons.spu.edu/pollard_papers/73.

21. C. William Pollard, "Speech at Drucker Education Seminar" (1991), *C. William Pollard Papers* 18, 2, https://digitalcommons.spu.edu/pollard_papers/18.

Clearly, the ServiceMaster model viewed profitability as a means to employ and serve people. ServiceMaster seemed to have recognized multiple stakeholders of the firm, though it primarily focused on employees. Pollard wrote, "People are not just economic animals or non-personal production units. Every person has their own fingerprint of personality and potential and wants to accomplish something significant and find meaning in their work."[22] In a service industry, this is even more important, as the work that employees conduct is interconnected with the product customers receive much more closely than with the manufacturing of tangible goods. In contrast, Henry Ford is reputed to have remarked, "Why is it that I always get the whole person when what I really want is just a pair of hands?"[23] ServiceMaster looked at ways to engage the whole person and provide dignity and motivation for their work as stakeholders toward the end goal of the company: to develop people and honor God.

From a stakeholder theory perspective (not a shareholder theory perspective) the main stakeholders include customers, employees, local communities, suppliers and distributors, and shareholders. Interestingly, all of these stakeholder groups are present in the Proverbs 31 wisdom-based business model. The Proverbs 31 leader had merchants buying her products (customers), had servant girls (employees), fed the poor and needy (local community), and bought food and flax from outside suppliers (suppliers and distributors). We can assume the Noble Woman's primary shareholder was her husband, as she lived in a time when women didn't hold property rights and were most likely not buying and selling on a large scale in the marketplace like she was. Similarly, ServiceMaster worked toward a mission that included stakeholders beyond the CEO, focusing on employee care and serving people beyond shareholders.

The End Goal: For Christ and His Kingdom

If profit isn't the end goal, what is? Profit is clearly important for the sustainability of a company. In a 2008 meeting with Herman Miller, Pollard's notes reflected on the importance of stewardship and profit.[24] Pollard's notes on

---

22. C. William Pollard. "Mission as an Organizing Principle" (1999), *C. William Pollard Papers* 65, 7, https://digitalcommons.spu.edu/pollard_papers/65.

23. Rodd Wagner and Jim Harter, "The Fifth Element of Great Managing," *Gallup Business Journal* (September 13, 2007), https://news.gallup.com/businessjournal/28561/fifth-element-great-managing.aspx.

24. C. William Pollard, "Reflections for the Herman Miller Board" (2008), *C. William Pollard Papers* 72, 6, https://digitalcommons.spu.edu/pollard_papers/72.

Psalm 24 indicated that ownership is central to the Christian faith. God owns everything; we are not the owners, we are just stewards. Pollard then spoke on the parable of the talents in Matthew 25:14–30.

In the passage in Matthew 25, Jesus teaches on the kingdom of heaven in three parables. One tells of ten virgins and the oil in their lamps as they await their groom (vv. 1–13), one about profit and stewardship (vv. 14–30), and one about caring for the poor and needy (vv. 31–46). In the middle parable, the story about profit and stewardship, Jesus taught the disciples that the kingdom of heaven would be like a man going on a journey. He called his servants to him and entrusted his wealth to them. He gave to each servant according to his ability and then left for his journey. When he returned, he asked his employees to give an account of his investment in them. The first employee doubled his five talents to ten. The second employee had doubled his two talents to four. However, the third employee was so fearful of losing the money that he buried it and returned to his master exactly what he had been given. The master condemned the third employee for not even putting the money in the bank to receive at least a minimum interest. While the parable has much broader meaning than business and money, it reflects a principle that whatever God entrusts us with, he wants us to sow and water and harvest more. In business, the surplus is profit, and it fits with God's economy of abundance.[25]

The master calls the first and second employees "good and faithful servant." They weren't just praised for the monetary value of their return, but also for their faithfulness with the few things they were entrusted with. The first and second employees were put in charge of many more things and invited to share in their master's happiness.

This parable is in the middle of two other parables also talking about the kingdom of heaven. In the preceding parable, Jesus tells a story of ten bridesmaids, five foolish and five wise. The foolish ones didn't take enough oil for their lamps to burn through the night, but the lamps of the wise ones had plenty of oil. The wise bridesmaids were able to follow the bridegroom to the wedding, while the foolish bridesmaids were locked out.

In the final parable in this series, Jesus talks about his own return in glory when the righteous will be rewarded in eternity. This time he doesn't focus primarily on their abundance (like the oil and talents) but praises them for their use of surplus or abundance. He calls the righteous "sheep," who gain access to

---

25. C. William Pollard, "Reflections for the Herman Miller Board" (2008), *C. William Pollard Papers* 72, 6, https://digitalcommons.spu.edu/pollard_papers/72.

heaven, and the unrighteous "goats," who do not. The righteous fed him, gave him a drink, clothed him, and nursed him when he was hungry, thirsty, naked, and sick. While the parable of the talents is used most frequently to exemplify the virtue of profit, all three parables have something to offer business leaders regarding wisdom and profit. In fact, we see this same use of profit in the wisdom-based business model presented by the Noble Woman in Proverbs 31:10–31.

In Proverbs 31:18, the Noble Woman sees her trading is profitable, and her lamp does not go out at night. This reflects her faithfulness and stewardship with what she was given, similar to the parable of the talents. Her abundant resources allow her to burn oil twenty-four hours a day. Unlike the foolish bridesmaids in Matthew 25, she is wise and has oil for her lamp all night long. She remains vigilant in her leadership. Proverbs 31:20 says, "She opens her hand to the poor, and reaches out her hands to the needy." Jesus's parables in Matthew 25 are strikingly similar to attributes of the Proverbs 31:10–31 Noble Woman, only he expands these characteristics from wisdom in the marketplace to explain the coming of the kingdom of heaven. Often we read the parable of the talents in Matthew 25:14–30 as an argument for business and profitability. However, the full context of all three parables in Matthew 25—which parallels the stewardship of the Noble Woman in Proverbs 31:10–31—reveals the kingdom of heaven worked out in business with wisdom and stewardship.

Pollard struggled with the challenge of serving two masters, both God and wealth.[26] However, the problem isn't with profit or wealth, it's the love of money that creates challenges with wealth.[27] It is a blessing to have abundance and surplus to serve God and others. With good stewardship and abundance, we can be good and faithful servants. The problem is the neoclassical economic theory of the firm. Throughout the 1980s and 1990s, business schools ramped up siloed teaching of neoclassical economics.[28] The economy was booming at that time, but it also came with a growing sense of separation of church and state and the decline of American Christian traditions in secular environments, exemplified by rejection of prayer in school and a growing divide between the sacred and secular in churches. Christian business leaders were

---

26. C. William Pollard, "The Virtue of Profit," in *Serving Two Masters?* (Lees Summit, MO: Delta One Leadership Institute, 2012), 138.

27. Luke 16:13–14: "'No slave can serve two masters; for a slave will either hate the one and love the other or be devoted to the one and despise the other. You cannot serve God and wealth.' The Pharisees, who were lovers of money, heard all this, and they ridiculed him."

28. Shelley L. Brickson, "Organizational Identity Orientation: Genesis of the Role of the Firm and Distinct Forms of Social Value," *Academy of Management Review* 32, no. 3 (2007): 864–88.

taught in business school that the role of the business was to generate returns for shareholders through profitability.

However, from the early 2000s to the economic downturn of 2008 the dark side of neoclassical business models was unmasked. Corporate scandals such as the Enron scandal in 2001 and the predatory mortgage lending that led to the 2008 housing market crash revealed the excessive self-indulgence that stemmed from the neoclassical assumption that self-interest is a reasoned and unavoidable basis for individual motivation.[29]

This brings us to the role of wealth in the kingdom of God. Many people reference Mark 10:17–31, the story of the rich young ruler, as an admonition against all profit or abundance. But the true problem revealed in this story is making profit the end goal. In this story, a rich man ran to meet Jesus. The Bible says he was righteous, and clearly, by the speed of his approach, he was excited to meet Jesus.

> "Good teacher," he asked. "what must I do to inherit eternal life?"
>
> "Why do you call me good?" Jesus answered. "No one is good—except God alone. You know the commandments: 'You shall not murder, you shall not commit adultery, you shall not steal, you shall not give false testimony, you shall not defraud, honor your father and mother.'" (vv. 17–19 NIV)

Many people who teach business ethics stop with Jesus's response in verses 18–19; he quotes all six socially oriented commandments in the Ten Commandments.[30] Over the years, I have taught business students that they should pursue business ethically. In general, business students are encouraged to avoid committing adultery and even in a secular setting, they are taught to avoid lying and defrauding. Clearly stealing and murder are off the table for Christians and non-Christians alike, even in a neoclassical economic system. Like many truly righteous Christian business leaders, the young man affirms that he adheres to this "Godly work ethic." He says, "Teacher, ... all these I have kept since I was a boy" (v. 20 NIV).

Jesus's response to the rich young ruler is beautiful. The rich young ruler exemplifies an ethical and upstanding businessperson today. He was *almost* righteous to the letter of the law. Jesus knew he was well intending, but he was missing the most important part of the law:

---

29. S. Ghoshal, "Bad Management Theories Are Destroying Good Management Practices," *Academy of Management Learning & Education* 4 (2005): 75–91.

30. Theology of Work Project, Inc., *Theology of Work Bible Commentary*, 1 vol. ed. (Peabody, MA: Hendrickson, 2015–2016), 62.

Jesus looked at him and *loved him*. "One thing you lack," he said. "Go, sell everything you have and give to the poor, and you will have treasure in heaven. Then come, follow me."

At this the man's face fell. He went away sad, because he had great wealth.

Jesus looked around and said to his disciples, "How hard it is for the rich to enter the kingdom of God!" (vv. 21–23 NIV, emphasis mine)

Jesus was not denigrating profit or wealth; he was recognizing the impossibility of humanity to look at an end goal beyond profit without the supernatural help of God. This conversation leads to the much-quoted verse 27, "With man this is impossible, but not with God; all things are possible with God" (NIV).

Two chapters later, in Mark 12, after discussing more business contexts—wages to employees and taxes due to Caesar—and the less business-oriented topic of marriage at the resurrection, Jesus is asked a pivotal question. A teacher of the law asks Jesus in verse 28 (NIV), "Of all the commandments, which is the most important?" In verses 29–31, Jesus answers:

The first is, "Hear, O Israel: the Lord our God, the Lord is one; you shall love the Lord your God with all your heart, and with all your soul, and with all your mind, and with all your strength." The second is this, "You shall love your neighbor as yourself." There is no other commandment greater than these.

In Matthew 22:40, Jesus says that all the Law and the Prophets hang on these two commandments. In Luke 10, he follows a conversation with an expert of the law about the two commandments to love God and neighbor with the parable of the Good Samaritan, defining the concept of neighbor.

This was the part of the law that the rich young ruler was missing. He followed all of the commandments except for the most important two. Deuteronomy 6:5 says to "love the LORD your God with all your heart and with all your soul and with all your *strength*" (NIV, emphasis mine). The word *strength* in the Hebrew is *meod*, which translates to "force," "might," and "abundance." He could love God with his heart and with his soul, but he could not love God with his abundance, with his profit and wealth. Unlike the good and faithful servants from Matthew 25, the rich young ruler was unable to give all he had earned back to his master. Further, he was unable to love his neighbor as himself by distributing his wealth among the poor and needy.

What is the lesson in these passages for business students who want to work in business for Christ and his kingdom? It seems as though profit is not a problem in and of itself. Jesus's parable of the talents praises the two servants who stewarded and grew the wealth they were entrusted with. You must have abundance in order to love God with it. However, profit is not the end goal. When profit becomes the end goal, it becomes difficult for the rich to enter the kingdom of God (Mark 10:23). Those who are welcomed into the kingdom of God in Matthew 25 are those who give food, drink, clothing, and medical assistance to the poor and needy out of their resources. They are like the Proverbs 31:10–31 Noble Woman who wisely recognizes the profit in her trade and then extends her hands to the poor.

In order to live this out, Christian businesspeople will need to move beyond the neoclassical economic business model to embrace a purpose of the firm beyond profit. Jesus indicates that to fulfill the law and the profits and to not become hindered by wealth and profit, we should love God and people with all of our hearts, souls, minds, and strength (might and abundance). As Christians, we need to adopt a stakeholder theory of the firm that looks beyond our shareholders to love and honor God and to love, honor, and develop the people God has entrusted us to lead and impact. This requires a long-term orientation that looks beyond short-term, quarterly profits and embraces a long-term view of profit that provides legacy for employees, suppliers and customers, and the community. Kingdom impact can only be achieved through a firm by loving and serving all of the firm's stakeholders, including the poor and needy in our communities. In doing this, we reflect the heart of God and love and honor him and others with all we do in business.

Business Research Support

While the neoclassical economic view of the firm definitely dominated academic research into the early 2000s, the corporate social responsibility and stakeholder theory literature continued to develop throughout the 1980s and 1990s. In 1984, Darden School of Business philosophy professor Dr. Freeman first published his seminal piece, *Strategic Management: A Stakeholder Approach*.[31] This book led to thousands of publications on stakeholder theory, stakeholder orientation, and stakeholder management over the last thirty years. However, the literature stream was tempered with an apologetic acquiescence to profitability as the end goal, and research strove to demonstrate that

---

31. R. E. Freeman, *Strategic Management: A Stakeholder Approach* (Boston: Pitman, 1984).

advancing social welfare, environmental initiatives, and economic returns to shareholders are well aligned.[32] Thanks to this determination to show that stakeholder views of the firm did not detract from profitability and shareholder returns, the last thirty years have demonstrated that there are, in fact, many benefits of a shareholder view of the firm that start with, but are not limited to, profit.

As early as the mid-1960s, research in stakeholder theory revealed that 80 percent of surveyed upper-level managers regarded it as unethical to solely focus on the interest of shareholders and not that of customers and employees.[33] Jeanne M. Logsdon and Kristi Yuthas, organizational studies and accounting professors at the University of New Mexico, took things a step further by introducing a view of stakeholder orientation in which morality was also a factor. In their view, the morality of leadership and the expectations for moral development of employees drive employee engagement, strategy, and rewards, and ultimately create a moral community.[34]

In 2011, a group of top business scholars tested the impact of stakeholder orientation and social responsibility on firm outcomes.[35] They surveyed 115 high-level executives (presidents and vice-presidents) leading for-profit companies with a minimum of 500 employees regarding their stakeholder orientation (in the firm culture and behavior). They then measured the impact of the firm's stakeholder orientation on multiple outcome variables. Their data showed a significant relationship between stakeholder orientation and firm performance, including market performance, financial performance, reputation, and employee commitment.

While this research still models the ultimate business outcome as financial performance, it does provide evidence that a stakeholder view of the firm does not necessarily detract from financial performance. In his seminal work in 1984, Freeman defined a stakeholder as "any group or individual who can affect or is affected by the achievement of the organization's objectives."[36] A stakeholder orientation can then be described as the organizational "culture and behaviors that induce organizational members to continuously be aware

32. Brickson, "Organizational Identity Orientation," 864.

33. R. Baumhart, *An Honest Profit: What Businessmen Say about Ethics in Business* (New York: Holt, Rinehart and Winston, 1968), 34.

34. Jeanne M. Logsdon & Kristi Yuthas, "Corporate Social Performance, Stakeholder Orientation, and Organizational Moral Development," *Journal of Business Ethics* 16 (1997): 1213–26.

35. Isabelle Maignan, Tracy L. Gonzalez-Padron, G. Thomas Hult, and O.C. Ferrell, "Stakeholder Orientation: Development and Testing of a Framework for Socially Responsible Marketing," *Journal of Strategic Marketing* 19, no. 4 (2011): 313–38.

36. Freeman, *Strategic Management*, 46.

of and positively act upon a variety of stakeholder issues."[37] The stakeholder view balances the economic goals of financial and market performance and the more people-oriented goals of employee commitment and reputation.

The Means and End Goals of the Wisdom-Based Business Model

The five wisdom orientations introduced in chapter 1 all have a long history of empirical evidence supporting their impact on firm performance (primarily financial). I use the word *impact* to mean that each of these orientations are positively correlated with each other and the outcomes listed below (I would be hard pressed to prove causation based on current business research evidence).

The Bible-based servant leadership that drives these orientations is focused on both profitability and kingdom impact. We see the long-term orientation play out in the Gospels as Jesus rocks the disciples' expectations of his governance. While they expected him to literally sit on the throne in Israel as was prophesied in Zechariah 9:9, he choose instead to die on the cross so that more (all who believe) could be saved. He sacrificed the short-term gain of ruling in one lifetime for the long-term outcome of sitting at the right hand of the Father in heaven. History would be forever changed as he ushered in the kingdom of heaven.

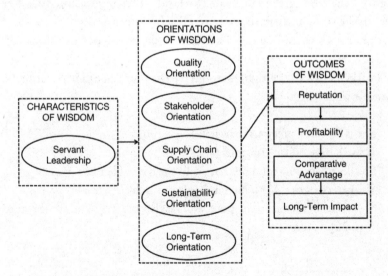

FIGURE 2.2: Wisdom-Based Business Model

---

37. Ferrell et al., "From Market Orientation to Stakeholder Orientation," 93–96.

The outcomes of wisdom found in the Noble Woman's work in Proverbs 31:10–31 are demonstrated in the figure above. Each outcome of wisdom can be captured in four categories of firm performance that are also found in business research. The first of the four outcomes of wisdom in action (servant leadership and wisdom orientations) is reputation. The Noble Woman and her husband are known and worthy of praise.[38] Second, reputation drives profitability. Five times in twenty-one verses, the Noble Woman demonstrates profitability.[39] Third, the combination of reputation and profitability are a reflection of wise skills that are hard to imitate, giving the firm a comparative advantage. The passage starts off with a claim that the Noble Woman is far more precious than jewels, and Proverbs 31:29 says, "Many women have done excellently, but you surpass them all." Finally, the impact of the servant leader in an environment that strives to honor God and all people will have eternal kingdom impact.

Organizational reputation is defined here as the stakeholders' cumulative judgments of a firm.[40] In Proverbs 31:10–31, the Noble Woman's direct stakeholders reinforce her reputation in verse 28: "Her children rise up and call her happy; her husband too, he praises her." In fact, her husband's reputation is also enhanced because he is connected to her, as demonstrated in verse 23: "Her husband is known in the city gates, taking his seat among the elders of the land." Her reputation goes beyond her direct stakeholders to include all who come and go in the marketplace through the city gates: "Let her works praise her in the city gates" (v. 31b).

Further, Proverbs 31 highlights and repeats the theme of her profitability in multiple ways:

"She is far more precious than jewels" (v. 10b).
"He will have no lack of gain" (v. 11b).
"She does him good and not harm, all the days of her life" (v. 12).
"She perceives that her merchandise is profitable" (v. 18a).
"She opens her hand to the poor, and reaches out her hands to the needy" (v. 20).

---

38. Proverbs 31:23, 28, 30, 31.
39. Proverbs 31:11—*shalal*, spoils/gain; Proverbs 31:16–31—*peri*, fruit, produce, shares; Proverbs 31:18—*tov*, valuable, pleasant, excellent; Proverbs 31:1, 29—*chayil*, strength, wealth.
40. Maignan et al., "Stakeholder Orientation," 320.

Financial performance is measured through indicators such as return on investments, return on assets, and profit growth. Based on these verses that indicate her growing wealth and ability to buy land and dispense her abundance to the poor, she demonstrates a profitable business.

Further, the language around her rarity and competitive strength in verses 10 and 19—"A capable wife, who can find? She is far more precious than jewels" (v. 10) and "She puts her hand to the distaff, and her hands hold the spindle" (v. 19)—indicate that she has resources and a skill set that are unique in her day. Unique resources are categorized in management literature as a comparative advantage, and this appears to be true of the Noble Woman. Traditional economics focuses on easy-to-replicate resources like capital, labor, and land. Unique resources that lead to a comparative advantage include relationships, organizational strategies, and brand reputation.[41] Compared to other capable women, she surpasses them all (v. 29). Wisdom is inimitable and unique. The Noble Woman has the right relationships to provide skills and methods that lead to financial success and effective engagement among the servants. She has a reputation that is acknowledged even beyond her immediate stakeholders (family) and is truly praiseworthy.

Finally, while it may seem somewhat tautological or repetitious to state that a long-term orientation leads to long-term outcomes, the longer-term vantage point in setting goals and objectives for the firm will most certainly lead to a kingdom impact on stakeholders of the firm and achieve kingdom purposes that are eternal (loving God and others, with righteousness, peace, and joy). The Noble Woman's care for her employees exemplifies this: "She is not afraid for her household when it snows, for all her household are clothed in crimson" (v. 21). Her lamp burns through the night as she is vigilant in her leadership (v. 18). She has all the contingencies of the future covered, and her household is well clothed.

Not only does she have the near future in mind, but as a righteous, noble woman (*ēšet ḥayil*), she would have an eternal perspective. Her fear of Yahweh and her lasting role as one of his people motivates a positive impact in the earth (Gen. 28:14). As a wise leader who remains vigilant, sows and reaps a profit, and provides for her stakeholders (her family, employees, and the poor), she looks a great deal like the five wise bridesmaids, the two faithful servants, and the sheep who gain entrance to the kingdom of heaven in Matthew 25.

---

41. Hunt and Morgan, "The Comparative Advantage Theory of Competition," 1–15.

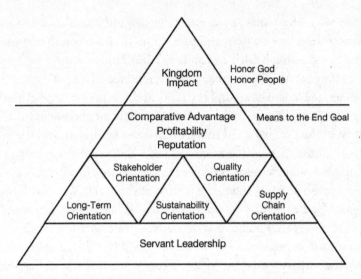

FIGURE 2.3: Proverbs 31:10–31 Means-End Hierarchy

In reflection, servant leadership is an attribute of a firm that drives its orientations, which are means to the end goal of kingdom impact. Servant leadership paired with biblical orientations of a firm have been studied extensively. Research has provided evidence that servant leadership, as well as the biblically based orientations that follow, positively impact performance outcomes. The marketplace cares most about profitability and competitive advantage, and while profit is an important outcome of a firm's orientation and leadership, the end goal of wisdom is greater. Profitability can be a means to the true end goal of wisdom: to honor God and people and to impact the world for the kingdom of heaven.

Reflection Questions

1. How would you draw your personal means-end hierarchy for business? What are your end goals?
2. Do you believe there is biblical support for the value of profitability? If so, provide Scripture references. If not, why not?
3. Can you think of examples of companies other than ServiceMaster that have a goal or purpose beyond profit? How do they achieve their goals? What are the means they focus on?

CHAPTER 3

THE FOUNDATION OF
SERVANT LEADERSHIP

The heart of her husband trusts in her,
> and he will have no lack of gain.

> *—Proverbs 31:11*

"Let the greatest among you become as the youngest, and the leader as one who serves."

> *—Luke 22:26 ESV*

We continuously strive to create a better, more innovative and compelling place to shop and to work, for the near and long term success of our company. That includes a relentless focus on doing what's right for ALL of our stakeholders by operating our business through the lens of our Foundation Principles and a commitment to conscious leadership.

> *—Melissa Reiff, CEO,*
> *The Container Store 2015–Present[1]*

Kip Tindell, previous CEO and founder of The Container Store, joined the conscious capitalism movement soon after its founding in 2010. Tindell's University of Texas at Austin roommate and Whole Foods CEO John Mackey and Babson College professor Raj Sisodia started the conscious capitalism movement in response to the rising support for socially conscious capitalist

---

1. Marcel Schwantes, "The World's Top 10 CEOs (They Lead in a Totally Unique Way)," Inc.com (March 29, 2017), https://www.inc.com/marcel-schwantes/heres-a-top-10-list-of-the-worlds-best-ceos-but-they-lead-in-a-totally-unique-wa.html.

enterprises. Mackey had long challenged the Friedman ideal that the sole social responsibility of business is to increase profits:

> Conscious capitalism is defined as an emerging economic system that "builds on the foundations of capitalism—voluntary exchange, entrepreneurship, competition, freedom to trade and the rule of law. These are essential to a healthy functioning economy, as are other elements of conscious capitalism including trust, compassion, collaboration, and value creation."[2]

A practitioner of conscious capitalism, Tindell founded his company with purpose beyond profit in mind. Along with other conscious leaders, Tindell, Sisodia, and Mackey imagined businesses that were born out of a dream about how the world could and should be.[3] They imagined businesses that could outlive them and deliver real value to everyone they touched, businesses their parents and children would be proud of—forces for good that enhanced the health and well-being of society. The business leaders engaged with conscious capitalism talk about their businesses within the context of love and care for all stakeholders involved.

Conscious leadership became the framework that captured the servant heart of many business leaders involved in the movement toward responsibility beyond profit, including ServiceMaster, Medtronics, Starbucks, TDIndustries, Southwest Airlines, Ritz-Carlton, SAS, Zappos.com, Intel, and Marriott. They rejected a zero-sum tradeoff orientation (if one entity gains, another loses) and embraced a mindset of analytical, emotional, and spiritual intelligence.

For Kip Tindell of The Container Store, the mindset of servant leadership was learned from a very young age. Tindell's fifth grade art teacher, Ann McGree-Cooper, laid for him the foundation of servant leadership. She continues to be an advocate of servant leadership as she has moved from the grade school classroom to become an expert in creative approaches for companies like Southwest Airlines, TD Industries, and The Container Store. The culture and leadership style at The Container Store modeled this others-first version of leadership as Tindell grew the company many years later. Tindell built a corporate culture that fostered "love rather than fear"[4] and servant leadership by

---

2. The Arthur W. Page Center/Public Relationship Ethics, Penn State University, "Conscious Capitalism: A Definition," https://pagecentertraining.psu.edu/public-relations-ethics/corporate-social-responsibility/lesson-2-introduction-to-conscious-capitalism/conscious-capitalism-a-definition/.

3. Raj Sisodia and John Mackey, *Conscious Capitalism* (Boston: Harvard Business School Publishing Corporation, 2014), 30–31.

4. Kip Tindell, *Uncontained* (New York: Grand Central, 2014), 247.

openly promoting an environment of listening and deeply investing in training (an unusual tactic in the retail industry).

After he founded The Container Store, Tindell became familiar with Robert Greenleaf's work on servant leadership and realized that it mirrored the way The Container Store does business with a leadership focus on listening, empathy, humility, and serving others. The Container Store was founded in 1978, and Greenleaf's experiment at AT&T exploring servant leadership was first published in an essay in 1970.[5]

In the book *Uncontainable: How Passion, Commitment, and Conscious Capitalism Built a Business Where Everyone Thrives,* Tindell tells the story about how he fell in love with retail and its potential benefits to employees, vendors, and communities. In keeping with Tindell's priorities, "Communication IS Leadership" was coined by current CEO, Melissa Reiff. This principle of listening and communication embodies a servant mindset. By starting with listening, this form of leadership promotes an orientation toward others. According to Reiff, the communication of leaders should not only be courteous and thoughtful, it should also be compassionate. The Container Store website states:

> Conscious businesses are led by *servant leaders* who are more concerned about the collective good and success of everyone at their company than their own personal gain. Conscious businesses also have conscious cultures that are trusting, authentic, innovative and caring—employees feel that working at a conscious company is not only professionally fulfilling, but that it truly makes them a better person! We're always astonished when our employees say that not only do they love working at The Container Store, but the experience has made them a better mother, wife, friend, or neighbor.[6] (emphasis mine)

Tindell is a strong advocate for women in leadership, believing that women have a natural tendency toward the two most crucial leadership qualities: communicating and listening.[7] Tindell purposefully elected women to the board and hired women to high levels of management, stating in an interview with *Business Insider,* "What's more important in a leader is emotional intelligence. That's why I think women make better executives than men."[8] He initially

---

5. Robert K. Greenleaf, *The Servant as Leader* (Westfield, IN: Greenleaf Center for Servant Leadership, 1970).

6. See http://standfor.containerstore.com/page/conscious-capitalism.

7. Tindell, *Uncontained,* 4.

8. Jenna Goudreau and Kip Tindell, "The Container Store CEO Says Women Make Better Executives Than Men," *Business Insider,* https://www.businessinsider.com/container-store-ceo-kip-tindell-leadership-women-success-2014-10.

met Reiff when she was a national sales manager at Crabtree and Evelyn in the mid-1990s. Tindell and his wife Sharon became good friends with Reiff and her husband, and he eventually hired her to run strategic marketing at The Container Store. Reiff was drawn to The Container Store because of the principles and values on which it operated. Tindell believed that employees should be compensated fairly and should be treated with affection and respect. His business methodology went beyond fair pay and engendered loyalty and success from his employees. His story is marked with friendships with the people he encountered throughout his journey of growing The Container Store. Tindell states in his book that while he does not apply his concept of love out of religious motivation, he recognizes that many of his philosophies align with religious concepts of loving others and the golden rule of treating others as you want to be treated. He states, "How can someone have one set of values in their personal life and a looser set of values in their business? Why shouldn't they be the same, since business is just one aspect of life."[9]

The result of this people-oriented leadership made The Container Store a remarkable place to work. Although they have had to make some major changes since going public in 2013, they weathered the 2008 economic downturn without having to lay off any employees.[10] In 1999, The Container Store entered *Fortune* magazine's 100 Best Workplaces competition and landed at number one.[11] Since that time, they have spent eighteen years on *Fortune*'s Best Workplaces list and have continued to be a "best of the best" of the "Best Workplaces for Women."[12]

The Container Store invests in its employees with high pay and intensive training. In the retail industry where the average training for new hires is around eight hours, The Container Store averages more than 200 hours of training and pays their sales people more than the industry average. Further, they have an incredibly low turnover rate: around 10 percent, compared to retail industry standards around 60 percent.[13] Like ServiceMaster, The Container Store is an employee-first culture that seeks to treat *all* of the organization's stakeholders with responsibility, respect, and dignity. Just as it was unique for ServiceMaster to inventively dignify the manual labor of the many cleaners

---

9. Tindell, *Uncontained*, 41.

10. "No Layoffs—Ever! The Container Store; Best Company Rank 21," *Fortune*, January 24, 2011, https://archive.fortune.com/galleries/2011/pf/jobs/1101/gallery.no_layoffs.fortune/6.html.

11. Tindell, *Uncontained*, 141.

12. Tindell, *Uncontained*, 141.

13. Kip Tindell, "The Container Store's CEO on Finding and Keeping Front-Line Talent," *Harvard Business Review* (2014), https://hbr.org/2014/11/the-container-stores-ceo-on-finding-and-keeping-front-line-talent.

they employed in the field, The Container Store looked to dignify the work of retail cashiers and salespeople compared to other retail chains. Over the years, The Container Store has been featured in *Harvard Business Review* articles and case studies for business students to explore stakeholder-based leadership.[14]

Reiff has gone beyond the stakeholder and employee mantra to also explore ways to become more sustainable as an organization. The Container Store implements sustainability initiatives across environmental and social initiatives. Reiff has found win-win opportunities to implement recycling programs, increase rail utilization, and replace inefficient air conditioners and lighting to boost both the company's environmental impact and long-term bottom line. She has also developed social initiatives in the communities around stores to donate 10 percent of grand-opening sales to a local nonprofit, providing containers to those in need, and offering discounts to educators.[15] Reiff's leadership and conscious, servant mentality has not only helped to maintain the success of The Container Store in a highly competitive retail industry but has also landed her among the top ten servant-oriented CEOs in the world.[16]

Servant Leadership

Just as profit is a means to the end goal of developing people and honoring God, servant leadership is a foundational means of a company that results in increased profitability to impact the end goal of loving God and people. Servant leadership is applied in multiple types of organizations and is taught in business schools, military training, and churches around the world. Servant leadership has gained momentum in business as a means by which organizational performance can be enhanced through people-centric orientation.[17]

It is not a new concept. Jesus frequently highlighted the importance of the greatest leader taking on servanthood over 2,000 years ago. However, it has had growing or renewed recognition in business over the last forty years. In 1970, Robert Greenleaf, former director at AT&T, founded the modern

---

14. Zeynep Ton, "Why 'Good Jobs' Are Good for Retailers," *Harvard Business Review* (January-February 2012), https://hbr.org/2012/01/why-good-jobs-are-good-for-retailers; Tatiana Sandino, Zeynep Ton, and Aldo Sesia, "The Container Store," *Harvard Business School Case* 116–120, published April 2016, revised December 2016, https://store.hbr.org/product/the-container-store/116020?sku=116020 -PDF-ENG.

15. Conscious Capitalism, "Melissa Reiff, The Container Store: Hero of Conscious Capitalism," n.d., https://www.consciouscapitalism.org/heroes/melissa-reiff.

16. Schwantes, "The World's 10 Top CEOs."

17. D. Jones, "Servant Leadership's Impact on Profit, Employee Satisfaction, and Empowerment Within the Framework of a Participative Culture of Business," *Academy for Studies in Business* 3, no. 2 (2011): 35–49.

servant leadership movement in response to the prominent power-centered authoritarian leadership style that seemed to be failing institutions. He redefined effective leadership as servant leadership:

> The servant-leader is servant first. . . . It begins with the natural feeling that one wants to serve, serve first. Then conscious choice brings one to aspire to lead. He is sharply different from the person who is leader first, perhaps because of the need to assuage an unusual power drive to acquire material possessions. The leader-first and the servant-first are two extreme types. . . . The difference manifests itself in the care taken by the servant-first to make sure that other people's highest priority needs are being served.[18]

A more succinct definition of servant leadership has emerged in recent years. Eva et al. define servant leadership "as an (1) other-oriented approach to leadership (2) manifested through one-on-one prioritizing of follower individual needs and interests, (3) and an outward reorienting of their concern for self towards concern for others within the organization and the larger community."[19] As such, servant leadership promotes the concept that the organization exists for the person as much as the person exists for the organization. This overlaps with and captures a stakeholder-oriented view of the organization or a manager's ability to give priority to the needs of multiple stakeholders beyond himself or herself. Servant leadership is outworked in the following ways to affect multiple stakeholders, including the leader's direct followers:

- forming relationships with subordinates
- empowering subordinates
- helping subordinates grow and succeed
- behaving ethically
- having conceptual skills
- putting subordinates first
- creating value for those outside of the organization

Greenleaf believed that if there was a theology of the individual, there should also be a theology of institutions. For Christians, the theology of the individual is broadly conceptualized in systematic theology as the *imago Dei*,

---

18. Greenleaf, *The Servant as Leader*, 1.
19. Nathan Eva, Mulyadi Robin, Sen Sendjaya, Dirk van Dierendonck, and Robert C. Liden, "Servant Leadership: A Systematic Review and Call for Future Research," *The Leadership Quarterly* 30, no. 1 (2019): 114.

which directly translates into "image of God." The theology of the individual as the image of God is drawn from the biblical creation story. In Genesis 1:26 (NIV), God states, "Let us make mankind in our image, in our likeness, so that they may rule over the fish in the sea and the birds in the sky, over the livestock and all the wild animals, and over all the creatures that move along the ground." God creates 'adam, humankind, in relationship with him, in relationship with each other, and in relationship with creation. In short, the theology of the individual as *imago Dei* encourages the relational reflection of humanity created in reflection of God's Trinitarian plurality.[20] However, Greenleaf believed a theology of persons is inadequate to account for both persons relating to persons and the leadership necessary to navigate the social, political, and economic pressures of modern-day institutions.

He framed his ideas of the theology of institutions within the context of the church. He purported that to lead effectively, church leaders needed a theology of institutions that shifts church membership and current leader styles to the regenerative force of servanthood. This aligns with biblical representations of leadership as personified by Wisdom in Proverbs 31:10–31. As portrayed by the Noble Woman and conceptualized in business research, servant leadership is leadership that is focused on serving the needs of others and is characterized by personal integrity, selflessness, and a strong moral compass.[21] In the New Testament, Jesus proposes in Matthew 20:26–27 (NLT) that "whoever wants to be a leader among you must be your servant, and whoever wants to be first among you must become your slave." Recent research, conducted by my logistics colleagues, has provided evidence that servant leadership is a unique leadership style that drives organizational commitment, operational performance, and financial performance in many organizations.[22]

While leadership research in general tends to focus on the individual, research suggests that servant leadership also drives change at the group level.[23]

---

20. Karl Barth, *Church Dogmatics*, vol. III.1, ed. G. W. Bromiley and T. F. Torrance (Edinburgh: T&T Clark, 1956–77), 193.

21. Robert K. Greenleaf, *Servant Leadership: A Journey into the Nature of Legitimate Power and Leadership* (New York: Paulist Press, 1977); R. S. Peterson, D. B. Smith, P. V. Martorana, and P. D. Owens, "The Impact of Chief Executive Officer Personality on Top Management Team Dynamics: One Mechanism by Which Leadership Affects Organizational Performance," *Journal of Applied Psychology* 88, no. 5 (2003): 795–808; M. G. Ehrhart, "Leadership and Procedural Justice Climate as Antecedents of Unit-Level Organizational Citizenship Behavior," *Personnel Psychology* 57, no. 1 (2004): 61–94; B. J. Avolio, and W. L. Gardner, "Authentic Leadership Development: Getting to the Root of Positive Forms of Leadership," *The Leadership Quarterly* 16, no.3 (2005): 315–38.

22. Overstreet et al., "Bridging the Gap between Strategy and Performance," 136–49.

23. R. C. Liden et al. "The Role of Leader-Member Exchange in the Dynamic Relationship Between Employer and Employee: Implications for Employee Socialization, Leaders, and Organization," in *The Employment Relationship, Examining Psychological and Contextual Perspectives*, ed. J. A.-M.

One of the most interesting findings in the supply chain research by Overstreet et al. is that servant leadership not only drives profitability, but it also impacts the day-to-day organizational commitment of employees and the operational performance of the company.[24] Because servant leadership encompasses the style and actions of leadership as well as the moral character of leadership, it bolsters reputation and provides long-term relationships with employees and external stakeholders. Servant leadership holds the key to performance and impact moving forward. In fact, according to Jesus, it is our key to greatness![25] When guided by a servant leader, businesses and business employees can flourish by taking on both the characteristics of the servant leader and the actions inspired by the servant leader, motivated through wisdom-guided philosophies or orientations.

After his career in management research, development, and education at AT&T, Greenleaf retired and launched the Greenleaf Center for Servant Leadership. After Greenleaf passed on in 1990, the center was led for seventeen years by Larry Spears, who built on Greenleaf's original conceptualization of servant leadership to include ten characteristics of a servant leader. Interestingly, many of the themes of servant leadership build on concepts introduced in the biblical wisdom books:

Characteristics of Servant Leadership	Spears' Description[26]	Wisdom Literature Description (NIV)
Listening	Identify the will of a group and help clarify that will.	Prov. 11:14: For lack of guidance a nation falls, but victory is won through many advisers.
Empathy	Understand and empathize with others, accept others and recognize them for their own special and unique spirits.	Prov. 21:13: Whoever shuts their ears to the cry of the poor will also cry out and not be answered.
Healing	The potential for healing one's self and one's relationship to others, wholeness.	Prov. 12:18: The words of the reckless pierce like swords, but the tongue of the wise brings healing.

Coyle-Shapiro, L. M. Shore, S. M. Taylor, and L. E. Tetrick (Oxford: Oxford University Press: 2004), 226–50.

24. Overstreet et al., "Bridging the Gap between Strategy and Performance," 143.

25. Luke 22:26.

26. Larry C. Spears, "Character and Servant Leadership: Ten Characteristics of Effective, Caring Leaders," *The Journal of Virtues & Leadership* 1, no. 1 (2010): 25–30.

Awareness	General and self-awareness strengthen the servant leader.	Prov. 21:2: A person may think their own ways are right, but the LORD weighs the heart.
Persuasion	The leader's ability to convince rather than coerce compliance in others.	Prov. 20:5: The purposes of a person's heart are deep waters, but one who has insight draws them out.
Conceptualization	Broad based conceptual thinking beyond day-to-day tasks to dream dreams.	Ps. 119:130: The unfolding of your words gives light; it gives understanding to the simple.
Foresight	Ability to foresee the likely outcome of a situation.	Prov. 12:26: The righteous choose their friends carefully, but the way of the wicked leads them astray.
Stewardship	Holding something in trust for another.	Prov. 16:3: Commit to the Lord whatever you do, and he will establish your plans.
Commitment to the growth of people	Belief that people have intrinsic value beyond their tangible contributions as workers.	Prov. 22:6: Start children off on the way they should go, and even when they are old they will not turn from it.
Building Community	Ability to identify some means for building community among those who work within an institution.	Prov. 27:17: As iron sharpens iron, so one person sharpens another.

TABLE 3.1: 10 Characteristics of Servant Leadership

Later research reduced these ten characteristics to seven dimensions. The final dimensions include *emotional healing*, or being sensitive to the personal setbacks of followers, *creating value for the community*, such as encouraging followers to engage in beneficial activities in the community, *conceptual skills*, or the problem solving and task knowledge that helps followers, *empowering, helping subordinates grow and succeed, putting subordinates first, and behaving ethically.*[27]

27. R. C. Liden, S. J. Wayne, J. D. Meuser, J. Hu, J. Wu, and C. Liao, "Servant Leadership: Validation of a Short Form of the SL-28," *The Leadership Quarterly* 26 (2015): 254–69.

Servant leaders see themselves as stewards of organizations[28] who seek to grow the resources, financial and otherwise, that have been entrusted to them.

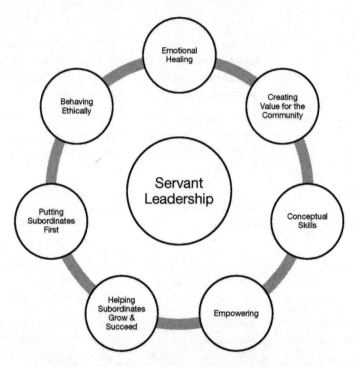

FIGURE 3.1: 7 Dimensions of Servant Leadership

By the end of Proverbs, wisdom, personified as the Noble Woman, captures all ten of the original servant leader characteristics as she works on behalf of her husband. She is serving him, her family, and her household with all the works of her hands. Proverbs 31:11–12 says that he trusts in her and has no lack of gain as she does him good and not harm all the days of her life. We see her empathy reflected in her care for the poor and the needy (v. 20). Her strength in verse 17 connotes physical health. She provides tasks for her maids (v. 15) and teaches/conceptualizes kindness (v. 26). She has foresight in her care for her household (v. 27) and stewards her husband's resources as she considers and buys land (v. 16). Her commitment to others is evident in her care for her servants and family, even working through the night (v. 18). Finally, all those immediately around her, her husband and children, rise up and call her

---

28. D. van Dierendonck, "Servant Leadership: A Review and Synthesis," *Journal of Management* 37 (2011): 1228–61.

blessed or happy (v. 28). In the New Testament, Jesus Christ himself becomes the power and wisdom of God.[29] Jesus sets an example similar to Proverbs 31:10–31 to demonstrate for us the picture of a servant leader.

Jesus's Example of Servant Leadership

There is a link in the writings of David in Psalms between kingship and servanthood that leads up to the prophetic foretelling of the Messiah's arrival in Isaiah. In Psalm 89:3–4, David references the words the Lord spoke to Nathan the prophet before the Lord made his covenant with David. Rather than referring to David as the king he established on the throne of Israel for all generations, the passage reads: "'I have made a covenant with my chosen one, I have sworn to my servant David: 'I will establish your descendants forever, and build your throne for all generations.'"

This theme of servant kingship begins in the historical books of the Old Testament in 2 Samuel 7:8–16 and continues into the Psalms and on into the major and minor prophets. Throughout the Old Testament, kingship is discussed in the context of servanthood. Psalm 119 is a beautiful meditation on the law of God (Torah) and an example of the attitude of David as the servant of God rather than as the appointed king. David does not refer to himself once in the passage as king, but calls himself God's servant over a dozen times, closing the passage in Psalm 119:176 with, "I have gone astray like a lost sheep; seek out your servant, for I do not forget your commandments." This theme continues from Psalms to Isaiah.

The first half of Isaiah focuses on the evil kings of Assyria and Egypt compared to the righteous king prophesied to come in Isaiah 32. From Isaiah 32–44, it becomes clear that the king in which Israel should put their hope is the Lord himself, the God and King of Israel. However, in Isaiah 42–53, the language of kingship shifts into servanthood. Recognized by biblical scholars as the Servant Songs,[30] Isaiah 42:1–4; 49:1–6; 50:4–7; and 52:13–53:12 all describe the coming Messiah as a suffering servant, compared to Israel the rebellious servant. The kingly redemption and salvation of Israel shifts to rest on a servant who will suffer. The ministering servant in Isaiah, who foreshadows the Messiah, is obedient, sensitive, and suffers unjustly on behalf of others to restore divine order to the world. Isaiah 42:1 (ESV) describes this servant chosen by God: "Behold my servant, whom I uphold, my chosen, in whom

---

29. 1 Corinthians 1:18–2:16.
30. J. G. McConville, *A Guide the Prophets* (Downers Grover, IL: InterVarsity Press, 2008), 28.

my soul delights. I have put my Spirit upon him; he will bring forth justice to the nations."

Generations later, these words are echoed at the baptism of Jesus captured in Matthew 17:5 and at the transfiguration of Jesus captured in Luke 9:35. In each passage, a voice comes down from heaven to proclaim over Jesus, "This is my Son, the Beloved, with him I am well pleased; listen to him" and "This is my Son, my Chosen; listen to him!" When the disciples heard these words, they may have remembered the coming of the chosen one in Isaiah 42:1—"Here is my servant, whom I uphold, my chosen, in whom my soul delights." In most Bibles, Luke and Matthew both reference the passage in Isaiah. In the Gospels, however, the word *servant* is transposed for the word *son*. Jesus hints at his role as suffering servant throughout the Gospels, but perhaps demonstrates it most clearly in the narrative captured by his disciple John.

Jesus Washes the Disciples' Feet

Jesus knew that the Father had put all things under his power, and that he had come from God and was returning to God; so he got up from the meal, took off his outer clothing, and wrapped a towel around his waist. After that, he poured water into a basin and began to wash his disciples' feet, drying them with the towel that was wrapped around him.

He came to Simon Peter, who said to him, "Lord, are you going to wash my feet?" Jesus replied, "You do not realize now what I am doing, but later you will understand." "No," said Peter, "you shall never wash my feet." Jesus answered, "Unless I wash you, you have no part with me." "Then, Lord," Simon Peter replied, "not just my feet but my hands and my head as well!" Jesus answered, "Those who have had a bath need only to wash their feet; their whole body is clean. And you are clean, though not every one of you." For he knew who was going to betray him, and that was why he said not every one was clean. When he had finished washing their feet, he put on his clothes and returned to his place. "Do you understand what I have done for you?" he asked them. "You call me 'Teacher' and 'Lord,' and rightly so, for that is what I am. Now that I, your Lord and Teacher, have washed your feet, you also should wash one another's feet. I have set you an example that you should do as I have done for you. Very truly I tell you, no servant is greater than his master, nor is a messenger greater than the one who sent him. Now that you know these things, you will be blessed if you do them. "I am not referring to all of you; I know those I have chosen. But this is to fulfill this passage of Scripture: 'He who shared my bread has turned against me.' "I am telling you now before it happens, so that when it does happen you will believe that I am who I am. Very truly I tell you, whoever accepts anyone I send accepts me; and whoever accepts me accepts the one who sent me." (John 13:3–20)

A New Commandment

A new command I give you: Love one another. *As I have loved you*, so you must love one another. By this everyone will know that you are my disciples, if you love one another.

—*John 13:34–35, emphasis mine*

Through the washing of his disciples' feet, Jesus demonstrates in action what it looks like for a leader to be a servant first to those who follow. Even in that day, it was awkward for the disciples to have their leader washing their feet. Peter tried to reverse the order and serve Jesus their leader, but Jesus was firm that they could have no part in him if they did not receive his service to them. Then he tells them to go and do likewise. The passage closes with a new commandment. This commandment shifts the Levitical commandment from "love your neighbor as you love yourself" to "love each other as Jesus loves you." In this way, our love becomes not a reflection of ourselves, but a reflection of our leader, who demonstrated servanthood in foot washing and ultimately on the cross.

Jesus exemplifies Spears' definition of servant leadership. Jesus sets an example of servant leadership through his discipleship and constant training and *growing* of his disciples. He *listened* to their debates and answered their questions. He *empathized* with the disciples and his other followers, *meeting their needs* both physically and spiritually. He is *healing* personified both in his life and in his death. Multiple times in the Gospels, Jesus healed *all* who were sick.[31] He led the disciples in *awareness* of themselves and a slow revelation of who he was. He *conceptualized* the kingdom of heaven and *prophesied* about the kingdom come and the kingdom to come. Upon Jesus's death and resurrection, the kingdom had already come and was yet still coming. He committed all of his life to God the Father and was obedient, even to death on the cross, as a true *steward* of all God had entrusted him to do. His followers became a *community* of Christians that continued through his life, death, and resurrection even until now. More than anyone else in history, Jesus was the perfect servant leader. Further, he called the disciples and future believers to follow his example and love others with obedience and humility, even suffering on behalf of others.

---

31. Matthew 8:16; 19:2; Luke 4:40; 6:19.

Twenty Years of Servant Leadership Research

A quick search of electronic databases of peer-reviewed academic journals reveals over 400 articles written on servant leadership in the last twenty years (1999–2019), with 100 articles published in the last four years alone.[32] In the past twenty years, more than 156 empirical studies of servant leadership have been conducted across thirty-nine countries, with the majority (44%) coming from North America (N=64) and China (N=25). As servant leadership has evolved as a concept, it has competed with other leadership models, such as transformational leadership, authentic leadership, and ethical leadership. However, servant leadership is unique in its focus on followers as an end goal, its propensity for self-awareness and others-awareness, and the tie between servant leadership and the concept of stewardship.[33] Spears viewed stewardship (the willingness to take responsibility on behalf of another) as a distinct component of servanthood.[34] As stewards of God's creation, the marketplace is one arena of many where Christians have an opportunity to be fruitful and multiply good work.

Unique to the concept of servant leadership is the antecedent of compassionate love. While love seems like an odd overlay for business practices, it is foundational to others-oriented leadership. The concept of love is dominant in the language of organizations like The Container Store. Greenleaf wrote that love is central to servant leadership, that love is indefinable, yet it has infinite manifestations.[35] Compassionate love is "an attitude toward others, either close others or strangers or all of humanity; containing feelings, cognitions, and behaviors that are focused on caring, concern, tenderness, and an orientation toward supporting, helping, and understanding the others, particularly when others are perceived to be suffering or in need."[36]

This others-oriented love defined as compassionate love captures the essence of Jesus's new commandment in John 13:34. Compassionate love is an essential component of servant leadership and of wisdom. Definitions of wisdom in the *Journal of Business Ethics* are directly linked to servant leadership and love.[37] Thus, servant leaders have a unique set of priorities; unlike other leaders,

---

32. Eva et al., "Servant Leadership," 111–32.
33. van Dierendonck, "Servant Leadership," 1228–61.
34. van Dierendonck, "Servant Leadership," 1234.
35. Greenleaf, *Servant Leadership*, 75.
36. S. Sprecher and B. Fehr, "Compassionate Love for Close Others and Humanity," *Journal of Social and Personal Relationships* 22, no. 5 (2005): 629–51.
37. D. van Dierendonck and Kathleen Patterson, "Compassionate Love as Cornerstone of Servant Leadership: An Integration of Previous Theorizing and Research," *Journal of Business Ethics* 128 (2015): 119–31.

they tend to focus on others first, organizations second, and themselves last.[38] Outcomes of servant leadership in business research have been explored in terms of follower outcomes, organizational outcomes, and leader-related outcomes.

Follower Outcomes of Servant Leadership

Nathan Eva et al. provide an in-depth systematic review of servant leadership research in *Leadership Quarterly*.[39] Eva et al. categorize follower outcomes as behavioral and attitudinal. As of 2019, over thirty research projects have explored behavioral outcomes of servant leadership, including organizational citizenship, helping, and proactive behaviors. Further, servant leadership reduces leadership avoidance and deviant behavior. The impact of servant leadership on individual behavior is augmented by leader-follower relationship development/exchange (LMX), trust, communication, lack of fear, employee self-identity and self-efficacy, psychological capital, positive organizational climate, team cohesion, satisfaction, engagement, and commitment. Of the three dozen articles exploring attitudinal outcomes, employee engagement, job satisfaction, thriving, reduced turnover, work-family balance, and organization commitment were dominant outcomes. These were increased by empowerment, access to resources, justice, and the fit of the employee for the organization.

In 2010, management professors at Arizona State University conducted a research study collecting data from 815 employees and 123 immediate supervisors in seven multinational companies operating in Kenya exploring the impact of servant leadership on follower behavior.[40] The 815 employees completed the servant leadership survey items about their work group supervisor, including statements like "My work group supervisor spends the time to form quality relationships with employees." They rated statements about confidence to do the job (self-efficacy), emotional attachment to their supervisor (commitment to leader), consistency of procedures (procedural justice climate), and organizational support of superior work and service (service climate).[41] The findings indicated that servant leadership directly affects individual outcomes in the workplace. Servant leadership boosts the confidence of followers to do their jobs well and increases their sense of commitment to their leader. In addition, servant leadership affects employees' sense of justice and service,

38. S. Sendjaya, *Personal and Organizational Excellence through Servant Leadership: Learning to Serve, Serving to Lead, Leading to Transform* (Switzerland: Springer, 2015), 114.

39. Eva et al., "Servant Leadership," 111–32.

40. F. O. Walumbwa, C. A. Hartnell, and A. Oke, "Servant Leadership, Procedural Justice Climate, Service Climate, Employee Attitudes, and Organizational Citizenship Behavior: A Cross-Level Investigation," *Journal of Applied Psychology* 95 (2010): 517–29.

41. Walumbwa, Hartnell, and Oke, "Servant Leadership," 522.

which increases citizenship behavior in the organization. Organizational citizenship behavior is defined as "discretionary behavior that is not recognized by the formal reward system and promotes the effective functioning of the organization."[42]

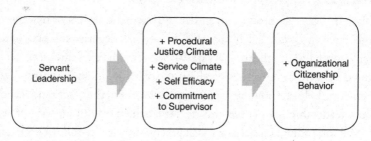

FIGURE 3.2: Servant Leadership and
Follower Behavior Research

In 2014, a group of management researchers[43] from the University of London and Monash University in Australia explored the impact of servant leadership on employee attitudes and organizational citizenship behaviors. They explored the attitudes and motivation of 446 employees to perform tasks in a large Chinese state-owned enterprise through matched surveys (supervisor and subordinate). The Chinese SOE has more than 90,000 employees, generating 80+ billion-yuan revenue/year (about $11.5 billion US dollars). They measured servant leadership, leader member exchange (LMX), psychological empowerment, proactive personality, and organizational citizenship behavior. Followers with a proactive personality felt more empowered than less proactive followers. Empowerment includes the competence, self-determination, and impact of an individual's intrinsic motivation to perform work tasks. Servant leadership was found to lead to greater feelings of empowerment in followers, but LMX had the greatest impact on organizational citizenship behavior. This research demonstrates that servant leadership is effective in fostering citizenship behavior through high-quality leader relationships and empowerment. Thus, interpersonal relationships are globally essential to the positive organizational citizenship behaviors motivated by servant leadership.

---

42. D. W. Organ, *Organizational Citizenship Behavior: The Good Soldier Syndrome* (Lexington, MA: Lexington, 1988), 4.

43. A. Newman, G. Schwarz, B. Cooper, S. Sendjaya, "How Servant Leadership Influences Organizational Citizenship Behavior: The Roles of lmx, Empowerment, and Proactive Personality," *Journal of Business Ethics* 145 (2017): 49–62.

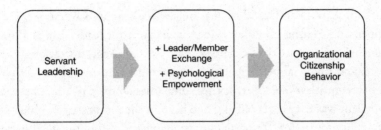

FIGURE 3.3: Servant Leadership & Follower Attitude Research

Organizational Performance Outcomes of Servant Leadership

Organizational outcomes, such as social impact and profitability, are much less explored in servant leadership research. Individual outcomes, such as organizational commitment, creativity, and service performance, have all been explored in multiple organizational contexts and cultures. However, another research study conducted across 154 teams in Chinese and Indonesian companies by the faculty at Monash University[44] demonstrated the impact of servant leadership on team innovation. Leaders who embody the norms, values, and beliefs of a team or group of people are prototypical of the group. Servant leaders will have a higher level of prototypicality because they have the best interest of the team at heart above their own self-interest. Leaders who embrace and reflect the norms, values, and beliefs of a group of people will create an atmosphere of empowerment that is important for self-efficacy (an individual's confidence in their abilities). Empowerment and self-efficacy are essential for innovation. This research demonstrates that managers who build connections with employees will increase the level of innovation their employees can contribute as a group.

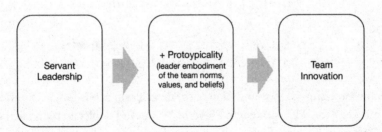

FIGURE 3.4: Organizational Performance Outcomes

---

44. D. T. Yoshida, S. Sendjaya, G. Hirst, and B. Cooper, "Does Servant Leadership Foster Creativity and Innovation? A Multi-Level Mediation Study of Identification and Prototypicality," *Journal of Business Research* 67 (2014): 1395–1404.

The research conducted by my logistics colleagues Overstreet, Hazen, Skipper, and Hanna provided evidence that servant leadership is a unique leadership style that drives organizational commitment, operational performance, and financial performance in many organizations.[45] Rob Overstreet and his team surveyed 158 trucking companies across the US. The average respondent was fifty years old and had been in the motor carrier industry for over twenty-four years. The trucking companies surveyed included national, regional, and international companies of many sizes with a range of truck fleets from 102 to 16,216 trucks. While the size of the company had a direct impact on the company's performance (better performing firms tend to be larger), servant leadership had a similar impact on employees of companies of every size.

This is an interesting finding in the trucking/logistics industry. The logistics industry tends to draw from military logistics practices, and a servant leadership style could prove somewhat counter cultural. However, servant leadership was found to be a plausible style of leadership to motivate commitment and operational performance in employees. Thus, servant leadership does not just build employee commitment and organizational citizenship, it also boosts the bottom line.

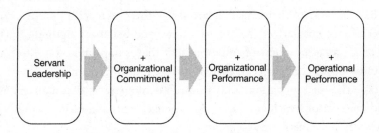

FIGURE 3.5: Company Performance

Servant Leadership as a Means to the End Goal of Wisdom

Servant leadership is the foundation of the description of wisdom personified in the marketplace. The passages in Proverbs 3–9 and 31 depict an individual who lives to better the lives of others. Those who find wisdom have an income that is better than silver and revenue better than gold.[46] Wisdom provides long life to those who find her and creates happy followers. Wisdom calls out in Proverbs

---

45. Overstreet et al., "Bridging the Gap between Strategy and Performance," 136–49.
46. Proverbs 3:14.

8:4–36 and reflects all the elements of servant leadership: wisdom empowers, heals and gives life, creates value, promotes justice and ethics, attains knowledge, promotes subordinates in favor with God, and grows all who follow. The seven elements of servant leadership are demonstrated in wisdom throughout Proverbs and accumulate in Proverbs 31:10–31. The key to servant leadership is our view of subordination and how we put subordinates first and help them grow.

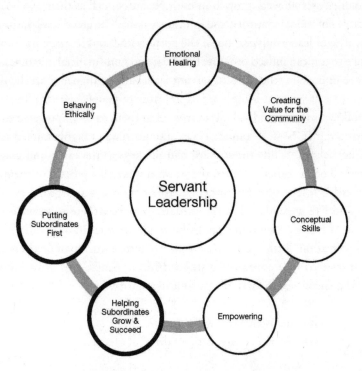

FIGURE 3.6: 7 Dimensions of Servant Leadership—Subordinates

In 1 Peter 2:18–25 and 3:1–22, the word ὑποτάσσω (*hupotassō*) is often translated as "submission," however, *hupotassō* is a Greek military term for "subordination."[47] Peter encourages believers, whether slaves or wives, to be subordinate to leaders, the authorities in their Greco-Roman society. However, he further encourages all believers to have unity of spirit, sympathy, love for one another, and a humble mind. Peter then quotes a passage of wisdom from Psalm 34:12–16 and encourages the believers to be wise and to pursue good,

---

47. Gene L. Green, *Jude and 2 Peter,* Baker Exegetical Commentary on the New Testament (Grand Rapids: Baker Academic, 2008), 260.

peace, and righteousness. Since we have been given authority and leadership as Christians, we should be like Christ. Christ, through his own righteousness, put us first, helped us grow, healed us, created a community, gave us knowledge, and empowers us to take up his authority and be like him.

Contrary to other leadership approaches that are focused on advancing the company's bottom line in both financial or non-financial outcomes, servant leadership focuses on followers' growth in multiple areas, such as their psychological wellbeing, emotional maturity, and ethical wisdom. The great news is, the result of this style of leadership *does* boost the bottom line, and research has provided evidence that it can indeed promote financial and non-financial outcomes.

More important, the focus of servant leadership is aligned with the notion of stewardship. Servant leaders act as stewards of people. Servant leaders put their followers first as individuals entrusted to them to be empowered to grow and succeed.[48] In New Testament times, a steward was a highly ranked servant in the household. While the steward had the keys to the castle and may have directed all of the other servants, the steward was still a servant to the master. A steward is responsible for someone else's employees and property. When Adam and Eve were placed in the garden, they were there to steward God's creation. When we are given responsibility in our roles in our work, it is not our own creation. Rather we carry on the Eden stewardship of God's creation. Servant leadership is a means—a stewardship of people—to grow followers, teach, and encourage them in the pursuit of security.

> Those who listen to me will be secure
> and will live at ease, without dread of disaster.
>
> —*Proverbs 1:33*

Reflection Questions

1. How would you define servant leadership? How do you impact the people who follow you?
2. What biblical support do you perceive for servant leadership (provide Scripture references)?
3. Can you think of examples of companies other than The Container Store that have leaders who put their employees first?
   a. What is the culture of their company like? What are their employees like?

---

48. Eva et al., "Servant Leadership," 114.

CHAPTER 4

THE ORIENTATIONS
OF WISDOM

All a person's ways seem pure to them,
   but motives are weighed by the LORD.
Commit to the LORD whatever you do,
   and he will establish your plans.

   —*Proverbs 16:2–3 (NIV)*

Our goal is to be one of the world's top 10 dairy enterprises by 2015.
We have made much progress but have much further to go.

   —*President Pan Gang, Yili Group,*
   HBR Case[1]

In China, a nation without a history of dairy consumption compared to Western markets, Yili Group overcame incredible odds to achieve the goals of president Pan Gang to become one of the world's top ten dairy enterprises. The long-term goal of the Yili Group was to build on their success as the top dairy enterprise in China to become the "most trusted health-food provider around the world."[2] In order to achieve this goal, they needed to develop core values that would enable the execution of their strategy. The Yili Group not only wanted to have a high-quality product, but they also wanted to create an international comparative advantage over long-standing dairy companies.

---

1. Regina M. Abrami, William C. Kirby, F. Warren McFarlan, and Tracy Yuen Manty, "Inner Mongolia Yili Group: China's Pioneering Dairy Brand," *Harvard Business School Case* 308–052, January 2008, revised December 2011, 1, https://hbsp.harvard.edu/product/308052-PDF-ENG.
2. William C. Kirby and Nancy Hua Dai, "Yili Group: Building a Global Dairy Company," *Harvard Business Review*, October 25, 2016, *https://store.hbr.org/product/yili-group-building-a-global-dairy-company/317003.*

In 2008, an article in the *China Daily* newspaper read, "Melamine found in more milk."[3] The article reported that 1,250 infants died of kidney failure due to melamine contamination in baby formula produced by dairy competitor Sanlu. However, the epidemic of melamine additives to milk products wasn't limited to baby formula alone. Traces of melamine were also found in the milk products of Yili Group in both ice cream and milk samples. As dairy farmers and suppliers to the Sanlu organization were arrested and imprisoned, they rationalized their choice as an attempt to raise the protein content of the milk. Sanlu's actions impacted buyers throughout their supply chain. New Zealand company Frontera had a 43 percent stake in Sanlu and ultimately reported the event after Sanlu refused to enact a recall during the 2008 Beijing Olympics. With Chinese consumer confidence in Chinese produced milk at an all-time low, Yili had a strategic opportunity to act fast and gain the trustworthy milk brand narrative. The Chinese dairy industry was in need of "quality enhancement to rebuild consumer confidence, market orientation, vertical integration, and international cooperation."[4]

President Pan Gang had only been in leadership of the Yili Group for three years when the melamine scandal occurred. While a relatively young CEO at the age of thirty-eight, he was well connected with the Chinese People's Party. Pan also served in multiple other government organizations, including a short tenure as the president of the China Youth Entrepreneurs Association. During that time, China shifted from state-owned enterprises to shareholding enterprises. From 2006 to 2011, Pan led the Yili Group to become a national leader, and by 2010, they were one of the top twenty dairy companies in the world.

The path to Yili's emergence as a dairy industry leader was due to Pan's strategy to create brand differentiation through sponsorship of the 2008 Olympics and Chinese athlete endorsements that established Yili as a high-quality product. Pan extended this strategy to develop national market coverage, with high-quality suppliers and a national logistics and distribution system. Yili had a market orientation that included a deep understanding of consumers' needs in the face of a national dairy crisis. He then pursued quality and supply chain strategies that would enable the market share of the Yili Group to grow while maximizing profitability. Yili worked closely with suppliers and distributors in the 2008 crisis and accepted returned products at a loss in order to build longer-term partnerships with upstream dairy farm and distribution suppliers and downstream retail and distribution customers. Yili invested in developing

---

3. Zhe Zhu and Louise Ho, "Melamine Found in More Milk," *China Daily*, September 9, 2008, http://www.chinadaily.com.cn/china/2008-09/17/content_7032353.htm.

4. Kirby and Hua Dai, "Yili Group."

suppliers by launching a dairy school to help dairy farmers improve their quality control and systems efficiency.

Yili's sourcing and quality strategies paid off. By 2015, Yili became a top ten global dairy company, earning revenues around $9.7 billion with net profits around $747 million. Yili's sourcing and quality strategies were scalable to the international market, and Yili moved into global sourcing. Yili built out its international strategy by partnering with international universities such as the Wageningen University in the Netherlands, Lincoln University in New Zealand, and the Wharton School and Cornell University in the US. Yili leaned into these university partnerships to develop research and development (R&D) for dairy products. Further, Yili partnered with the Wharton School on a research project to develop talent for business innovation.

The Yili group recognized the importance of innovation for remaining competitive. Pan Gang stated in a talk,

> No innovation, no future.
>
> Through cooperation with the world's top institutions in innovation, we will continuously develop innovative products to serve the Chinese market.
>
> This is Yili's unique "reverse innovation."[5]

Through a commitment to their quality and sourcing strategies, the Yili Group was able to become innovators in China, setting industry standards through their dairy research institute. Innovation became a driver of Yili's development. By 2019, Yili grew to $27.9 billion in revenue and was listed as one of the world's best employers in 2018. Yili Group was also noted as one of the most innovative companies in the world in 2014, though it dropped off in 2015. As Yili gained global market share, the Yili Group established Innovation Centers in Europe and New Zealand with their academic partners.

The *Harvard Business Review* cases published in 2011 and 2016 demonstrate how innovation and a clear strategy propelled Yili Group to international leadership. Yili's investment in R&D and customer relationships helped them develop new products. The strategies the Yili Group developed from 2005 to 2019 were largely based on the R&D conducted by their innovation centers. Over the years, Yili expanded its focus beyond quality and sourcing to include stakeholder development, long-term investment in R&D, and sustainability. In 2007, President Pan acknowledged the importance of integrating sustainability into the corporate strategy:

---

5. Kirby and Hua Dai, "Yili Group."

As a leader in the industry, we have an obligation to help the development of the industry. In the past few years, there were a lot of price wars, advertising wars ... that really hurt the industry. This is not a healthy situation. I think for dairy we need to be cooler in our thinking and focus more on management. Since 2005 Yili decided to make our foundation solid and raise its management skills. We are not trying to grow fast blindly, chasing volumes and scale. We are focusing on "Green" production and brand development with environmental protection. We want to make sure all parties-farmers, government, and consumers work together because we all have a stake in this. Recently, the government issued eight guidelines for the industry that skewed the policy toward large companies to make them more efficient and to protect the interest of the farmers. These have been tenets that Yili has promoted and we believe we are obliged to follow, to build a more healthy and sustainable dairy industry in China.[6]

In business literature, the underlying strategies held by a firm that influence its tactical decisions are called orientations. Firms tend to have multiple strategies in play at all times. President Pan started out with two guiding strategies: build brand and quality perceptions, and develop the Yili Group's supply chain partnership through sourcing and customer relationships. As the Yili Group gained market advantages through the quality control of its products, which boosted its brand reputation, it also gained better control over its supply chain and sourcing opportunities. As firms become more efficient and effective, there is a natural progression from a total cost perspective to a customer-value market orientation.[7] For most firms, a combined orientation that focuses on supply chain management, markets, and customers provides superior customer value.

The Yili Group is just one corporate example of an organization that adopted multiple orientations. When the Yili Group emerged as a world leader in the dairy industry, it adopted a more proactive stakeholder orientation as it engaged suppliers in dairy training and university partners in R&D and product innovation. By creating corporate tactics that achieved its quality, supply chain, and stakeholder strategies, the Yili Group became the largest dairy company in the world.[8] As the Yili Group looked to longer-term strategies, it incorporated sustainability initiatives that built on its partnerships to achieve environmental protection and green product and brand development. Quality and supply chain orientations may have preceded the Yili Group's other strategies, but by the time the Yili Group gained a comparative advantage over

---

6. Abrami et al., "Inner Mongolia Yili Group."
7. Minn, Metzer, and Ladd, "Market Orientation."
8. Kirby and Hua Dai, "Yili Group."

most of its competition, it had adopted and integrated multiple stakeholders, sustainable initiatives, and a longer-term orientation into its strategic outlook. The orientations that made the Yili Group successful are the same strategies that enable many other companies to become world leaders.

A 2015 *Harvard Business Review* article on corporate strategy acknowledged the plethora of strategies available to business leaders. The authors recommend a strategy palette that can be matched to specific parts of the business over time.[9] Regardless of a leader's approach to corporate strategy, it is clear that strategy and the orientation or philosophy of the firm will drive the tactics that get implemented in the marketplace. A single orientation will not be sufficient for a firm to achieve the outcomes of profitability, reputation, comparative advantage, and a long-term kingdom impact. Yili's journey details the adoption of multiple strategies as it grew.

Our Belief: "Yili" Represents the Highest Quality.

Quality is as precious as life itself (based on the highest principles).

Quality represents 100 percent devotion, 100 percent attention to safety, 100 percent health-enhancing dedication (reflecting the most stringent standards).

Everyone is a creator of quality (demonstrating the finest behavior).

Our Vision: Becoming the Most Trusted Health-Food Provider Around the World.

Delivering the finest products and services to the world.

Advocating a healthy lifestyle for the benefit of everyone.

Leading the industry's development on the world stage.

Fulfilling social responsibilities, with diligence and devotion.

Our Core Values: Excellence, Accountability, Innovation, Win-Win

Excellence: Exceeding expectations continuously.

Accountability: Wholeheartedly embracing responsibility.

Innovation: Inventing and progressing each and every day.

Win-Win: Progressing hand in hand for collective strength and superior results.

---

9. Martin Reeves, Knut Haanaes, and Janmejaya Sinha, "Navigating the Dozens of Different Strategy Options," *Harvard Business Review*, June 24, 2015, https://store.hbr.org/product/navigating-the-dozens-of-different-strategy-options/H025UU.

> **The Spirit of Yili**
>
> With a strong ownership mindset, Yili people molded its unique core competitive advantages, including a spirit of accountability, outstanding execution capabilities, and exceptional qualities in the pursuit of excellence.
>
> Be loyal, trustworthy, grateful, and value emotions.
> Be courageous in meeting challenges, diligent in overcoming them.
> Be extremely disciplined, highly efficient in execution.
> Be vigilant, ever-innovative.
> Be self-disciplined and self-reflective, fostering a virtuous atmosphere.[10]

The Path: How a Firm Orients Its Path to Find the Way to Reach Its Vision

It is essential that firms have a vision. Management schools teach that vision is the starting place of a firm's mission, strategy, and tactics. Yili president Pan Gang had a vision of Yili Group becoming one of the top ten dairy providers in the world. In order to achieve that vision, Yili Group needed a plan to get there. Companies are faced with a lot of different ways of achieving their goals. The vision of the firm is shaped by the orientation of the firm's leaders and objectives that they most value.

Building on the orientation literature reviewed in this chapter, an orientation is defined here as an underlying philosophy or strategy held by all members of the organization that influences and flavors their strategic and tactical decisions and actions for continuous superior performance. From a means-end standpoint, the orientation defines the end goals of the organization and the means required to attain each end goal. The underlying philosophy of the firm will direct the necessary consequences/outcomes and performance measures that will drive the achievement of organizational goals. End goals capture the outcomes of the philosophy of the firm that impact organizational priorities. Different business orientations are the result of varying perspectives of organizational priorities, such as how the customer is viewed and how the firm defines its reason for being in business. Writers on business strategy, such as

---

10. "Spirit of Yili," cited from Yili.com, accessed May 10, 2020, http://www.yili.com/en/rest /reception/articles/list?categoryId=36. Also available at https://image.yili.com/upload/usrFiles/2016 1028193728515.pdf.

Reeves, Haanaes, and Sinha,[11] have long recognized the paramount importance of strategic business orientation for business development, innovation, and strategic success.

I have had the opportunity to observe the emergence of the strategic orientations of the Yili Group and the Chinese dairy industry from a distance over the past twenty years. This makes Yili Group an interesting case example for me personally. As a Chinese language student at the Beijing Language and Culture University (北京 语言 大学), I had the opportunity to travel to many towns and cities around Beijing. It has been a long time since my undergraduate days; pre-Beijing Olympics and pre-2008 financial crisis. I was in China during the heyday of the economic reforms. The dot-com bubble had burst, and Asia was just coming out of its own financial crisis of the late 1990s. American manufacturing was shifting to China, a shift that has cost the US 3.2 million manufacturing jobs since 2001. As an international political economics and Mandarin major with a minor in Asian studies at Carthage College, I was particularly interested in the economic development of China and the industries that were observably booming. It was clear that construction was booming. It was also apparent that foreign investment was increasing. Even in the early 2000s, there were new Starbucks stores everywhere, and Western brands were fairly easy to find.

Toward the end of my semester at BLCU, I spent a long weekend in Inner Mongolia. Several classmates and I took a train from Beijing to Hohhot, China. At that time, Hohhot, the capital city of Inner Mongolia, was a far cry from the bustling modernization of Beijing. We spent a few days in the city and then ventured out of Hohhot for a very touristy excursion into Nèi měng gǔ (the Mandarin pinyin name for Inner Mongolia). I rode horses across the Hulunbuir grasslands for several days before we swapped them for camels and ventured into the Gobi Desert. I saw a lot of horses, camels, and even goats, but I don't remember seeing a single cow. I saw even fewer dairy products in the markets, university cafeterias, and restaurants. Lactose intolerant myself, I was happy to be a culinary tourist in a nation with a predominant predisposition against lactose. Little did I know that throughout the 1990s China was poised to become the most dynamic sector in the global dairy market. In 2017, China was second only to the US in output and is projected to pass the US in 2022. The growth of the dairy industry in China was in part due to the orientation of dairy companies in response to changes in the Chinese and international marketplace.

---

11. Reeves, Haanaes, and Sinha, "Navigating the Dozens of Different Strategy Options."

In 2008, when the dairy industry took a huge hit from the melamine scandal, the first orientation that became paramount in the dairy industry was quality. Once the Chinese government started to promote milk as a healthy dietary product, the Chinese dairy industry had bigger challenges to face than lactose intolerance. The strategic quality orientation of the Yili Group came in response to government regulations cracking down on illegal producers and enforcing new regulations to better ensure the safety and quality of domestic dairy products in China. As the Yili Group grew, its orientations needed to expand to encompass a larger customer and supplier base with a much larger global footprint impacting multiple environmental ecosystems (literally involving cows and pastures) and local communities. Management literature has explored strategic orientations and has found that over time, strategic orientations drive innovation and performance.[12]

The Role of Wisdom in the Philosophy of the Firm: Strategic Orientation

I stayed in your presence, you grasped me by the right hand;
You will guide me with advice, and will draw me in the wake of
    your glory.
Who else is there for me in heaven? And, with you, I lack nothing
    on earth.[13]

Biblical scholar Walter Brueggemann classifies an entire genre of wisdom psalms as "Psalms of Orientation."[14] Psalms of Orientation speak of creation, wisdom, and the favor of God. Just as David as leader of Israel oriented himself toward God, we as Christians in business are called to continuously orient ourselves toward a Maker we know and to whom we belong. Out of this orientation toward God, we find an understanding of the kingdom of heaven (our new creation), practical wisdom, and a right relationship with God that guides us in our deliberations. Practical wisdom is the intellectual virtue of reasoning. It is the ability of an individual to reason and act with regard to the things that are good or bad for people. Called *phronesis* in its original Greek, practical wisdom was defined by Aristotle as a means for

12. Hubert Gatignon and Jean-Marc Xuereb, "Strategic Orientation," *Journal of Marketing Research* (February 1997): 77–90.

13. Psalm 73:23–25 New Jerusalem Bible.

14. Walter Brueggemann, *Praying the Psalms: Engaging Scripture and the Life of the Spirit* (Eugene, OR: Wipf & Stock, 2007).

deliberating as to what a good end is, identifying the right means, and doing so in a timely way.[15]

The end goal of Wisdom Literature in the Hebrew Scripture, the Old Testament of the Bible, was to honor others and to honor God, to *yare* ("be in awe of or fear") God. Love of God and love for others ultimately fulfill the great commandment. An application of the practical wisdom of the Old Testament identifies the end goal of loving and fearing God and demonstrates the means to achieving that end goal in all aspects of life. The practical wisdom of Wisdom Literature features the virtues of righteousness and the actions that follow (the duties we are called to conduct—for example, fear God, love others, give to the poor, work diligently, and more). The straight course of the righteous presented in Proverbs defines wisdom in terms of ethics. The writers of Proverbs encourage the reader to turn aside from evil and keep to the straight path of humility, justice, and mercy that reflects a love of God and others. The end goal of the way of the wise is to guard closely all paths that allow people to love God and others.

In business, if superior performance is the end goal, the firm must decide the *ways* it will adopt to achieve that end goal (the strategies). An overarching business philosophy may be to achieve long-term/kingdom impact by loving others and loving God. ServiceMaster provides a great case example of an end goal of service to God and others. This business orientation (philosophy of the firm) will inform the strategies and tactical outworking of the firm. Business ethics literature draws from philosophy to understand the compass that should guide the decision science of the firm.

Within the discipline of ethics, moral theories guide our choices of what we ought to do (deontic theories). Deontology, *deon* (duty) and *logos* (science or study of), literally means the "study of duty." Other moral theories guide what kind of person we should be (such as virtue theory). The three main classical moral theories in the Western tradition conceptualize wisdom uniquely across the lenses of the pragmatic wisdom virtue in virtue theory,[16] relational wisdom in deontological theory,[17] and outcomes-based wisdom as a utility in the utilitarian theory.[18]

In my research, reading, and experience, I have found that Christian business leaders have a general understanding of what kind of person a Christian

---

15. Aristotle, *Nicomachean Ethics: On Practical Wisdom*, book VI.5, 1140a-b.

16. Aristotle, *Nicomachean Ethics*, book VI.5, 1140a-b.

17. Immanuel Kant, *Groundwork of the Metaphysic of Morals*, trans. H. J. Paton (New York: Harper and Row, 1964).

18. John Stuart Mill, *The Collected Works of John Stuart Mill*, ed. John M. Robson (Toronto: University of Toronto Press; London: Routledge and Kegan Paul, 1963–91).

should be. Maybe their views would echo Aristotle's categories of virtues: courage (bravery), temperance (self-control), liberality (charity), magnificence (radiance), pride (self-satisfaction), honor (respect), good temper (level-headedness), friendliness (sociability), truthfulness (candor), wit (humor), friendship (companionship), and justice (fairness). The four cardinal virtues that were eventually adopted by Plato across virtue ethics included wisdom (phronesis), courage, temperance, and justice.[19]

However, these virtues do not necessarily inform what a person should do and how their decisions should be guided in business. According to the *Stanford Encyclopedia of Philosophy*, the number-one objection to virtue ethics is that they are more concerned with *being* rather than *doing*.[20] My classes on business ethics throughout my business education leaned heavily on the utilitarian ethic, focusing on the outcome more than the action itself. Only deontic ethics (duty ethics) provides a lens for the right action and what we should do. Thomas Aquinas was one of the few philosophers who combined virtue ethics with deontological ethics to say that we are called to be righteous. However, the Law itself is summed up not in who we are, but in what we do: to love God and love others as Christ loved us. This ethical philosophy of an individual and a group of individuals in an organization (employees of a company) includes the end goal of the organization as well as the activities (the action/duty) required to achieve the end goal.

Plans, Paths, and the Way

The word *strategy* is never used in the Hebrew Old Testament. Instead, Scripture discusses counsel for war versus strategy for war (*etsah*—counsel). The concept of strategy was introduced by the Greeks. However, Old Testament Scripture does speak to our plans, paths, ways, and purposes. In fact, the concept of *the way* is a dominant concept in Hebrew tradition. דרך *derekh* is the Hebrew word for a "way, road, path," a "journey" or "manner, custom" of life, and "the way." Within Wisdom Literature, there are two paths that are constantly at odds: the way of the wise and the way of the fool. The way (the direction and orientation of an individual or company) may be crooked or straight as it leads to tragic consequences for many fools or prosperity and

19. David Carr, "The Cardinal Virtues and Plato's Moral Psychology," *The Philosophical Quarterly* 38, no. 151 (1988): 186–200.

20. Rosalind Hursthouse and Glen Pettigrove, "Virtue Ethics," *The Stanford Encyclopedia of Philosophy* (Winter 2018), Edward N. Zalta, ed., https://plato.stanford.edu/archives/win2018/entries/ethics-virtue/.

blessing for the wise. Even though there are many examples of the wicked flourishing, it is a short-term outcome. The long-term outcome is always blessing for the righteous, as the wicked prosper for a season:

> Do not fret because of those who are evil
>> or be envious of those who do wrong;
> for like the grass they will soon wither,
>> like green plants they will soon die away.

> Trust in the LORD and do good;
>> dwell in the land and enjoy safe pasture.
> Take delight in the LORD,
>> and he will give you the desires of your heart.

> Commit your way to the LORD;
>> trust in him and he will do this:
> He will make your righteous reward shine like the dawn,
>> your vindication like the noonday sun.

> Be still before the LORD
>> and wait patiently for him:
> do not fret when people succeed in their ways,
>> when they carry out their wicked schemes. (Psalm 37:1–7 NIV)

The concept of the way pervaded Jewish culture and was a clear metaphor for a righteous way of life when Jesus taught his parable of the seeds that fell on the path or on the way.[21] Much later, the philosophy of Rabbi Samson Raphael Hirsch (1808–1888) engaged the concept of *derekh* in his mantra, "*Torah im derekh eretz*" (Torah with the way of the land), as he built on the virtue and duty ethics of Kant.[22] Hirsch referred to the way of the land as the way of secular wisdom and sought to integrate Torah with concepts derived from intellectual philosophy and virtue ethics. Hirsch believed that Torah could be integrated with all elements of secular study and knowledge and that Torah is central to knowledge and our understanding of right and wrong in the world around us.

The concept of *derekh* is prevalent throughout the Torah (the first five books of the Old Testament). It is mentioned 187 times in the Wisdom books,

---

21. Mark 4:1–20; Luke 8:4–15.
22. Max Levy, "From Torah im Derekh Eretz to Torah U-Madda: The Legacy of Samson Raphael Hirsch," *Penn History Review* 20, no. 1 (2013): 72–93.

and it appears 69 times in 26 of 31 chapters of Proverbs and 64 times in the book of Psalms. Throughout Wisdom Literature, we see the way of the righteous, the way of the wise, and the way of the ungodly unfold. In Wisdom Literature, the way was the orientation of an individual toward God. After all, it is God who determines our way, and wisdom found in the fear and awe of God will orient us to every good path (emphases mine):

> Proverbs 2:6–8 NIV: The LORD gives wisdom; from his mouth come knowledge and understanding. He holds success in store for the upright, *he is a shield to those whose way of life is blameless, for he guards the path of the just and protects the way of his faithful ones.*
>
> Proverbs 3:17–18 NIV: *Her ways are pleasant ways and all her paths are peace.* She is a tree of life to those who take hold of her; those who hold her fast will be blessed.
>
> Proverbs 3:5–6 NIV: Trust in the LORD with all your heart and lean not on your own understanding; *in all your ways* submit to him, and he will make your *paths straight.*
>
> Proverbs 4:26 ESV: Watch the path of your feet And *all your ways* will be established.
>
> Proverbs 6:20–23 ESV: My son, keep your father's commandment, and forsake not your mother's teaching. Bind them on your heart always; tie them around your neck. When you walk, they will lead you; when you lie down, they will watch over you; and when you awake they will talk with you. For the commandment is a lamp and the teaching a light and the reproofs of instruction are *the way of life.*

Proverbs 6:20–23 provides insight into the integration of Torah with our day-to-day life. The way is action and duty oriented. The fool acts in one way, and the wise act in another way. Torah represents the Law and provides us the actions and duties we are called to and called not to do. The Ten Commandments provide a list of things we shall (honor your father and mother) and shall not do (murder). Jesus states that the entire Law can be summed up in two great commandments: to love God and to love our neighbor.[23] These two commandments are a call to duty and action. Our love for God and our love for others orients us as we walk. Our love for God centers us on the path, and our love for others propels us along the way. The Old Testament closes with Malachi's promise of a messenger coming to prepare the way before the Lord:

---

23. Matthew 22:36–40; Deuteronomy 6:5; Leviticus 19:18.

"I will send my messenger, who will prepare the way before me. Then suddenly the Lord you are seeking will come to his temple; the messenger of the covenant, whom you desire, will come," says the LORD Almighty."[24]

Here *the way* refers literally to the procession of the king, but biblical scholars believe that in the Gospel of John, Jesus picks up *the way* language from Malachi to refer to his own task of preparing a place for his disciples. He tells his disciples that they now know the way to where he is going. Jesus flips the language in Malachi from the procession *of* the king to the procession *to* the king when he states in John 14:6: "I am the way, the truth, and the life. No one comes to the Father except through me."[25]

Hebrew tradition understood *the way* as ushering the king to earth. Jeremiah prophesied and John the Baptist preached about preparing the way of the coming king. But *the way* Jesus referred to ushers us *to* the king. Jesus became the way for us to know God and serve God more fully in righteousness. Jesus encourages the disciples and whoever believes in him to do the works that he did and even greater works. He says that whoever believes, whoever asks anything in his name, he will do it. He then refers back to the Torah in his statement, "If you love me, keep my commands,"[26] and promises the coming of the Holy Spirit.

100+ Years of Orientation Research

Over the past 100 years, starting with the industrial revolution and an orientation centered on production, firms have created corporate strategies based on competition, differentiation, and the innovation of new processes and models for doing business. The three traditional business orientations were production, sales, and market orientations, with a later addition of the entrepreneurial orientation.

First, the industrial revolution initiated the production orientation. The end goal of many companies in that era was to maximize profitability through the production of standardized, high-value products that required very little promotional efforts. All competing firms, suppliers, and even customers were treated with an adversarial posture. Information and raw materials were scarce because this was before the invention of the telephone, the personal computer, or the internet.

---

24. Malachi 3:1.
25. N. T. Wright, *How God Became King: The Forgotten Story of the Gospels* (San Francisco: HarperOne, 2012), 91.
26. John 14:15 NIV.

The original model-T is a great example of the production orientation. Henry Ford optimized the assembly-line production process and created a unique product in the marketplace. Henry Ford is fabled to have said, "If I had asked people what they wanted, they would have said faster horses."[27] The production orientation of Ford allowed him to mass-produce cars with little customer engagement and competition. Cars were offered to customers in any color they wanted . . . "so long as it is black."[28] The production orientation propelled many firms through the industrial revolution to great success. However, as competitors gained production capabilities, it was no longer sustainable to compete based on production capabilities alone.

This introduced a new era of sales orientation. The sales era forced a slightly more externally focused orientation that shifted the emphasis toward increasing sales volume with a focus on selling products, not necessarily serving customer needs. Ford's competitive advantage of assembly-line production capabilities eroded as General Motors and Chrysler gained their own production capabilities and began differentiating their cars based on innovative features and luxury options. They also provided customers with financing options. The competitive focus in the auto industry was to persuade customers to buy products instead of understanding customer needs. Emphasis was on advertising and developing aggressive sales tactics. The product and production capabilities still preceded customer needs. Some industries—including the auto industry, insurance, and apparel—still function with a sales orientation. However, many leading industries have shifted from a focus on driving sales volume of an existing product to focus on designing and selling a product mix that meets the expressed desires and needs of the customer.

The orientation toward understanding and meeting the needs and desires of customers through a strategic product mix was first defined in the early 1950s as the market orientation. The market orientation is the organization-wide information generation, dissemination, and appropriate response related to current and future customer needs and preferences. A market orientation requires the firm to have a customer and competitor orientation, as well as inter-functional coordination. A customer orientation of a firm would indicate that the members of the firm make decisions through the lens of the customer's desired outcomes. A competitor orientation requires firms to constantly assess their strengths and weaknesses relative to their competitors. In order to have an organizational philosophy that includes a focus on the market, firms need

---

27. Patrick Vlaskovits, "Henry Ford, Innovation, and That 'Faster Horse' Quote," *Harvard Business Review* 29, no. 8 (2011): 2011.

28. Famous quote attributed to Henry Ford—may or may not be true.

to understand both the customer and the competition in the marketplace. However, those orientations are not sufficient if they happen in a silo. Customer and competitive information need to be integrated across all the functions of the firm in order for the tactical production, pricing, and sourcing of materials to align with customer needs and create differentiation from competitors.

The most dominant orientation in business research over the years has been the market orientation. As early as 1955, Peter Drucker stated that "there is only one valid definition of business purpose: to create a customer."[29] Over 1,500 articles were published during the growing popularity of the market orientation concept from 1990 to 2010. However, the world changed a lot between 1990 and 2010. For instance, in 1990 only 15 percent of US households had a computer at home. By 2010, 77 percent of US households had a computer,[30] and information became easier to share and could no longer be considered scarce. From 1990 to 2010, manufacturing in the US was increasingly outsourced, moving US production capabilities overseas, largely to Asia. This also meant that the production orientation model was no longer as relevant for most US-based companies.

Marketing and supply chain researchers have explored how orientations are complementary to one another and how firms combine them for superior customer value. For instance, marketing researchers Slater and Narver demonstrated the relevance of combining customer orientation, competitor orientation, and inter-functional coordination in producing superior customer value.[31] Thus, many researchers have argued that firms must adopt multiple orientations to enhance firm performance. No single orientation is sufficient to ensure success. The timeline in the table below highlights the evolution of firm orientations and details how they are defined in current business research.

Consequently, it is not surprising that a timely *and* timeless business framework described in Proverbs 31 would provide the following five orientations: **quality** (shifting the internal production orientation to an external quality orientation), **stakeholder** (including shareholders, customers, employees, competitors, suppliers, government agencies, and society), **supply chain** (engaging a global network of suppliers and customers), **sustainability** (creating positive financial, environmental and social initiatives), and **long-term orientations** (pursuing initiatives that do not only reap short-term benefits).

29. P. F. Drucker, *The Practice of Management* (New York: Harper & Brothers, 1954), 37.

30. Camille Ryan, "Computer and Internet Use in the United States: 2016," US Census Bureau, August 8, 2018, p. 5, https://www.census.gov/library/publications/2018/acs/acs-39.html.

31. Stanley F. Slater and John C. Narver, "Market Orientation and the Learning Organization," *Journal of Marketing* 59, no. 3 (1995): 63–74.

YEAR	Orientation	Definition
	Organizational Orientation—Peterson, 1989, Fred J. Borch, 1957, President of GE	• A firm's philosophy that defines the scope of the business domain. • An internal set of operating "beliefs and norms," management's philosophy of business
	Strategic Orientation— Narver and Slater, 1990	Strategic directions implemented by a firm to create behaviors for continuous superior performance
1850s	**Production Orientation**— Peterson, 1989	A firm focus on producing standardized, high-value products, with minimum promotion
1930s	**Product Orientation**— Voss and Voss, 2000	A firm commitment to integrate innovative product development and the marketing process
1950s	**Sales Orientation**— Zikmund and D'Amico, 1986	An external focus on increasing sales volume and selling products, not serving customer needs
1950s– Today	**Market Orientation**— Payne, 1988, Kohli and Jaworski, 1990	• The organization-wide information generation, dissemination, and response related to current and future customer needs and preferences. • Customer orientation, competitor orientation, inter-functional coordination
1950s– Today (cont.)	**Customer Orientation**— Levitt, 1964; Kotler and Levy, 1969; Deshpande, Farley, and Webster, 1993, p. 27	• A knowledge of customer's needs and wants. • The firm's sufficient understanding of its target buyers to create superior value. • Putting the customer first
	Competitive Orientation— Narver and Slater, 1990	The ability and will to identify, analyze, and respond to competitors' actions
	Quality Orientation— Miles et al., 1995	Organizational commitment to developing a competitive advantage based on a quality focus
1970s– Today	**Stakeholder Orientation**—Yau et al. 2006	A multidimensional construct with four orientations: customer, competitive, shareholder, and employee orientations

	Entrepreneurial Orientation—Miles and Arnold, 1991; Lumpkin and Dess, 1996	The organizational processes, methods, and styles that firms use to act entrepreneurially
1990s–Today	**Resource Orientation**—Barney, 1991	An internal orientation focused on the development and deployment of unique bundles of firm resources that are immobile and heterogeneous
	R&D/ Innovation Orientation—Manu 1992, Siguaw, Simpson, and Enz 2006	The learning philosophy, strategic direction, and transfunctional beliefs within an organization that define and direct the organizational strategies and actions toward specific innovation-competencies and processes
	Environmental Orientation—Miles and Munilla, 1993	The ecologically-oriented business philosophies of environmentally sensitive organizations
	Technological Orientation—Gatignon and Xuereb, 1997	The ability and will to acquire a substantial technological background and use it in the development of new products
	Supply Chain Orientation—Mentzer, 2001, p. 4	The recognition by a company of the systemic, strategic implications of the activities and processes involved in managing the various flows in a supply chain
2000s–Today	**Sustainability Orientation**—Crittenden et al., 2010	A firm's sustainability orientation is a function of its DNA—deeply rooted values and beliefs that provide behavioral norms that trigger or shape its sustainability activities
	Long-Term Orientation—Bearden et al., 2006	The cultural value of viewing time holistically, valuing both the past and the future rather than deeming actions important only for their effects in the here and now or the short term

TABLE 4.1: Timeline of Firm Orientations in Business Literature (with Academic Definitions)

Orientation toward the End Goal

The orientation of the firm defines the end goal. There is no kingdom orientation or wisdom orientation defined in business literature, but based on Proverbs 31:10–31, it starts with an awe of God. A wisdom orientation would contain a combination of stakeholder (reflecting love for others), quality (reflecting honesty in the benefits versus cost of a product), supply chain (engaging others in creative activity), sustainability (in stewardship of creation and love for others), and long-term orientations (in response to our anticipation of his return). An orientation of the firm that draws from ancient Near East Wisdom Literature is based on both pragmatic and deistic wisdom. Biblical wisdom starts with a fear of God, thus the foundation of wisdom is knowing and loving God.

I define a wisdom orientation of the firm as the set of beliefs that prioritizes a love for God (faith) and others as the end goal; this love-centered philosophy will direct organization strategies toward:

- understanding the needs of **stakeholders;**
- viewing time holistically in the **long-term**, valuing the past and the future;
- co-creating **quality** products;
- recognizing and strategically managing the various flows of products through the **supply chain;**
- and balancing the **sustainability** of economic health, social equity, and environmental resilience.

FIGURE 4.1: Wisdom Orientation Conceptualized

Wisdom is the penultimate resource that motivates the human ability to achieve good ends. Fortunately, God gives wisdom freely and generously to all who lack wisdom and ask him for it.[32] Wisdom Literature as a genre calls us to draw from pragmatic wisdom as a necessary virtue without dependence on faith.[33] However, true wisdom only comes from love for and awe of God. Divine wisdom is relational; it is the result of loving and understanding that God is, that God knows all, and that God's will should be reflected on earth as it is in heaven. Divine wisdom enables us to achieve the Ten Commandments and the Great Commission. Divine wisdom demonstrates to us in the eternal and daily scope of life the way to love God, to love others, and to keep the entire law as we take up our cross and follow Christ as his disciples. Without wisdom, we are self-centered, pursuing empty goals of wealth and prosperity without peace. Without wisdom, there is no kingdom impact and no love for others.

Wisdom is the path to all blessing and all of the extravagant promises of God for those who listen and respond. This orientation is exemplified in Proverbs 31:10–31 as wisdom personified as the Noble Woman demonstrates fear of the Lord and love for others as she sees to all their needs. Through wise purchasing and manufacturing, wisdom provides a product fit for royalty to merchants in a way that is profitable. The result of wisdom is the provision of resources for her household (including her family and servants/employees). Wisdom fairly sources flax, food, and land from suppliers. Wisdom cares for the community and the environment and looks to the future with confidence.

Over the years, firms have responded to the demand of the market environment to shift from one strategic orientation (originally production orientation) to embrace multiple strategic orientations. As firms grow in resources, market share, and profitability, they gain greater impact and responsibility. For example, as the Yili Group's market share grew, they no longer had enough domestic supply to meet demand. Thus, they adopted a supply chain orientation. As the Yili Group grew its international market and established more international partners, a greater need for stakeholder and sustainability orientations followed. However, with wisdom as the guide, the ultimate goal is not to be the best, but to deliver righteousness, justice, and fairness. The next five chapters will explore the five orientations that contribute to a wisdom orientation. Each chapter will demonstrate how the five orientations work in synergy with each other while driving profitable business practices that create beneficial long-term outcomes.

---

32. James 1:5.
33. James L. Crenshaw, *Old Testament Wisdom: An Introduction* (Louisville: Westminster John Knox, 2010), 373.

For the LORD gives wisdom;
> from his mouth come knowledge and understanding.
He holds success in store for the upright,
> he is a shield to those whose walk is blameless,
for he guards the course of the just
> and protects the way of his faithful ones.

Then you will understand what is right and just
> and fair—every good path. (Proverbs 2:6–9 NIV)

Reflection Questions

1. Read and reflect on Proverbs 31:10–31.
   What are the activities highlighted in the passage?
   What are the outcomes of the activities?
2. Describe the orientation of the Noble Woman in your own words.
3. Can you think of other examples of companies that have shifted their orientations and strategies over the years? What do you believe drove their change in focus?

CHAPTER 5

STAKEHOLDER
ORIENTATION

"Then the King will say to those on his right, 'Come, you who are blessed by my Father; take your inheritance, the kingdom prepared for you since the creation of the world. For I was hungry and you gave me something to eat, I was thirsty and you gave me something to drink, I was a stranger and you invited me in, I needed clothes and you clothed me, I was sick and you looked after me, I was in prison and you came to visit me.'"

—*Matthew 25:34–36 NIV*

At The Giving Keys, we want to inspire the world to pay it forward, so we've built it into how we do business. Through our social impact employment model, every product you purchase supports job creation for people transitioning out of homelessness.[1]

The summer of 2018 was a whirlwind. I returned to Asia for the first time in fifteen years to teach an executive MBA marketing class in Ho Chi Minh City for Kairos University. The following month, I spent two weeks in the library at Seattle Pacific University where I began working on this book with the financial support of a Bill Pollard Faith and Business Fellowship. As I headed south to Biola University to attend the Praxis Academy hosted every year by the Crowell School of Business, I was overloaded with ideas—with global business and church experiences and a new appreciation for the theological development of the literature on faith and work over the past 100 years to which I had just recently been introduced.

---

1. The Giving Keys, "About Us," https://www.thegivingkeys.com/pages/about-us.

Praxis Labs is "a creative engine for redemptive entrepreneurship, supporting founders, funders, and innovators motivated by their faith to renew culture and love their neighbors."[2] Praxis Academy is one of Praxis Labs' annual events that gathers college students and young entrepreneurs for a week-long learning experience with keynote addresses from founders and leading practitioners, roundtables, breakouts, and workshops. During one of the keynote sessions, Brit Gilmore, president of The Giving Keys, took the stage and began to tell the story of an organization that exists solely to employ individuals transitioning out of homelessness in Los Angeles to make inspirational jewelry and accessories.

I was jetlagged, distracted, and multi-tasking throughout the sessions that morning, but the message Brit Gilmore shared caught my attention and has stuck with me over the past few years. The Giving Keys was founded by Caitlin Crosby in 2008. As an actor, artist, and musician, Caitlin was passionate about inspiring people, especially women, to love themselves. In 2008, she launched "Love Your Flawz" and paid a locksmith to engrave keys with "love your flawz" as a wearable inspirational reminder. Caitlin began having keys engraved with other words like *love*, *strength*, and *let go* as reminders to be adopted and then passed on. Engraved keys began as an organic product line with orders kept in her journal and filled individually as they came in. Pretty soon Caitlin was making keys around the clock, and they were outselling her albums.

Homelessness is rampant in Los Angeles, and in 2009 Caitlin met and began building a relationship with a young couple who were living on the streets. She took them to dinner and, upon learning their story, was inspired to hire them to engrave the keys that she had been paying a locksmith to stamp. She bought the equipment and hired them. A year later, The Giving Keys was launched as a social impact company with a social impact employment model. Not only do the products provide inspiration and awareness of others for customers, but every product purchased also supports job creation for people transitioning out of homelessness. In 2012, Caitlin asked Brit Gilmore to join the team as production manager. Soon, the Giving Keys began hiring more employees as they expanded into bigger retail stores like Altar'd State and Kitson. The Giving Keys has gone on to provide over seventy job opportunities to people transitioning out of homelessness while simultaneously impacting lives through the power of its products.

---

2. See www.praxislabs.org.

Brit Gilmore took the Praxis Academy stage and shared the powerful story of a for-profit company that creates products that provide opportunities for positive social impact for multiple stakeholders, including customers, employees, and the local community. The Giving Keys collects the stories of their customers and the keys they purchase, then share the stories of how different customers wear and meditate on their symbolic word and then pass it on once they meet someone who needs the word more. Brit told the story of a daughter who bought her mother a *strength* key to wear during her cancer treatments. Once in remission, the woman paid her key forward to another woman she met in treatment.

In an essay for the *Praxis Journal*,[3] Brit discussed the call to love others in Matthew 22. She also reflected on our call to demonstrate Jesus's heart for the unimportant and unlikely in our communities. Jesus taught that he was the fulfillment of the Isaiah 60 servant anointed by the Spirit of the Sovereign Lord to bring good news to the poor, to comfort the brokenhearted, and to proclaim that captives will be released and prisoners freed.

The Giving Keys exemplifies this call to renew all things, starting in our local communities. By offering a quality product that brings value to the customer, The Giving Keys has the profit margin to grow and employ individuals who need grace, good news, and hope. Work and employment offer dignity and hope. By creating a working environment that promotes hope and acceptance, renewed hope for life can emerge.

The Giving Keys has been featured on *The Today Show*, in *O, The Oprah Magazine*, *The New York Times*, and *Us Weekly*, as well as fashion blogs and magazines over the past ten years. In 2012, *Teen Vogue*[4] featured Caitlin's journey from making key necklaces as a side gig to her music and acting career and turning it into a profitable company with a social mission. The article highlighted some of the achievements of the company: more than fifteen employees, necklaces sold at Fred Segal and forty stores around the country, with employees making around $40,000 from the sales of roughly 8,000 keys. The jewelry side gig became a social movement. When Brit Gilmore was featured in the *Forbes 30 Under 30–Social Entrepreneurs* in 2017, The Giving Keys had sold more than 500,000 keys with their engraved inspirational messages. With stability, identity, and community as the keys to unlocking potential, it is easy to see the community thread throughout The Giving Keys' purpose statements.

---

3. See https://journal.praxislabs.org/brit-gilmore-the-giving-keys-6152cb1d731f.
4. Sierra Tishgart, "Giving Back: Caitlin Crosby of The Giving Keys," *Teen Vogue*, June 29, 2012, https://www.teenvogue.com/gallery/caitlin-crosby-the-giving-keys.

Social entrepreneurs like Brit Gilmore and The Giving Keys are sometimes poised to make a larger scale impact than their nonprofit counterpart organizations. Without donor funding, social enterprises must create
a profit that provides marketable value. This also provides opportunities
throughout the supply chain of the social enterprise for an exchange to take
place with an impact that balances profit and purpose. There is growing
recognition that society's most challenging problems cannot be solved by
governments and nonprofits alone. In a TED Talk on "Why Business Can
Be Good at Solving Social Problems," Harvard strategy guru Michael Porter
said the following:

> I'm a business school professor, but I've actually founded, I think, now, four
> nonprofits. . . . That was the way we've thought about how to deal with
> these issues. But I think at this moment, we've been at this for quite a while.
> We have decades of experience with our NGOs and with our government
> entities, and there's an awkward reality. The awkward reality is that we're
> not making fast enough progress. We're not winning.[5]

B-Corporations (B-Corp: corporations that are legally licensed based on
social and environmental performance, public transparency, and legal accountability to balance profit and purpose) are one solution to gaining the benefits
of capitalism while structuring companies to balance the interests of investors,
employees, customers, and the community. There are currently over 3,000
B-Corp certified companies in 150 industries across 71 countries with one
unifying goal: to balance purpose and profit. Certified B-Corp companies are
legally required to consider the impact of their decisions on their workers, customers, suppliers, community, and the environment. By considering the impact
of business decisions on shareholders and multiple stakeholders, B-Corp offers
a model for people using business as a force for good. Cabot, Eileen Fisher,
Patagonia, New Belgium Brewing, Stonyfield Organic, and Klean Kanteen
are just a few of the highly successful companies that have legally adopted a
B-Corp model of doing business. Business models like the social-impact model
of The Giving Keys and B-Corp businesses are all part of a growing global
movement of people using business as a force for good. While some focus on
different areas of sustainable development goals, all are focused on creating
meaningful work with dignity and purpose.

---

5. Michael Porter, TED Talk (2013), "Why Business Can Be Good at Solving Social Problems,"
https://youtu.be/0iIh5YYDR2o.

Stakeholder Orientation

An ounce of information is worth a pound of data.
An ounce of knowledge is worth a pound of information.
An ounce of understanding is worth a pound of knowledge.

—Russell Ackoff[6]

Competitive models of profit maximization have dominated business thinking over the last century. Starting with Milton Friedman's model defining business as markets and the maximization of shareholder value, the predominant mindset is that business is not about social responsibility, it is about capitalism. According to Friedman, the responsibility of a business is to "use its resources and engage in activities designed to increase its profits so long as it stays within the rules of the game, which is to say, engages in open and free competition without deception or fraud."[7] Businesses should invest in the community, Friedman said, but only out of corporate self-interest. Friedman believed that profit maximization is the sole driver and outcome of a successful business.

Stakeholder theory emerged as a way of thinking about the organization beyond economic and financial impact to explore value creation for all stakeholders. Instead of business as shareholder value maximization or competitive advantage through win-lose value creation, stakeholder theory suggests business is about how customers, suppliers, employees, financiers, communities, and managers interact to create value when viewed through a stakeholder lens. With a stakeholder mindset, serving all stakeholders is viewed as the best way to produce long-term results and create a growing, prosperous community. A stakeholder approach to business is about creating as much value as possible for stakeholders without resorting to trade-offs.

The concept of a "stakeholder" first originated at the Stanford Research Institute in an internal memo in 1963.[8] A stakeholder was originally defined as "those groups without whose support the organization would cease to exist." From the original ideas that emerged from Stanford, the concept of stakeholder was integrated into business strategy literature. The work of systems theorists such as Russell Ackoff, corporate social responsibility literature, and organizational theory integrated stakeholder theory more broadly across business fields.

---

6. R. L. Ackoff, *Ackoff's Best* (New York: John Wiley & Sons, 1999), 170–72.

7. Milton Friedman, *Capitalism and Freedom* (Chicago: University of Chicago Press, 1962), 133.

8. R. Edward Freeman, Jeffery S. Harrison, Andrew C. Wicks, L. Bidhan, Simone De Colle Parmar, *Stakeholder Theory: The State of the Art* (Cambridge: Cambridge University Press, 2010), 30–62.

Perhaps the first-ever ethics-based theory of the firm, stakeholder theory had the following premises:

1. The effects of a company's actions on itself *and* others must be taken into account.
2. In order to understand effects, companies must understand stakeholder behaviors, values, and contexts.
3. Well-defined ways of thinking about company strategy should be presented from a stakeholder perspective.
4. Stakeholder relationships need to be understood at three levels: firm (organizational) level, process or operational level, and transactional level.
5. Strategic planning needs to take all stakeholders into account.
6. Stakeholder interests should be balanced and re-balanced over time.[9]

Stakeholder orientation is defined as the organizational culture and behaviors that induce organizational members to continuously be aware of, and positively act upon, a variety of stakeholder issues. This orientation moves beyond the early market orientation to recognize that the shareholder and the customer are not the only relevant market participants. Stakeholders also include competitors, suppliers, and buyers and influencing forces such as governments and NGOs.

A database search across academic journals for articles that utilize the stakeholder concept returns nearly two million articles. Stakeholder theory has been acknowledged or applied in nearly 75,000 of them, while stakeholder orientation makes up another 10,400 academic research articles. In a Web of Science database search for stakeholder theory in business research, it is clear that its application has increased from 2011 to today.

The stakeholder orientation is perhaps the most encompassing orientation of the five orientations discussed in this book. The stakeholder model of the firm includes the supply chain (employees, customers, and suppliers) as well as shareholders and communities as primary stakeholders. Secondary stakeholders include the organizations that are one tier removed from the day to day operations of the firm. Because the stakeholder model captures all of the engaged participants in firm transactions and decision making, a stakeholder orientation impacts all other corporate orientations and strategies (if the orientation is viewed as the philosophy and the strategy is the resulting plan for action).

---

9. Freeman et al., *Stakeholder Theory*, 30–62.

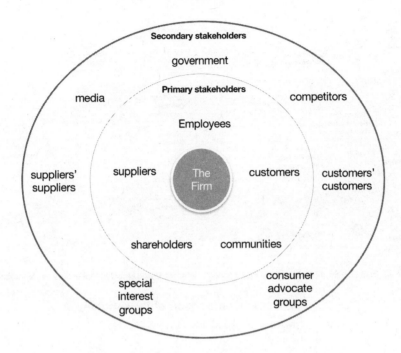

FIGURE 5.1: Stakeholder Model of the Firm[10]

Built by sociologists and philosophers, the stakeholder model of a business is less about antecedents and outcomes and more about capturing the ecosystem that is necessary to the existence and survival of the firm. However, later work conducted by researchers at Boston University and the University of Washington[11] proposed that the stakeholder orientation is the primary orientation that drives secondary orientations of the firm. While their model explored the role of a stakeholder orientation in driving corporate strategy, I would argue that a stakeholder orientation drives the prioritization of other orientations of the firm. The models tested by Berman, Wicks, Kotha, and Jones utilized data from the top 100 Fortune 500 companies. They found that a stakeholder orientation has both a direct and indirect effect on firm performance but did not directly guide firm strategy. Thus, across the top 100 Fortune 500 firms in 1999, Berman and the team found that stakeholder relationships had a direct impact on increased firm financial performance *and* increased the impact of a firm strategy on firm financial performance.

10. Adapted from Freeman et al., *Stakeholder Theory*.

11. Shawn L. Berman, Andrew C. Wicks, Suresh Kotha, and Thomas M. Jones, "Does Stakeholder Orientation Matter? The Relationship between Stakeholder Management Models and Firm Financial Performance," *Academy of Management Journal* 42, no. 5 (1999): 488–506.

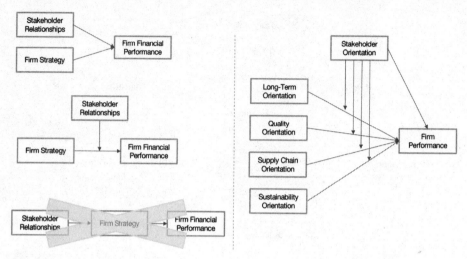

Berman et al. 1999 Models of Stakeholder → Performance   Wisdom-Based Model of Stakeholder → Performance

FIGURE 5.2: Comparison of Stakeholder Model to Wisdom-Based Model

I realize not everyone is familiar with reading the academic boxes and arrows that make up the theoretical models that we test statistically. (I'll spare you the mathematical model.) Each arrow represents a hypothesis between the two boxes it connects; thus in Berman's models we have the following hypotheses:

Hypothesis 1a. Both strategy variables and stakeholder relationship variables will have direct and separate effects on firm financial performance.

Hypothesis 1b. Strategy variables will have a direct effect on firm financial performance, which will be moderated by stakeholder relationship variables.

Hypothesis 2. Managerial commitment to stakeholder interests will drive strategic decision making, which in turn will affect firm financial performance. (This hypothesis was not proven significant and was rejected by Berman et al. 1999.)

The main difference between the models presented by Berman et al. 1999 and the model I am presenting through a lens of wisdom is the outcome of performance and the incorporation of firm strategy into multiple orientations. The fundamental premises of a wisdom-based view of the firm include the following:

- Performance is a balance between economic, social, and environmental outcomes. The ultimate goal is not firm financial performance; it is to honor and glorify God through the stewardship of all resources in creation, which includes the garden (environment), the people (social), and the fruitfulness of the people and the garden (economic).
- Stakeholder orientation and servant leadership (not included in this model) are central to wisdom, which is based on the fear of God and leads to loving God and others.
  - Only the stakeholder theory/orientation includes all others, not just shareholders who have a financial investment, but also the employees, suppliers, customers, and community who will be directly impacted positively or negatively by the actions of the firm.
  - Without a stakeholder orientation, all other orientations will have a weaker impact on firm performance.
- A stakeholder orientation will both directly impact firm performance and indirectly increase the impact of all other orientations on firm performance (moderating effect).

Freeman's view of stakeholder theory challenges the dichotomy between capitalism and ethics. Through a stakeholder lens, business and ethics should be put together conceptually and practically. Stakeholder theory suggests that if we adopt a unit of analysis as the relationship between a business and the stakeholder groups and individuals who can affect or are affected by the business, we will have a better chance of integrating business and ethics. Essentially, the concept of loving your neighbor may be the most important way of overcoming popular notions about business ethics as an oxymoron. Freeman sees a delineation between the moral ethics of Aristotle and Aquinas and the business ethics that reside in the business academy today. While Aquinas and Aristotle both saw profit as immoral, Freeman argues that moral principles are necessary to introduce charity and social responsibility to legitimize profit-seeking to balance self-interest. On ethics and strategy, Freeman and Gilbert have stated,

We cannot connect ethics and strategy unless there is some point of intersection between the values and ethics we hold and the business practices that exemplify these values and ethics. In order to build strategy on ethics and avoid a process that looks a lot like post hoc rationalization of what we actually did, we need to ask "What do we stand for?" in conjunction with our strategic decisions.[12]

---

12. M. Freeman and D. R. Gilbert, *Corporate Strategy and the Search for Ethics* (Englewood Cliffs, NJ: Prentice Hall, 1988), 70–71.

For moral principles to guide business strategy, "What do we stand for?" questions need to be asked up front. Wisdom Literature provides the answers to some of the questions that may guide our business ethics without an adverse position on profitability. When Aristotle wrote his treatise *Nicomachean Ethics* in 350 BC, he was hardly concerned with profitability.[13] Aristotle was born to a medical family. His father, Nicomachus, served as a court physician to King Amyntus III of Macedonia. As a teen, he went to Athens and enrolled in Plato's Academy, where he spent twenty years, initially as a student and later as a teacher and philosopher. In 342 BC, Aristotle was summoned to Macedonia, where he tutored the future Alexander the Great at the request of King Philip II. He essentially lived as a courtesan, a sage of the kings and society.

In his view, pleasure was the goal of the base, whereas the noble viewed wealth only for the sake of virtue. Aristotle focused on cardinal virtues, central to which were two kinds of wisdom: *phronesis* and *sophia*. Practical wisdom, as defined by Aristotle, is the development of plans and solutions that are well reasoned and capable of action concerning matters that are good or bad for humanity. *Sophia* was viewed as theoretical, and *phronesis*, or prudence, was viewed as practical wisdom or the ability to perceive good or bad outcomes of a decision.[14] *Sophia* seems to capture the ability to create a bridge from information to knowledge to understanding to wisdom. In Aristotle's writings, practical wisdom is attainable by anyone. However, it is *Sophia,* or intellectual wisdom, that truly seems to enable people to achieve the good life (*eudaimonia*).

Applied business ethics research has moved in the direction of practical wisdom but with the hope of somehow moving the needle toward achieving the good life for humanity. As a core concept of the field of transformative consumer research (TCR), practical wisdom is the guide to the good life. A leading thinker in this space, Nicholas Maxwell[15], has advanced what he calls "aim-oriented empiricism" that pursues, first and foremost, valuable truth. He disqualifies the value of knowledge and inquiry without integration with society's needs and priorities. The principle task of such inquiry is the application of reason with the enhancement of practical wisdom. This wisdom, he asserts,

13. History.com editors, "Aristotle," August 22, 2009, https://www.history.com/topics/ancient-history/aristotle.

14. Claudius Bachmann, André Habisch, and Claus Dierksmeier, "Practical Wisdom: Management's No Longer Forgotten Virtue," *Journal of Business Ethics* 153, no. 1 (2018): 147–65.

15. N. Maxwell, *From Knowledge to Wisdom: A Revolution in the Aims and Methods of Science* (Oxford, England: Basil Blackwell, 1984); N. Maxwell, "Is Science Neurotic?," *Metaphilosophy* 33, no. 3 (2002): 1036–68; N. Maxwell, "From Knowledge to Wisdom: the Need for an Academic Revolution," in *Wisdom in the University*, ed. R. Barnett and N. Maxwell (London: Routledge, 2008), 1–19.

includes knowledge and understanding but goes beyond them in also including the desire and active striving of what is of value, the ability to see what is of value, actually and potentially, in the circumstances of life, the ability to experience value, the capacity to help realize what is of value for oneself and others, the capacity to help solve those problems of living that arise in connection with attempts to realize what is of value, [and] the capacity to use and develop knowledge, technology, and understanding as needed for the realization of value.[16]

While it is encouraging to see the central role that practical wisdom is playing in the growing field of transformative consumer research, it is still lacking *sophia*, intellectual wisdom and moral-based discernment. From a faith perspective, *sophia* is not just intellectual; it is divine and provides insights based on living in awe of an awesome God.

The Wisdom of Loving Stakeholders

"You shall love the Lord your God with all your heart and with all your soul and with all your mind. This is the great and first commandment. And a second is like it: You shall love your neighbor as yourself. On these two commandments depend all the Law and the Prophets."

—Matthew 22:37–40 ESV

Wisdom is introduced almost immediately in Proverbs 1:20 personified as an individual engaged in the public square. She is calling out in the public square and calling people from their simple ways, rebuking the fools for hating knowledge. Wisdom does not just seek to teach the priests and kings. By being in the public square and calling out in the streets, it is a call to all of humanity and society to be wise, to seek instruction, knowledge, and wisdom. Interestingly, this challenge is highlighted in secular business research today by thought leaders like Russell Ackoff and Nicholas Maxwell. We seek knowledge in the academic spheres, but not wisdom.

Proverbs 2 teaches that when we turn our ears to wisdom and apply our hearts to understanding and insight, we will understand the fear of the Lord and will find the knowledge of God. This knowledge arguably provides the kind of true value that Maxwell is seeking with his transformative consumer research paradigm that seeks to integrate practical wisdom to improve society's

---

16. Nicholas Maxwell, *From Knowledge to Wisdom*, 2nd ed. (London: Pentire, 2007), 79.

well-being. The kind of wisdom offered in Proverbs, however, is the wisdom given by God with knowledge and understanding.[17] This wisdom provides understanding of what is right and just and fair—every good path. Seemingly, this providential distribution of wisdom provides an avenue to achieve the good life, or at the very least, every good path.

Unlike Aristotle, Proverbs 3 does not stray away from the role of wealth and profitability. Referencing Numbers 18:12, Proverbs 3:9 encourages the listener to honor the Lord with the first fruits of any wealth, and goes on to talk about the blessing that comes to those who find wisdom in later verses:

> Happy are those who find wisdom,
>   and those who get understanding,
> for her income is better than silver,
>   and her revenue better than gold.
> She is more precious than jewels,
>   and nothing you desire can compare with her.
> Long life is in her right hand;
>   in her left hand are riches and honor.
> Her ways are ways of pleasantness,
>   and all her paths are peace.
> She is a tree of life to those who lay hold of her;
>   those who hold her fast are called happy. (Proverbs 3:13–18)

In this passage, we see that Wisdom brings blessings: financial blessing in terms of resources but also long life, honor, and peace. Whenever Wisdom is in action in the first 9 chapters of Proverbs, she is engaging the community, calling them to a better life and inviting them to her table. In Proverbs 9, we see Wisdom in action again, calling all in the community to leave behind their simple ways of life to embrace her and have insight:[18]

> Wisdom has built her house,
>   she has hewn her seven pillars.
> She has slaughtered her animals, she has mixed her wine,
>   she has also set her table.
> She has sent out her servant girls,
>   she calls from the highest places in the town,

---

17. Proverbs 2:6.
18. Proverbs 9:1–6.

"You that are simple, turn in here!"
To those without sense she says,
"Come, eat of my bread
and drink of the wine I have mixed.
Lay aside immaturity, and live,
and walk in the way of insight."

Interestingly, as consumer research has grown as an academic discipline, so have calls for a more transformative consumer research paradigm. The TCR paradigm strives to encourage, support, and publicize research that benefits quality of life for all beings engaged in or affected by consumption trends and practices around the world.[19] TCR is an attempt by business research to correct itself today by countering hedonic, conspicuous, and overconsumption behaviors probably encouraged by marketing with a more transformative consumption model that engages the needs and priorities of multiple stakeholders. However, this model was being promoted nearly 3,000 years ago by Wisdom in the public square.

In the passage above, Wisdom is providing food and wine for consumption, but more important, she is encouraging the simple to learn a new way of life that brings blessing, longevity, and peace. After the introduction to the characters of Wisdom and Folly in chapters 1–9, the book of Proverbs offers twenty-one chapters of proverbial sayings that compare wisdom and folly or demonstrate the outcomes of wisdom versus folly.

Lazy hands make for poverty,
but diligent hands bring wealth.[20]

Folly → Outcome   Wisdom → Outcome

Throughout the proverbial sayings, a common theme relates to the treatment of neighbors, customers, suppliers, and multiple stakeholders in the ancient Near East community and economic life:

Whoever derides their neighbor has no sense,
but the one who has understanding holds their tongue.
(Proverbs 11:12 NIV)

---

19. David Glen Mick, Simone Pettigrew, Cornelia Pechmann, and Julie L. Ozanne, eds., *Transformative Consumer Research for Personal and Collective Well-Being* (New York: Routledge, 2012), 5.
20. Proverbs 10:4 NIV.

One person gives freely, yet gains even more,
>   another withholds unduly but comes to poverty.
A generous person will prosper,
>   whoever refreshes others will be refreshed.
People curse the one who hoards grain,
>   but they pray God's blessing on the one who is willing to sell.
>   (Proverbs 11:24–26 NIV)

Whoever oppresses the poor shows contempt for their Maker,
>   but whoever is kind to the needy honors God. (Proverbs 14:31 NIV)

A friend loves at all times,
>   and a brother is born for a time of adversity. (Proverbs 17:17 NIV)

Whoever is kind to the poor lends to the LORD,
>   and he will reward them for what they have done. (Proverbs 19:17 NIV)

Employees (servants), neighbors, customers, suppliers, and the poor are all given attention throughout Proverbs. The wise come to the rescue of neighbors, are honest with customers, promote skillful workers, pay an honest price to suppliers, and give with the excess of their profit to the poor. Prosperity and wealth are not the goals, as Proverbs acknowledges that even the foolish and ungodly have wealth. Rather, the goal of Proverbs and Wisdom Literature in general is to instruct those who are simple and those who are wise in living a life guided by the fear of Lord. Throughout Proverbs, this life is characterized by peace, longevity, and honor to the individual and to God himself. In our pursuit of wisdom through loving and honoring God, we find the good life for ourselves and have the resources to extend this good life to the spheres of people entrusted to us and around us.

Stakeholder Orientation Research

Morality or moral norms serve as one of the means to override self-interest that wages against the positive outcomes possible through capitalism. The moral norms put forward throughout Scripture encourage us to put the interest of others before ourselves. It appears that faith increases the potential for a moral norm of altruism to be attained. Altruism is the moral practice of concern for the happiness of other human beings. Outside of faith, altruism seems less likely and more difficult to attain. Of all business theories, stakeholder theory has provided multiple ways through which moral development can be attained.

In the early 2000s, Harvard sociologist Robert Putnam repopularized the concept of social capital in his book on *Bowling Alone*, where he discussed the negative impact of the individualistic focus of US culture on social capital.[21] Social capital is a central concept in network theory (a theory that is closely related to stakeholder theory). Social capital captures the value of social ties to others and the impact of those connections on outcomes in life. While Putnam originally thought the concept of community was being lost in US culture, a later study that he published in his book *American Grace* highlighted the role of religion and worship in bringing people together and creating a sense of community that had seemed lost. Research conducted across the US between 2004 and 2006 found that people who attend worship services are more likely to give to charities and the homeless, more likely to donate blood, more likely to help a neighbor, offer a seat to a stranger, or help someone find a job.[22] This is great news for people of faith in respect to culture, but there is also ample evidence to demonstrate that an others-oriented mind-set is also good for business performance. Research conducted over the last twenty years has demonstrated the impact of stakeholder orientation on quality, long-termism, sustainability initiatives, and supply chain performance.

In 1997, professors Jeanne Logsdon and Kristi Yuthas at the University of New Mexico proposed that by combining the theory of moral development with stakeholder theory, a firm adopting a stakeholder orientation would encourage both individual and organizational moral development. In a longitudinal study conducted in India across 206 pharmaceutical companies,[23] stakeholder-oriented firms entering the market forced down the prices of high-end incumbents and increased the prices of low-end incumbents while stabilizing quality. The price of pharmaceuticals is a hotly debated issue in business ethics, as pharmaceutical products are an essential product for many consumers. Pharmaceutical companies are predominantly thought to be caught in short-termism due to the cost of R&D and their ability to raise prices

21. Robert D. Putnam, *Bowling Alone: The Collapse and Revival of American Community* (New York: Simon and Schuster, 2000).

22. Robert D. Putnam and David E. Campbell, *American Grace: How Religion Divides and Unites Us* (New York: Simon and Schuster, 2012).

23. Arzi Adbi, Ajay Bhaskarabhatla, and Chirantan Chatterjee, "Stakeholder Orientation and Market Impact: Evidence from India," *Journal of Business Ethics* 161, no. 2 (2020): 479–96.

while protected from competition upon initial entry into the market with patents. The long-term value creation perspective of stakeholder-oriented firms motivates them to refrain from short-termism to provide quality products at a reasonable price.

A study conducted in 2019 by French professors Brulhart, Gherra, and Quelin[24] across 188 food, beverage, and personal and household products companies explored the impact of stakeholder orientation and environmental proactivity on firm profitability. They found that in these industries the immediate effect of a stakeholder orientation negatively impacts profitability in the short run. However, a stakeholder orientation increased environmental proactivity, which in turn increased short-term profitability. They discovered a win-win relationship between environmental proactivity and profitability, while stakeholder orientation has an indirect effect on profitability.

Finally, Vivek Soundararajan, professor at the University of Bath, Jill Brown at Bentley University, and Andrew Wicks at the University of Virginia offer a framework to predict the positive impact of a stakeholder orientation on sustainability initiatives and global supply chain performance.[25] Stakeholder orientation is increasingly being explored in the global context. The work by Soundararajan et al. builds a global model, while the work of Cheung, Tan, and Wang explore stakeholder orientation at the national level of analysis. Cheung et al. explore the relationship between corporate social responsibility (CSR) and bank loan pricing by the degree of national stakeholder orientation. They found that firms with superior CSR have lower loan costs in more-stakeholder-oriented countries versus less-stakeholder-oriented countries. Their sample included 1,462 loan facilities in twenty countries with data spanning 2008 to 2012.

Countries with a higher level of stakeholder orientation have higher expectations of a firm's engagement with employees, consumers, government, and community. The work of Cheung built on previous research by Maignan,[26] which found that consumers in France and Germany are more likely to value social responsibility over economic responsibility of a company compared to

24. Franck Brulhart, Sandrine Gherra, and Bertrand V. Quelin, "Do Stakeholder Orientation and Environmental Proactivity Impact Firm Profitability?," *Journal of Business Ethics* 158, no. 1 (2019): 25–46.

25. V. Soundararajan, J. A. Brown, and A. C. Wicks, "Can Multi-Stakeholder Initiatives Improve Global Supply Chains? Improving Deliberative Capacity with a Stakeholder Orientation," *Business Ethics Quarterly* 29, no. 3 (2019): 385–412.

26. Isabelle Maignan, "Consumers' Perceptions of Corporate Social Responsibilities: A Cross-Cultural Comparison," *Journal of Business Ethics* 30, no. 1 (2001): 57–72.

consumers in the US. A 2016 case study[27] in the global textile supply chain further explored the role of suppliers as stewards of social standards in the supply chain and providing evidence for the importance of buyer-supplier relationships in achieving stakeholder goals and interests.

Stakeholder Orientation as a Means to the End Goal of Wisdom

Stakeholder theory provides a way of thinking about the role of the firm in meeting the needs of multiple corporate neighbors. Corporations impact the lives of many people, including shareholders and employees, especially as their operations span global borders. The stakeholder orientation positions the leadership of the firm to view the end goal of their firm with the goals and interests of multiple individuals (stakeholders, including shareholders, employees, customers, suppliers, communities, and government agencies) in mind. Servant leadership seems like a natural antecedent to a stakeholder orientation. Servant leadership is rooted in ethical and caring behavior motivated to serve others, including employees, customers, and community.[28] Characterized by providing direction, empowering and developing people, demonstrating humility, authenticity, interpersonal acceptance, and stewardship, servant leadership is a recognized mechanism for a stakeholder orientation to be adopted by a firm.

Wisdom guides a servant leader. By definition, servant leadership will have a stakeholder orientation. The outcomes of servant leadership and stakeholder orientation will lead to honoring and serving others. However, only with faith can any individual or organization create a culture that will ultimately honor God and serve people. While it ends up looking complicated, I believe the relationship between wisdom, business strategy, faith, and honoring God looks something like this:

1. Awe/Fear of God
2. Fear of God → Wisdom
3. Wisdom → Servant Leadership

---

27. Michael S. Aßländer, Julia Roloff, and Dilek Zamantili Nayir, "Suppliers as Stewards? Managing Social Standards in First- and Second-Tier Suppliers," *Journal of Business Ethics* 139, no. 4 (2016): 661–83.

28. Robert K. Greenleaf and Larry C. Spears, *Servant Leadership: A Journey Into the Nature of Legitimate Power and Greatness* (New York: Paulist, 2002), 4.

4. Servant Leadership ➜ Stakeholder Orientation + Long-Term, Quality, Supply Chain, and Sustainability Orientations of the Firm
5. Stakeholder Orientation ➜ + Firm Performance
6. Long-Term, Quality, Supply Chain, and Sustainability Orientation ➜ + Firm Performance
7. Stakeholder Orientation ➜ > Other Orientations➜ + Firm Performance
8. Wisdom, Servant Leadership, and Stakeholder Orientation ➜ Greatest Commandments to Love God and Love others.
9. Firm Performance + Faith ➜ Greatest Commandments

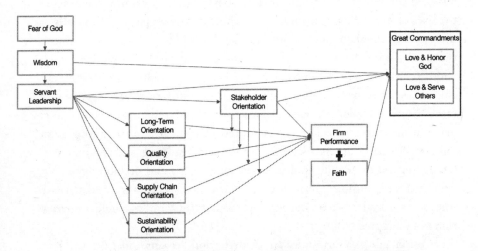

FIGURE 5.3: The Moderating Effect of Stakeholder Orientation on Other Wisdom Orientations

If the ultimate goal is to love, honor, and glorify God and to love and serve others, the fear and awe of God is the revelation on which everything else rests. Without awe of God, no one can ever be wise. Without wisdom, servant leadership will not honor God; it will ultimately provide self-gratification to the leader.

Stakeholder orientation—the organizational culture and behaviors that induce organizational members to continuously be aware of, and positively act upon, a variety of stakeholder issues—is just a means to attaining the end goal of loving and honoring God and others. It positively impacts firm performance, which is just another means of honoring God and others. Maybe more simply, stakeholder orientation is driven by servant leadership to augment the impact of all wise orientations toward the ultimate goal of honoring God.

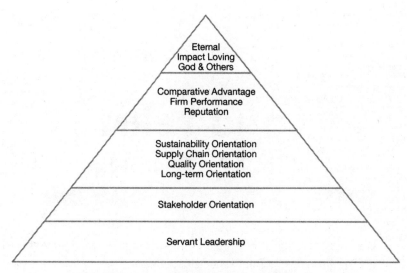

FIGURE 5.4: Stakeholder Orientation as a Means to Wisdom Orientations

Each of the means must ladder on top of each other and be grounded in wisdom. It does not take faith to be a servant leader, to have a stakeholder, sustainability, supply chain, quality, or long-term orientation, or to have a comparative advantage through firm performance and reputation. However, it does take faith to do all of these things with the end goal of loving God and others. Business research has provided evidence that a stakeholder orientation will improve firm performance. However, if firm performance (economic, environmental, and social) is the end goal, the overall impact of the firm will be good but not great. It will have a positive temporal impact, but the potential impact for the kingdom of heaven (which is eternal) may be lost.

Reflection Questions

1. What do you see as the biggest difference between Friedman and Freeman's models of firm responsibility?
2. Why is it important to think beyond self-interest in order to achieve good? Can good be achieved through self-interest?
3. What other examples does the Bible provide of someone acting in the interest of others at the expense of self-interest?

CHAPTER 6

LONG-TERM
ORIENTATION

Our responsibility to our region and sustainable management
approaches are important aspects of our work.

—Helmuth Neuner, former Business
Director of the Admont Abbey[1]

A recent study by McKinsey & Company found the average lifespan of
companies listed in the Standard & Poor's 500 was ninety years in 1935.
In 2010—only seventy-five years later—it was less than fourteen years.[2] The
US has a short-termism crisis that has increasingly become a talking point of
business thought leaders. Larry Fink, CEO of BlackRock, the world's largest
investment firm, recently urged CEOs to resist "the powerful forces of short-
termism afflicting corporate behavior."[3] Few firms remain with a history of
more than fifty years. As of 2019, only fifty-two companies have remained on
the Fortune 500 list since 1955.[4] The vast majority of businesses will be gone in
less than twenty years. Few firms represent the impact a long-term orientation
can have on the lifecycle of a business over time.

---

1. See https://www.stiftadmont.at/en/enterprises-projects/commercial-enterprises.

2. Christopher Handscomb and Shail Thaker, "Activate Agility: The Five Avenues to Success," *McKinsey
Organization Blog*, February 1, 2018, https://www.mckinsey.com/business-functions/organization/our
-insights/the-organization-blog/activate-agility-get-these-five-things-right.

3. Matt Turner, "Here Is the Letter the World's Largest Investor, BlackRock CEO Larry Fink, Just
Sent to CEOs Everywhere," *Business Insider*, February 2, 2016, https://www.businessinsider.com/black
rock-ceo-larry-fink-letter-to-sp-500-ceos-2016-2.

4. Mark J. Perry, "Only 52 US Companies Have Been on the Fortune 500 Since 1955, Thanks to
the Creative Destruction that Fuels Economic Prosperity," *AEIdeas Blog*, May 22, 2019, https://www.aei
.org/carpe-diem/only-52-us-companies-have-been-on-the-fortune-500-since-1955-thanks-to-the-creative
-destruction-that-fuels-economic-prosperity/.

The few brands and companies that have stood the test of time to make an impact over centuries and nearly a millennium are rare, hard to find outliers. The Oreo brand has sustained profitability globally for nearly 100 years now as a leading Unilever brand. Global leader Coca-Cola has been profitable for a solid century. One outlying organization in Europe, Admont Abbey, has maintained profitability for nearly 1,000 years.

The economic structure of the Admont Abbey in Austria is so unique that it has been studied as a Harvard Business case on long-term orientation and is one of the few case studies that demonstrates a working faith-based code of ethics implemented into an organizational culture.[5] It is amazing to think that the Benedictine monastery of Admont created multiple profitable business models in forestry, manufacturing, and wine nearly 950 years ago that remain viable today. A profitable organization with the social impact and longevity of Admont Abbey is rare. Founded by the financial contribution of Hemma of Gurk, Admont Abbey provides unique insights as to how companies can maintain social responsibility and sustainable profitability.

Hemma of Gurk (also known as Emma of Gurk) was born in AD 980 in Friesach, Austria, to a noble family of great wealth. She was educated in her grandfather, Henry II's, imperial court and became a lady-in-waiting to Saint Cunegundes (also Empress Saint Cunigunde).[6] Hemma's paternal grandmother Imma was vested with minting rights at her estates in Lieding by Emperor Otto II in 975 and was wealthy in her own right. The Bollandist's Vita recorded that Hemma had a happy arranged marriage to the Carinthian count William II of Friesach. Together they had two sons. Historical Jesuit records indicate that they enjoyed many years of happiness. They were known as virtuous in their regular attendance to mass and wise with their wealth.[7]

In a tragic uprising in their mining company, their two sons were murdered. William was grief-stricken. His immediate impulse was to hold the miners accountable for the murder of his sons. He plotted revenge. Hemma pleaded with him for mercy, and he repented of his initial rage. In penance, William went on a pilgrimage to Rome, leaving Hemma to govern all of their businesses and lands. During his return from Rome, William became sick and died.

5. Guillaume Mercier and Ghislain Deslandes, "There Are No Codes, Only Interpretations: Practical Wisdom and Hermeneutics in Monastic Organizations," *Journal of Business Ethics* 145, no. 4 (2017): 781–94. Dietmar Sternard, "Long-term Orientation in the Benedictine Monastery of Admont," *Harvard Business Case Study*, March 21, 2016, https://store.hbr.org/product/long-term-orientation-in-the-benedictine-monastery-of-admont/W16144.

6. Edmund Kern, "Counter-Reformation Sanctity: The Bollandists' Vita of Blessed Hemma of Gurk," *Journal of Ecclesiastical History* 45, no. 3 (July 1994): 412.

7. Kern, "Counter-Reformation Sanctity," 412

The murder of her sons and the untimely death of William left Hemma a wealthy widow.[8]

Sainted in the history books, Saint Hemma of Gurk was also a CEO and philanthropist. Unlike her husband, she did not react in anger to the deaths of her sons. Nor did she immediately remarry after the death of her husband (as a wealthy landowning woman, this was unusual). Instead, Saint Hemma focused on the long-term instead of being shortsighted as she committed herself to serving God. She could have easily remarried, but she chose to commit her life to investing her wealth in caring for the poor and the development of religious houses.

Widowed and now childless, Hemma withdrew from society. She devoted her life to God. She used her fortune to fund charity and gave generously to the poor. She also founded nearly a dozen religious houses and churches, including Gurk Abby and the monasteries of Admont and Seiz. She was venerated as a saint during her lifetime for her generosity and impact on the region. She later found solace in the Gurk Abbey Benedictine convent and is thought to have retired there a nun.

After she passed away, her wealth financed the construction of the Admont Abbey and the Diocese of Gurk-Klagenfurt. Many years later, Saint Hemma was canonized as the patron saint of the Diocese of Gurk-Klagenfurt, as well as the patron saint of the Austrian state of Carinthia. Her intercession is sought for health in childbirth and healing from diseases of the eye. For the past 300 years, the pious have made pilgrimages from Slovenia and Turia to her tomb in Gurk Cathedral. The Bollandist community of Jesuit scholars, philologists, and historians later wrote the Vita of Blessed Hemma of Gurk, describing her life and post-mortem veneration in a volume of the *Acta Sanctorum* issued in 1709.[9]

The religious houses she sponsored not only served as spiritual centers, but also served communities around Austria through education, medical care, and economic development. The Benedictine Abbeys created through Saint Hemma of Gurk's foundation were initially double monasteries (housing monasteries and convents). These medieval monasteries were rare hubs of spiritual, intellectual, and economic scholarship that empowered both men and women.

---

8. "Blessed Hemma of Gurk," CatholicSaints.info, https://catholicsaints.info/blessed-hemma-of-gurk/.

9. Kern, "Counter-Reformation Sanctity," 412.

FIGURE 6.1: Image of a nun preaching from a
12th Century manuscript produced at Admont[10]

In the book *Women as Scribes*,[11] Alison Beach describes the nearly 500 years of theological and educational contributions made by the monks and nuns of Admont Abbey. It became a center of spiritual, intellectual, educational, health, and economic development for all of Bavaria. Admont Abbey produced books on a wide range of topics. The Admont community also began to record collective histories of the region.[12] They wrote economic books and books serving the community's legal needs. Today, the library at Admont Abbey is the largest monastic library in the world, and it houses the largest archive of twelfth-century manuscripts.

As Admont Abbey flourished in intellectual life, it also expanded into the economic development of forestry and vineyards in the local community. These economic endeavors to create employment opportunities for the surrounding community and resources for the abbey grew into hugely profitable businesses. The initial generous endowment of Saint Hemma of Gurk took place in the year 1074.[13] Nearly 1,000 years later, the abbey is still thriving as a spiritual, cultural, and economic center of international prominence.[14]

---

10. Alison I. Beach, *Women as Scribes: Book Production and Monastic Reform in Twelfth Century Bavaria* (Cambridge: Cambridge University Press, 2004), 74.

11. Beach, *Women as Scribes*, 65–103.

12. Beach, *Women as Scribes*, 75.

13. See https://www.stiftadmont.at/en/the-abbey/monastery/history.

14. See https://www.stiftadmont.at/en/the-abbey/monastery/history.

The motto of the Benedictines is *"ora et labora et lege"* (pray and work and read). For hundreds and hundreds of years, the Admont Abbey has provided jobs for local Austrians who have created products that have been sold to customers around the world. The Admont Abbey lumber division became one of the largest door suppliers in Europe before it outgrew their scalability and was eventually sold off. A visit to the website today illustrates a diverse business portfolio that includes:

- Manufacturing: Wooden floorboards
- Real Estate
- Vineyards
- Flowers + Wine
- Forestry
- Agriculture
- Services
- Construction
- Energy[15]

How does an organization sustain profitable growth for nearly 1,000 years? The economic development and sustainability that grew out of the monastery had its foundation in leaders committed to service. Monks and nuns committed their lives to God and humanity. In an extreme example of servant leadership, they withdrew from society and material wealth, taking vows of celibacy. They followed the Benedictine Rule, written by founder Benedict of Nursia, to provide direction for the management and spiritual well-being of a monastery. It integrated prayer, manual labor, and study into the day-to-day lives of adherents. The Admont Monastery reflected this integration of spiritual life, intellectual pursuits, and economic growth to benefit the community and eventually all of Austria. The incredible longevity of Admont Abbey's financial sustainability has highlighted the Benedictine Rule as a potential business practice guide.[16]

The Benedictine Rule is a unique corporate code of ethics. Secular corporate codes of ethics have had limited ability to foster ethical behavior.[17] However, the integration of spirituality, intellectualism, and work advocated by the Benedictine Rule has sustained spiritual life, scholarship, and profitability

---

15. See https://www.stiftadmont.at/en/enterprises-projects/commercial-enterprises.
16. Mercier and Deslandes, "There Are No Codes," 781–94.
17. Mark Schwartz, "The Nature of the Relationship between Corporate Codes of Ethics and Behaviour," *Journal of Business Ethics* 32, no. 3 (2001): 247–62.

for nearly 1,000 years.[18] Short-term views of life will reduce business strategy to quarterly, maybe annual, goals. However, viewing strategy in the scope of eternity provides accountability for the impact of our actions on the next generation and beyond.

An excerpt from the prologue of the Rule of Benedict reads: "While there is still time, while we are still in the body and are able to fulfill all these things by the light of this life, we must hasten to do now what will profit us in eternity."[19] People of faith are called to a long-term horizon in their decision making. Saint Hemma of Gurk, patron saint of childbirth and diseases of the eye, is predominantly sought by pilgrims praying for miracles in childbirth. Thus, the patronage of Saint Hemma impacts the next generation *and* the vision of her followers. Childbirth guarantees lineage to the next generation and the passing on of spiritual culture. The curing of eye diseases reflects the miracles attributed to Saint Hemma of enabling the blind to see. These miracles metaphorically speak to the need to both see in the present and look toward the future.

Futurity and the Role of Long-Term Orientation in Strategy

The concept of understanding and focusing on time to come is referred to as futurity, the state of being futuristic. Futurity plays a central role in the biblical wisdom books. The role of futurity in Wisdom Literature has a broad genesis beyond Jesuit traditions that shape modern Western thinking. The wisdom received by Solomon as a gift from God was divine wisdom. However, the Wisdom Literature that was written in the courts of Solomon was both practical (*phronesis*) and divine (*sophia*), as it offered everyday advice for integrating wise behavior and practical virtues within a divine cosmic order.[20] Although wisdom traditions from Mesopotamia, Egypt, and China differed from Hebraic literature in respect to the divine, much of their natural wisdom is similar.[21]

Throughout my undergraduate studies of Mandarin and Asian studies, I found there to be interesting overlap between Confucian writing and biblical wisdom principles. From the wisdom of Confucius we get the following analects that have shaped modern Eastern thinking:

---

18. Mercier and Deslandes, "There Are No Codes," 781–94.

19. *The Rule of Our Most Holy Father St. Benedict, Patriarch of Monks*, http://www.saintsbooks.net/books/St.%20Benedict%20-%20The%20Rule%20of%20-%20Latin%20and%20English%20Edition.pdf.

20. Bachman et al., "Practical Wisdom."

21. Bruce K. Waltke, "The Book of Proverbs and Ancient Wisdom Literature," *Bibliotheca Sacra* 136, no. 543 (1979): 221–38.

The Master said,
"There are three things constantly on the lips of the gentleman,
none of which I have succeeded in following:
'A man of benevolence never worries;[22] a man of wisdom is
never of two minds;[23]a man of courage is never afraid,'"
Tzu-kung said, "What the Master has just quoted is a description of himself."[24]

子曰。君子道者三、我無能焉

仁者不憂。知者不惑

勇者不懼

子貢曰。夫子自道也

The Master said,
"He who gives no thought to difficulties in the future
Is sure to be beset by worries much closer at hand."[25]

子曰。人無遠慮、必有近憂

The Chinese concept of 不憂 (bù yōu, never worrying), refers to a person's disposition toward the future. The concept 不惑 (bù huò, never confused) refers to an individual's ability to discern right and wrong without doubt and with full self-confidence. Confucius taught that the future is defined by the past. The foolish person is compared to the wise person to inspire filial piety (孝, xiào). Filial piety means to be good to one's parents; to take care of one's parents; and to bring a good name to one's family by showing love, respect, and deference to the elders in the family and ancestors from the past. 孝 (xiào) is one of the oldest characters/words in the written Chinese language. It is arguably the most important moral principle in Chinese culture. Xiào connects the decisions of young people to the reputation of the elderly and removes the tendency to live in the short term from Chinese culture. An individual's action will impact the reputation of the family in the past, present, and future.

In the 1980s and 1990s, the dominant emergence of Asian economies drew scholarly attention to the cultural differences between the East and the West. Organizational behavior expert Geert Hofstede specifically explored the Asian

---

22. Chinese translation of a concept about the future.

23. Chinese translation of a concept about right and wrong.

24. Confucius, *The Analects: Sayings of Confucius*, trans. D. C. Lau (New York: Penguin Classics, 1998), 14:28.

25. Confucius, *The Analects: Sayings of Confucius,* 15:12.

wisdom traditions in order to understand the cultural dimensions that drove Asian economic growth. Hofstede concluded that the dominant economic growth in Asia (faster growth than the US and Europe) was due to their long-term orientation. [26]

Initially dubbed the Confucian dynamic,[27] Hofstede's concept of long-term orientation emerged from Confucian values concerning time, tradition, perseverance, saving for the future, and allowing others to "save face." Long-term orientation was later defined as the "the cultural value of viewing time holistically, valuing both the past and the future rather than deeming actions important only for their effects in the here and now or the short term."[28] The concept of long-term orientation is widely recognized as the dichotomy between focusing on the "here and now" and holding a holistic view of the future and past.

Geert Hofstede developed this long-term orientation dimension at the individual level. In the early 1970s, IBM made their databank on international employee attitude surveys available for academic research. Hofstede had access to 116,000 employee surveys from 1967 to 1973 in twenty different languages from seventy-two countries. Hofstede utilized the data to develop four initial dimensions of cultures and organizations where he perceived significant differences. Over the years, researchers built on Hofstede's original work, adding two dimensions. The six dimensions include:

1. Collectivism vs. Individualism
2. Power Distance
3. Femininity vs. Masculinity
4. Uncertainty Avoidance vs. Tolerance
5. **Short-Term Orientation vs. Long-Term Orientation**
6. Indulgence vs. Restraint

When the concept of long-term orientation is shifted from the individual to the firm level, it captures the ability of the leaders of a firm to build a vision that directs resource allocation and inspires organizational members to achieve a competitive advantage in the future. Firms with a long-term orientation are more likely to invest in R&D, spot trends in consumer preferences that lead to new markets, and develop strategic resources without explicit short-term value.

---

26. Hofstede Geert and Michael Harris Bond, "The Confucius Connection: From Cultural Roots to Economic Growth," *Organizational Dynamics* 16, no. 4 (1988): 5–21.

27. Geert and Bond, "The Confucius Connection," 5–21.

28. William O. Bearden, R. Bruce Money, and Jennifer L. Nevins, "A Measure of Long-Term Orientation: Development and Validation," *Journal of the Academy of Marketing Science* 34, no. 3 (2006): 456–67.

Ultimately, firms with a long-term orientation will be more relational and strategic, whereas firms with a short-term orientation will be more transactional.

A textual analysis of the Rule of Benedict by Guillaume Mercier and Ghislain Deslandes in a 2016 article in the *Journal of Business Ethics* argues that the Benedictine Rule shapes a structured organization that ensures long-term sustainability through an emphasis on common work. The virtue of the participants in the community creates a moral community reflected in the restraint by Benedictine monks and nuns. At the Admont Monastery, this ensures a culture of long-term anticipation and removes the pressures of short-termism. Paired with a culture that was focused on reflecting on the past (the framework of Scripture) as it informs the future, the Admont Abbey is perhaps the longest living evidence that long-term orientation grounded in spiritual morality (or virtue-ethical organizations) may be the key to sustainable kingdom impact. Without futurity and a long-term orientation, firms will struggle to achieve sustainable economic growth with short-term strategies.

The Wisdom of Long-Term Orientation

> Therefore, since we are surrounded by so great a cloud of witnesses, let us also lay aside every weight, and sin which clings so closely, *and let us run with endurance the race that is set before us*, looking to Jesus, the founder and perfecter of our faith, who for the joy that was set before him endured the cross, despising the shame, and is seated at the right hand of the throne of God.
>
> —*Hebrews 12:1–2 ESV, emphasis mine*

The term *futurity* was coined by Shakespeare in Othello and later used by Benjamin Franklin to refer to what is to come: "futurities are uncertain."[29] *Futurity* is also defined as a race or competition in which the entries are made well in advance of the event. The writing of Paul in Hebrews 12:1–2 captures the essence of futurity. Here we are running a race that was chosen for us before we were born. This echoes the wisdom of King David in Psalm 139:16 (ESV), where he wrote: "Your eyes saw my unformed substance; in your book were written, every one of them, the days that were formed for me, when as yet there was none of them."

---

29. Noted in the Merriam-Webster "Did you know?" section in the entry for *futurity*, https://www.merriam-webster.com/dictionary/futurity.

As people of faith, we are a part of an unfolding story. Within this story, we are called to live with the knowledge of the past, understand our role in the present, and live in faith for the promises to be fulfilled in the future. In this section, I discuss the role of the past, present, and future; the role of faith, hope, and love; and the future fulfillment of all of God's promises.

Honor Your Father and Mother

The Old Testament mandate to "honor your father and mother, so that you may live long in the land the Lord your God is giving you"[30] is all about honoring the past in the present with a promise for the future. It's not altogether at odds with the practical wisdom of the concept of *xiào* (filial piety). When this commandment was given, it was part of the covenant established by God at Mount Sinai, later referred to as the Law. This is built on the covenant God had previously made with Abraham, in which he promised to make Abraham's offspring many nations and kings in the land he had given him. The covenant with Abraham was all about how the impact of righteousness in the present would bring favor to future generations.

The covenants in Scripture are long-term promises and were all fulfilled in future generations. None were completely fulfilled in the present. This is a foreign concept to me. I've grown up with anticipation and expectation for God to fulfill his promises today, in the present. At the time of the covenant on Mount Sinai, the nation of Israel was in the desert and had not reached the land that God had promised to give them. The promise was fulfilled in the very long-term. It took forty years and was only seen to fruition by two of the more than 500,000 people in the Israelite tribes wandering the desert.

The original call to Abraham included family, faith, and land. As Israel became a nation, they continuously recorded the mighty works of God. Psalms gives a continuous call to record the glorious deeds of God today for the next generation to know: "Let this be written for a future generation, that a people not yet created may praise the LORD."[31]

Similar to the Confucian analects, in Proverbs, Wisdom does not worry. Wisdom is not afraid of the next season or snow for her household. Wisdom laughs at the time to come.[32] Proverbs even indicates that with wisdom comes hope for the future: "Know also that wisdom is like honey for you: If you find it, there is a future hope for you, and your hope will not be cut off."[33]

---

30. Exodus 20:12 NIV.
31. Psalm 102:18 NIV.
32. Proverbs 31:21, 25.
33. Proverbs 24:14 NIV.

There have been many debates about the nature of the promises in Proverbs. A quick search online tells you that there are two camps on how Proverbs should be read: One believes that we should read it directly as a promise; the other believes it is an indication of the way things should be but often are not in a broken world. Both of these are only partially true. Like *all* biblical promises, it comes down to our anticipation of the timeline. In our Western, immediate-gratification consumerism, our anticipation of promise keeping is for immediate fulfillment. However, when we read the Bible holistically (as one book, read as an entire story), we realize that God makes a lot of promises that don't get fulfilled for one or two generations, forty years, 400 years. The challenge for Western-minded thinkers is short-termism and the expectation of immediate results. As stated by biblical scholars Gordon Fee and Douglas Stuart: "The particular blessings, rewards, and opportunities mentioned in Proverbs are likely to follow if one will choose the wise courses of action outlined in the poetic, figurative language of the book. But nowhere does Proverbs teach automatic success."[34]

The Role of Faith, Hope, and Love in Shaping our Long-Term Orientation

For all of the covenants and promises God makes to his people in Scripture, we should expect their fulfillment without wearying in the short term. Perhaps this is why faith and hope remain alongside love.[35] Paul is clear that love is the greatest; only love enables us to fulfill our side of the covenant to love God and to love others. But hope and faith are necessary as we wait for God to fulfill his part of the covenant. Faith (πίστις—pistis) implies that actions based on trust will follow. It is our continued trusting belief that God is faithful to his promises. Hope (ἐλπίς—elpis), on the other hand, captures our expectation.

In Romans 4, Paul writes to the Roman church about the promise realized through faith alone. He wrote that Abraham's faith saw his promises to fulfillment. The following passage demonstrates the role of faith and hope:

> It [righteousness] depends on *faith*, in order that the promise may rest on grace and be guaranteed to all his offspring—not only to the adherent of the law but also to the one who shares the *faith* of Abraham, who is the father of us all, as it is written "I have made you the father of many

---

34. Gordon Fee and Douglas Stuart, *How to Read the Bible for All It's Worth* (Grand Rapids: Zondervan, 2014), 220.

35. 1 Corinthians 13:13.

nations"—in the presence of the God in whom he believed, who gives life to the dead and calls into existence the things that do not exist. In *hope* he *believed* against *hope*, that he should become the father of many nations, as he had been told, "So shall your offspring be." He did not weaken in *faith* when he considered his own body, which was as good as dead (since he was about a hundred years old), or when he considered the barrenness of Sarah's womb. No *unbelief* made him waver concerning the promise of God, but he grew strong in his *faith* as he gave glory to God, fully convinced that God was able to do what he had promised.[36]

Belief (πιστεύω—pisteuō) in this passage captures hope in action. Paul says that our faith will also be counted to us as righteousness when we believe in the promise of Jesus who was offered up for our sins and raised up for justification. Where we go wrong when reading Proverbs is not that we believe the promises are true; it is that we believe the promises are always going to be fulfilled immediately. Proverbs scholar Bruce Waltke concludes: "The popular evangelical solution that these are not promises but probabilities, though containing an element of truth, raises theological, practical, and psychological problems by stating the matter badly. . . . A psychologically well person could scarcely trust God with all his heart[37] knowing that he usually, but not always, keeps his obligations."[38] Our anticipation that God will keep his obligations is important.

The evangelical solution also rests on the assumption that promises are fulfilled in our lifetime. Proverbs offers us the ideal of the kingdom of heaven. If we shift to an assumption that all the promises of God will be fulfilled in eternity, then we can shift our expectations to a long-term anticipation that what we sow today may impact our lives in the near term, but will definitely impact the next generation and the generations to follow.

The structure of each proverb either compares the wise (W) to the foolish (F) (W:F) or offers a condition and an outcome (O). Proverbs also compares the outcomes of the wise (W→O) and the outcomes of the foolish (F→O). Outcome variables measured in business are probabilities. For instance, based on business research, it is highly probable that servant leadership will lead to higher productivity and better financial performance of the company. However, I don't want to read the Word of God as mere probability; I believe it can be read as truth. We are mistaken if we believe the Word of God offers us

---

36. Romans 4:16–21 ESV, emphases mine.
37. Proverbs 3:5.
38. Bruce Waltke, *The Book of Proverbs, Chapters 1–15* (Grand Rapids: Eerdmans, 2004), 107–8.

promises as a short-term truth interpreted through our modern-day Western lenses. The problem with the prosperity doctrine isn't that God promises that we will prosper. The challenge with the prosperity doctrine is that we think prospering is only financial. Financial prosperity becomes the goal and the measured outcome, whereas God could be promising righteousness—right relationship with him through wisdom. Prosperity is gaining a relationship with God; the promised wealth is merely a means to love others.

Eventually, all of these promises will be fulfilled. Some of them may be realized in my lifetime, some will be realized in my children's lifetime, and some may be realized in the generations to follow me. It's a hard pitch to make to investors, but long-term thinking is essential for walking in faith, hope, and love. It is also essential to shape our motivation. Wisdom is not founded on the love of money or trust in money (which results in failure); it is founded on our love for God. If we are wise, our motivation is to love and serve God. The blessings and financial outcomes are not our motivation; they are resources that God entrusts us with to love and serve him and others. Out of faith, hope, and love, faith and hope pass away when all promises are fulfilled. Love will remain and should remain our primary motivation for all that we do in the short-term and long-term. With a long-term orientation and a wisdom orientation toward loving God and others, we can read with fresh expectation all of the outcomes of wisdom.

Proverb (NIV)	WISDOM	OUTCOME
3:5–6 Trust in the Lord with all your heart, and do not rely on your own insight. In all your ways acknowledge him, and he will make your paths straight	*Trust in the Lord*	*Straight paths*
10:4 Lazy hands make for poverty,	*Slack hand*	*Poverty*
10:4 but diligent hands bring wealth.	*Diligence*	*Riches*
11:24a One gives freely, yet grows all the richer;	*Generosity*	*Increasing riches*
11:28a Whoever trusts in his riches will fall,	*Trust in riches*	*Failure*
11:28b the righteous will flourish like a green leaf.	*Righteousness*	*Flourishing*
13:11a Dishonest money dwindles away,[39]	*Dishonesty*	*Dwindling money*

---

39. NIV, NRSV reads, "wealth hastily gotten will dwindle."

14:23a All hard work brings a profit,	Toil	Profit
14:23b but mere talk leads only to poverty.	Mere talk	Poverty
14:24a The wealth of the wise is their crown,	Wisdom	Wealth
14:24b but the folly of fools yields folly.	Folly of fools	Folly
15:27b but the one who hates bribes will live.	Hate bribes	Life

TABLE 6.1: Outcomes of Wisdom in Proverbs

Proverbs, if read in its entirety, encourages us to live in the long-term. We are not called to be hasty. We are called to plan diligently with the motivation of loving God and others. We are also called to vigilance in expectation. We should be watching and waiting for the promises of God to be fulfilled. We need to have a long-term view to better understand today. Just like Proverbs 20:13 (ESV) encourages us to be vigilant, to work hard, and persevere in our work: "Love not sleep, lest you come to poverty; open your eyes, and you will have plenty of bread," Jesus also encourages us to be watchful and alert for the future: "Therefore keep watch, because you do not know on what day your Lord will come. But understand this: If the owner of the house had known at what time of night the thief was coming, he would have kept watch and would not have let his house be broken into. So you also must be ready, because the Son of Man will come at an hour when you do not expect him."[40]

Await His Return and the Fulfillment of the Promise

Scripture has a prophetic call to balance the past with the future, to understand what God has already done in establishing his covenant and his kingdom on earth. The Abrahamic covenant was realized in Jesus. As he fulfilled the promise to the nation of Israel, he established God's kingdom on earth. Yet we still live in the already but not yet. The kingdom has already come through Jesus but has not yet been fully realized. We still look to the future for the kingdom to come as it will be fully realized in Jesus's triumphant return. In the meantime, God has called us to run a race that he perfected for us. This pattern seems to be new to us in the Christian church established after the resurrection and ascension of Jesus, but it reflects God's interactions with humanity throughout history. We are just part of the realization of God's covenant with his people. Each time, his covenant was made as a promise for the future, the long-term plan for humanity!

---

40. Matthew 24:42–44 NIV.

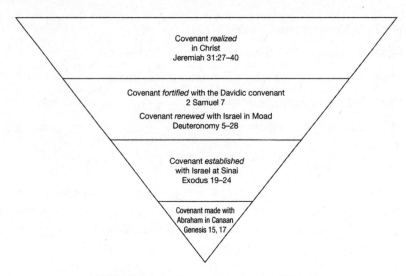

FIGURE 6.2: Covenants in the Bible[41]

As my New Testament professor, Nick Perrin, described it, the opening genealogy in Matthew highlights the importance Abraham and David had as receivers of important covenants in the lineage of Jesus. Abraham gets the promise of land/space and family. David was promised a descendant always on the throne, which translates into land/space and a ruling lineage—a kingdom for the people of God.

In the Lord's prayer, Jesus taught his disciples to pray, "your kingdom come, your will be done, on earth as it is in heaven."[42] People may wonder where the kingdom of God is or what space it occupies. If the kingdom of God is the space around Jesus, then you can see Jesus as the fulfillment of the Abrahamic covenant (space) and the Davidic covenant (royal lineage). It all converges in Jesus. Isaac, the son of Abraham, was the willing sacrifice. He was the preface to Jesus's atonement. He is the fulfillment of the covenants, and he is also the heir of God's covenant with his people. He earned both space (the whole earth) and rule. He gained his bride, the church, and a throne in heaven for eternity (now *that's* long-term).

What seems to have been lost in our long-term orientation in many Western countries is an awareness of the role we can play in the future of the story. Maybe we tend to think of salvation as being saved from sin and judgment. However, as New Testament scholar N. T. Wright notes, this leaves us

---

41. Adapted from Daniel I. Block, *Deuteronomy*, NIV Application Commentary (Grand Rapids: Zondervan, 2012), 1–314, 416–47, 598–620, 721–82, 805–18.

42. Matthew 6:10 NIV.

with a mindset of being saved *from* this world, not saved *for* life in this world.[43] A "saved from" mindset leaves us with nothing to do but wait for death and heaven. A "saved for" mindset gives us purpose in the unfolding story of the kingdom of God and his people. It beckons us toward a long-term orientation that looks to his return. Without this orientation, we have no great deeds to tell the next generation. Rather than sitting around waiting for heaven, we should expect God to answer our prayer requesting his kingdom come, his will be done on earth as in heaven *now*. This kingdom of heaven is now and not yet, present and future.

Evidence of the Impact of Long-Term Orientation in Business Research

Marketplace leaders have begun challenging their peers to move beyond the error of short-termism. BlackRock CEO Larry Fink's widely circulated annual letters to S&P 500 CEOs continuously call corporate leaders to move to longer-term purpose. A 2017 McKinsey Global Institute report measured the economic impact of short-termism by testing the impact of a Corporate Horizon Index on investment, growing earning quality, and management using a data set of 615 publicly listed companies from 2001–2015.[44] They found that companies classified as "long-term" outperformed their short-term peers on a range of key performance metrics (economic and financial):

- Performance Outcomes
  - 47% higher average growth in revenue
  - Less volatility
  - Earnings from 37% more on average over short-term firms
  - Profit grew by 81% more
- Long-term oriented firms invested more
  - 50% higher investments in R&D[45]

Over fourteen years of data, long-term oriented firms added 12,000 more jobs on average compared to short-term peers. The study suggested that if all

---

43. Wright, *How God Became King.*

44. Dominic Barton, James Manyika, Timothy Koller, Robert Palter, Jonathan Godsall, Josh Zoffer, *"Measuring the Economic Impact of Short-Termism: Discussion Paper,"* McKinsey Global Institute, February 2017, https://www.mckinsey.com/~/media/McKinsey/Featured%20Insights/Long%20 term%20Capitalism/Where%20companies%20with%20a%20long%20term%20view%20outperform %20their%20peers/MGI-Measuring-the-economic-impact-of-short-termism.pdf.

45. Barton et al., *"Measuring the Economic Impact of Short-Termism."*

US organizations adopted a long-term orientation, the US economy could have grown another $1 trillion, creating five million additional jobs.

Academic research has found similar results.[46] Research from 1975 to 2019 has explored the impact of long-term orientation on both individual and company outcomes. Research has been conducted everywhere, including the business school undergrad and MBA classrooms and in nearly every country in the world, establishing that a long-term orientation is essential for strategic thinking. Futurity and a long-term orientation play a crucial role in a firm's ability to plan for their future goals. Nevins, Bearden, and Money found that at the individual level, the long-term orientation of the individual drives frugality and personal ethics while reducing compulsive buying.[47]

At the company level, long-term orientation has multiple outcomes. A long-term orientation highlights effectiveness, whereas a short-term orientation will focus on efficiency. Research by MIT professor N. Venkatraman in the late 1980s surveyed 110 managers across five industries, including consumer goods, capital goods, raw materials, components goods, and service companies to explore the concept of strategic orientation. Venkatraman found that companies with a high propensity for futurity reflect a longer-term orientation in the resource allocation operations of the business.[48]

The research conducted by Wang and Bansal explored long-term orientation for new ventures. Most of the existing research either focused on long-term orientation at the individual level or on companies that are established in their industries. Across 149 new venture companies in eighteen different industries, Wang and Bansal found that a long-term orientation significantly increased corporate social responsibility activities and financial performance.[49] Corporate social responsibility included community engagement and giving, healthy employee relations, environmental initiatives, environmentally friendly

46. H. I. Ansoff, "Managing Strategic Surprise by Response to Weak Signals," *California Management Review* 18, no. 2 (1975), 21–37. G. Hamel, C. K. Prahalad, *Competing for the Future* (Boston: Harvard Business School Press, 1994); D. Miller and P. H. Friesen, "Innovation in Conservative and Entrepreneurial Firms: Two Models of Strategic Momentum," *Strategic Management Journal* 3, no. 1 (1982): 1–25; D. Miller and P. H. Friesen, "A Longitudinal Study of the Corporate Life Cycle," *Management Science* 30, no. 10 (1984): 1161–83; J. C. Narver, S. F. Slater, D. L. MacLachlan, "Responsive and Proactive Market Orientation and New-Product Success," *Journal of Product Innovation Management* 21, no. 5 (2004): 334–47; Wang Tiayuan and Pratima Bansal, "Social Responsibility in New Ventures: Profiting from a Long-Term Orientation," *Strategic Management Journal*, 33 (2012): 1135–53.

47. Jennifer Nevins, William O. Bearden, Bruce Money, "Ethical Values and Long-Term Orientation," *Journal of Business Ethics* 71, no. 3 (2007): 261–74.

48. N. Venkatraman, "Strategic Orientation of Business Enterprises: The Construct, Dimensionality, and Measurement," *Management Science* 35, no. 8 (1989): 942–62.

49. Taiyuan Wang and Pratima Bansal, "Social Responsibility in New Ventures: Profiting from a Long-Term Orientation," *Strategic Management Journal* 33, no. 10 (2012): 1135–53.

product design and production, and stakeholder awareness. While they found that a long-term orientation increased financial performance, corporate social responsibility actually came at a financial cost to most companies. The newness of the new ventures mitigated some of the positive effects. Time matters to corporate social responsibility; it is increasingly becoming recognized that new ventures need time to develop profitable products that are socially and environmentally responsible but also build value for all stakeholders. It is difficult to see short-term value in the strategies inspired by a long-term orientation.

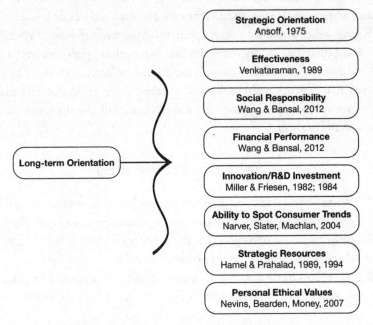

FIGURE 6.3: Outcomes of Long-term Orientation in Business Research

A multinational study conducted across 886 companies demonstrated that everywhere in the world, long-term orientation directs resource allocation and inspires organizational members to achieve a competitive advantage in the future.[50] Long-standing companies with a long-term orientation have the resources to engage in activities that do not necessarily generate immediate returns, such as investing in R&D,[51] spotting trends in consumers' preferences

---

50. P. Brews and D. Purohit, "Strategic Planning in Unstable Environments," *Long Range Planning* 40, no. 1 (2007): 64–83.

51. Miller and Friesen, "Innovation in Conservation"; Venkatraman, "Strategic Orientation of Business Enterprises," 198.

that may lead to new markets,[52] and developing strategic resources that do not have explicit short-term value.[53]

Long-Term Orientation as a Means to Establish the End Goal of Wisdom

The very concept of strategy is built on the assumption that firms are planning for a desired future. Futurity is essential in the process through which businesses plan to reach a desired state. Strategy is viewed by some scholars as the means, whereas goals are viewed as the end. However, other scholars encompass both goals (ends) and means as comprehensive parts of a strategy. Regardless of the view, a corporate strategy must include future ends (goals), means (actions), and conditions (contexts). Research conducted by Venkatraman in 1989 discovered that of the six dimensions of strategic orientation, futurity plays an important role in a firm's ability to establish end goals and the means through which to attain them.

Reflection Questions

1. What do you think the difference in long-term orientation would be if you viewed the world with practical wisdom versus divine wisdom?
2. How might a recognition that the kingdom is already, but not yet, shape your personal long-term orientation?
3. Are there any disadvantages to a short-term orientation? List potential disadvantages of a short-term orientation and long-term orientation.

---

52. Narver, Slater, and MacLachlan, "Responsive and Proactive Market Orientation."
53. Hamel and Prahalad, "Competing for the Future."

CHAPTER 7

QUALITY
ORIENTATION

As much as I love the mission, I can't buy the product if I can't sell the product. Similar to how we talk about our company to our customers. If we talk to a non-profit, we emphasize mission, if we talk to a cafe, we emphasize the quality. Mission is not the thing they're looking for, if our coffee doesn't taste good then they should not buy it.

—Pete Leonard, CEO, I Have a Bean[1]

I sat in the back room of the coffee roastery on a warm spring day. The smells of roasting coffee hung thick in the air. I spent the previous hour in a team meeting, learning the insights of the I Have a Bean team regarding the latest trends in coffee. With a background in logistics, I had spent plenty of time in warehouses and manufacturing plants, but not many were like this one. It wasn't the scale that impressed me, it was the fine-tuned science of the roaster, the call to mission that opened the day, and the general commitment of the employees to see a small start-up company succeed and scale. The success of the company was a part of each of the employees' personal story. The story of I Have a Bean and CEO Pete Leonard captures the impact of a quality orientation. Companies with a quality orientation not only produce products that delight the customer, but also bring out high-quality engagement from employees as they seek to empower employees to seek continuous improvement.

In order to achieve a quality product, companies must empower employees to innovate old processes and products to engage in continuous improvement until a unique product emerges that will delight the customer. The antecedent

---

1. Interview with Pete Leonard, May 23, 2019.

to Pete's story is his passion for and training in technology paired with his desire to love God and others. From disassembling radios to developing the technology that digitized medical records, Pete was on a trajectory to build a successful technology company. By nature, Pete was inventive and entrepreneurial. As he built projects for clients, he found that there was a shortage of skilled employees to execute the projects. Pete was about to discover a huge social need in his neighborhood. In the process of learning to love his neighbors well, he also discovered a new product that was desperately in need of quality improvement.

While he was scaling his technology company, Pete developed another passion: coffee. In January 2005, Pete and a group of men traveled from the west suburbs of Chicago to the rainy Brazilian tropics to volunteer in construction projects. Memories of the heat and humidity were trumped by an unexpected encounter Pete had with quality coffee. Until Pete arrived in Brazil, he never knew that humans roasted coffee. His lifelong coffee consumption had mainly consisted of mass-produced, modest quality arabica coffee. Arabica coffee beans make up 75 percent of the coffee bean market and are used by Folgers, McDonald's, Tim Hortons, Dunkin' Donuts, and Starbucks. The other 24 percent of the coffee market is the lower quality robusta coffee bean.

When it came to coffee, Pete's main concern was to find a café where he could order a mocha, ready in minute. His daily coffee source in Brazil was a local plantation owner. The local plantation owner roasted the coffee in a stainless-steel roaster as his wife fed sticks into the fire below. His first cup was the best cup of coffee he had ever tasted. It was brewed within minutes of being roasted and ground. The flavors were rich, nutty, fragrant, and had low acidity. He bought ten pounds to give away as gifts and ended up drinking most of them. After returning to the US, Pete went to a large coffee retail shop and bought a black coffee on his way to work. It was so bad that he spit it out and determined he needed a solution to his newfound love of freshly roasted coffee. Ever the inventor and engineer, Pete went to work figuring out how to roast his own coffee.

He conducted research, fabricated a roasting drum, and turned his backyard gas grill into a rudimentary roasting machine. Meanwhile, as Pete was slowly becoming a master taster (the coffee equivalent of a wine sommelier), Pete moved his technology company from the city to the suburbs and landed a huge project. The project required a skill set that wasn't broadly available in the market, and Pete was faced with the challenge of finding skilled employees and delivering the project on *time*.

Around the same time, a news story ran in Chicago featuring Pete's brother-in-law. He had run afoul of the law, had been arrested, and was in jail awaiting trial in another state. Pete's brother-in-law's boss was watching the news and immediately fired him from his job. But it just so happened that his brother-in-law had the programming and mathematical skill set Pete needed for his project.

Pete hired him. It took his brother-in-law a year to go to trial, get convicted, and go to prison. It took a year to complete the project. Pete believed the quality work his brother-in-law conducted was unusual among felons. He believed that there were few felons who had highly sought-after skill sets. When Pete's brother-in-law went to prison, Pete had to hire four people to do his work. When he got out, Peter brought him back to work for him again.

His company was using an outside payroll processing company that also handled their business and health insurance. After two weeks, they ran payroll and immediately got a call from the owner/founder of the payroll company. The conversation went a little like this:

Payroll company: Hey, Pete. This is Jeff. . . . Listen, we just ran your payroll, and something came up that I'm sure you didn't know. You have a convicted felon on your payroll!

Pete: Hey, Jeff. Yeah, I know I have a convicted felon on my payroll. He's been here for a couple of weeks.

Payroll company: Pete, you can't have a convicted felon on your payroll. While it is your company, they are not your employees. You get great insurance rates because the people who work at your company are part of a much larger pool of people who are actually *my* employees of record, and we do not hire felons. He's gotta go.

Pete: Jeff, I can't do that. I don't want to go home tonight and tell my wife, "Hi, hon! Listen, I . . . um . . . I fired your brother today."

Payroll company: I don't care who he is. He's gotta be gone by the end of the day or we are going to stop processing your payroll and drop your health insurance and your business insurance. If we do that, no one else will pick you up. You'll essentially be out of business.[2]

Pete called his brother-in-law into the office and the two of them made a plan. Pete fired him. Then his brother-in-law created a corporation. Pete's company was able to contract with his brother's company to do some programming work.

---

2. Interview with Pete Leonard, May 23, 2019.

This experience planted the seed in Pete's mind that there was a huge need in society to provide opportunities for quality workers who have been convicted of crimes and want to reintegrate into society after serving time. It's a challenging problem. For instance, laws vary by state. Often, convicted felons with a sex offense can't be around their own families. They can't be around children. They can't live near or even walk within 500 feet of a park or school. They can't live in a house or rent a room near a daycare. They can't live in an apartment complex where another sex offender lives. They can't get a temporary hotel room if another felon is staying there already.

Pete's brother-in-law was a quality worker—a database engineer with a genius-level IQ, expert programming skills, and accounting experience. Because of his felony, no one would hire him. Pete began looking for organizations that reintegrate returning felons. He learned that over 700,000 people are released from prison every year, and roughly 63 percent of them end up back in prison within three years. The world changes while they are in prison. They change while they are in prison. Many of them reemerge to find themselves no longer employable by many companies. This got Pete's attention. There were others like his brother-in-law—lots of others.

Meanwhile, Pete's backyard BBQ roastery was growing from providing coffee to his own household to developing a small market in his neighborhood. As his backyard roastery fired up, neighbors began making requests for his freshly roasted coffee beans. Pete realized he had an opportunity to build a unique company with a new set of rules about the product quality and the people it employed. He set to work developing a business plan for a new kind of coffee roasting company, one that would welcome and train the men living at a re-entry house in his community.

He had some challenges to launch his company. The business plan revealed that it was not possible to roast enough coffee in a homemade grill-roaster to make enough revenue to employ six people. You can't have pallets of green coffee beans delivered by freight truck to your garage. However, the biggest challenge facing the success of Pete's business was the training timeline to onboard a roaster. Reintegration programs last six, nine, or possibly twelve months, while learning to roast coffee properly can require a two-year apprenticeship. Trainees would not be around long enough to produce high-quality roasts. Pete began searching the market for a roasting machine that would allow a person with no previous roasting experience to consistently and perfectly produce high-quality coffee. He found no product on the market that came even close to meeting his specific needs, so he set to work inventing.

The highest advertised quality of bean sold on the market at that time was in the top 3 percent of the roasting scorings (think 97 percent perfection). Pete didn't settle until he created a process that delivered beans rated in the top 1 percent. The roasting machine Pete invented was 600 times more precise than anything else on the market at the time. While Pete was sourcing beans rated in the top 1 percent in the world and inventing a roasting process that was unmatched in the market, he sourced quality talent from a pool of people that most of society views as the bottom 1 percent of the workforce.

One of the most dynamic stories is told by an I Have a Bean employee who rose through the ranks from roaster to sales manager, Louis Dooley, in his book *Prison Saved My Life*.[3] Louis found personal faith in prison. His life was transformed, but when he was released most company policies wouldn't allow him to apply or said no upon receiving his application. The opportunity for employment at I Have a Bean started Louis's journey. Grateful for a job, Louis showed up thirty minutes early and stayed late daily. Over the year-and-a-half he worked at I Have a Bean, he learned the value of a quality product and how to interact with people of any socio-economic class. Louis now works as regional director for a nonprofit ministry that provides Bible training, educational resources and, through a network of volunteers, Bible training certifications to people in prison.

Another employee at I Have a Bean, Mike, spent a few minutes with us on his last day at work. In a full-circle redemption story, Mike had finally been offered an opportunity to move back into his original field of engineering. We sat in the offices off of the roasting area eating cake and, of course, drinking coffee as he shared his story. Before a felony conviction, Mike had earned a master's degree in mechanical engineering and had worked in various industries. Upon release, he applied for over 1,700 jobs over the course of three years and found himself with offers contingent on a background check.

During this discouraging process, he got involved with a Bible study that gathers people with past incarceration and families of people incarcerated. It was a safe space for him where he felt respected and treated like a normal human being. At one of those meetings, an employee at I Have a Bean gave a testimony. Mike followed up with him and was able to connect with Pete for an interview. He found a company that gave him a job offer contingent on his background check, but this time they were checking to make sure he *did* have a felony.

With a background in quality assurance, Mike did a little bit of everything

---

3. Louis Dooley and Heidi Gruber O'Very, *Prison Saved My Life* (Dubuque, IA: Emmaus International, 2018). I recommend it for everyone.

but sales. He found a culture at I Have a Bean where people could excel. There was no risk of being found out as a felon because people were known and treated as people instead. I Have a Bean offered acceptance and an opportunity to be a productive member of a quality brand. He was given the freedom to do quality work without judgment of his past.

Just before we met, Mike got a call back from one the 1,700 job interviews. He had a second interview with the CEO and had disclosed his background. The CEO didn't ask him much about technical engineering questions but focused on who Mike was as a person. The CEO called and offered him the job only to have human resources pull the offer a few days later. Mike followed up and thanked the CEO anyway. The CEO called Mike back and thanked him for following up. Through a series of events, the CEO decided to go ahead and hire him. Mike finished his time at I Have a Bean on the day of my visit and planned to start his new job just one week later. He trusted God to open the right door at the right time. Pete Leonard was there to partner with God in offering the opportunity for employment, providing recommendations, and journeying with Mike as he pursued his own redemption.

Quality Orientation

And whatever you do, whether in word or deed, do it all in the name of the Lord Jesus, giving thanks to God the Father through him.

—*Colossians 3:17 NIV*

A quality orientation is defined as the business goal of ensuring that the customer will be "totally satisfied with the product in every respect."[4] Miles et al. defined it simply as "an organizational philosophical commitment to developing and maintaining a competitive advantage based upon a quality focus."[5] All the products the Proverbs 31 Noble Woman sells are of fine quality—to a standard that was fit for royalty. In Proverbs 31:22 she makes bed coverings and clothing of fine linen and purple, which signified royalty. Purple has long been the color worn in royal courts because purple dye was expensive and difficult to make. Further, linen is one of the more expensive fabrics as it is inelastic and easy to break in production, making the cost of production higher than most other fabrics. In ancient Israel, priests were clothed in linen, and the curtain in

---

4. John L. Warne, "Developing a Quality Orientation," *Target* (Summer 1987), *http://* https://www.ame.org/sites/default/files/target_articles/87Q2A2.pdf.

5. Morgan P. Miles, Gregory Russel, and Danny R. Arnold, "The Quality Orientation: An Emerging Business Philosophy?," *Review of Business* 17, no. 1 (1995): 7–15.

the temple that separated the holy of holies was made of linen. Proverbs 31:24 states that the Noble Woman makes linen garments and sells them, so they are available for both her home and her customers. Further, the Proverbs 31 Noble Woman took great care to find the right roles for her employees, empowering them in their work and teaching them with kindness.[6]

To deliver a quality product, companies do not just need to understand the customer. They also need to empower employees to understand the best process to transform raw materials into a product that provides value to the customer. Customer value indicates that the customer feels as though the benefits of the product far outweigh the cost of the product's purchase. At I Have a Bean, the customer must be satisfied and delighted with the quality of the product. (Objective quality can be measured by the tangible attributes of the product, such as flavor and aroma.) Then, in many cases, customer loyalty can be solidified through an emotional connection to the mission of the organization to have a positive impact on society. (Perceived quality goes beyond tangible attributes to psychology and emotion.) The mission won't win the customer without a great product, but the combination of a great product and an inspiring mission enables both objective and perceived quality to be maximized.

Quality has been a consistent orientation of leading firms. With the advent of the industrial revolution and the conception of the assembly line, manufacturing and product creation underwent a revolution. However, over time, the production system introduced by innovators like Henry Ford could not keep up with both the product variety *and* the quality desired by customers. Competition emerged in the market to offer more products, and consumers had more choice. Ford worked to provide variety without also providing necessary incremental growth in quality.

Around this time (1930s to post-WWII), Kiichiro Toyoda and Taiichi Ohno at Toyota observed Ford's quandary and shifted their focus in manufacturing from machine utilization to the flow of the product through the entire process.[7] This transformed the mindset around product manufacturing from mass production to lean production and ushered in the era of quality management (eventually total quality management). The focus on the Toyota Production System (TPS) moved beyond total output to focus on continuous improvement and the quality of the output.

TPS took the lead for best in class manufacturing practices. Soon many companies began adopting the quality philosophy developed by Toyoda and

---

6. Proverbs 31:15, 26.
7. James P. Womack et al., *The Machine That Changed the World* (New York: Free Press, 1990).

Ohno. Concepts emerged from the quality philosophy to include lean management, continuous improvement, total quality management, and just in time manufacturing.

The central goal of TPS was waste elimination. One of the first drivers of waste to be eliminated in TPS was product quality issues in the manufacturing process. This meant that Toyota engages *every* employee in managing the transformation of products. Earlier in this book I quoted Henry Ford, "Why is it that I always get the whole person when what I really want is just a pair of hands?"[8] TPS refutes this mindset and seeks instead to engage the whole person in the manufacturing process. TPS found that engaged employees could flag defects early in the production process and were able to reduce quality defects to almost zero.

As TPS was adopted across different retail and supply chain sectors it became more popularly known as lean management. The concept of lean management came from the focus on waste elimination, including eight central wastes: defects, overproduction, waiting, not utilizing talent, transportation, inventory, motion, and excess processing. This created not only a reduction in inventory (finished products owned by a firm that are not yet sold) but also established new ways of viewing employees and the entire eco-system of the firm. Innovative firms with a focus on continuously improving to stay competitive quickly adopted lean strategies.[9] Because companies were more focused on not overproducing products (a default of mass production), they became more responsive to the needs and desires of the customer.

Research conducted by Rust et al. in the mid-1990s demonstrated that a quality orientation affects business performance either by reducing costs or improving customer loyalty and attracting new customers, which in turn influences profitability.[10] A market orientation is the philosophy of the firm that elevates insights into the customer and competition and coordinates those insights internally. A product orientation, on the other hand, is more focused on the production of a product that meets a customer need. Both a market orientation and a product orientation require an understanding of the customer. Where the orientations diverge is in the external focus of the market orientation on competition and the more internal focus of the quality orientation on continuous improvement in production.

---

8. Wagner and Harter, "The Fifth Element of Great Managing."

9. Diane Mollenkopf, Hannah Stolze, Wendy Tate, and Monique Ueltschy, "Green, Lean, and Global Supply Chains," *International Journal of Physical Distribution and Logistics Management* 40, no. 1–2 (2010): 14–41.

10. Roland T. Rust, Anthony J. Zahorik, Timothy Keiningham, "Return on Quality (ROQ): Making Service Quality Financially Accountable," *Journal of Marketing* 59, no. 2 (1995): 58–70.

Much has been written about quality orientation and total quality management (TQM) practices and the many benefits of these practices.[11] TQM has historically been emphasized in managerial circles.[12] However, a large body of scholarly academic research has emerged to explore the impact of quality orientations on business performance through increased efficiency, cost reduction, enhanced return on investment, market share, and sales growth.[13]

The original quality orientation (philosophy of quality) developed by Warne[14] argued that high quality is a powerful competitive weapon. Rust et al. found that a quality orientation affects business performance by reducing cost or by improving customer loyalty and attracting new customers (which grows revenue and profits).[15] The Proverbs 31:10–31 business framework seems to embrace this type of product quality, which gains the confidence and business of merchants and indicates a direct tie between quality management and reputation and profitability.

The Wisdom of Quality

So whether you eat or drink or whatever you do, do it all for the glory of God.

—1 Corinthians 10:31 NIV

Interestingly, the Bible has a lot to say about the quality of our work and the value we put on it. In order to provide a quality product, not only must the customer feel like the product's benefits are greater than the costs, but they should feel as though the benefits of the product far exceed the cost. The definition of customer value is simply objective benefits plus perceived benefits are greater than cost. When a product provides customer value, the value perceived by the customer accounts for the product quality, the service quality, and the price of the product. All three of these components must be in sync. A great quality product can provide a customer with a bad experience if delivered with poor service or if the customer doesn't know the product well and has a bad user experience. Great customer service will be devalued if the product

11. Joseph M. Juran and A. Blanton Godfrey, *Juran's Quality Handbook* (New York: McGraw-Hill, 1998).

12. Wuthichai Sittimalakron and Susan Hart, "Market Orientation Versus Quality Orientation: Sources of Superior Business Performance," *Journal of Strategic Marketing* 12, no. (2004): 243–53.

13. T. C. Powell, "Total Quality Management as Competitive Advantage: A Review and Empirical Study," *Strategic Management Journal* 16 (1995): 15–37; I. Mohr-Jackson, "Conceptualizing Total Quality Orientation," *European Journal of Marketing* 32, no. 1/2 (1998): 13–22.

14. Warne, "Developing a Quality Orientation."

15. Rust et al., "Return on Quality (ROQ)."

itself doesn't meet the customers' expectations. Finally, price is easily a go-to proxy for quality. We assume that more expensive wine is better quality, that the expensive imported chocolate bar is going to taste better than the regular Hershey's chocolate bar.

Proverbs 20 discusses the valuation of a product four times. It speaks to how we buy *and* sell products. Not only should we pay what the product is worth (see Proverbs 20:14, 17), but we should also charge what a product is worth (see Proverbs 20:10, 23). We should expect to pay what a product is worth (honoring the person selling us the product) and charge what a product is worth (honoring the person buying a product from us). In both of these scenarios, whether we are selling or buying, Proverbs has a standard of win-win exchange. Neither the supplier nor the customer should lose in a transaction with a wise person.

> Unequal weights and unequal measures
>   are both alike an abomination to the LORD. (Proverbs 20:10 ESV)

> "Bad, bad," says the buyer,
>   but when he goes away, then he boasts. (Proverbs 20:14 ESV)

> Bread gained by deceit is sweet to a man,
>   but afterward his mouth will be full of gravel. (Proverbs 20:17 ESV)

> Unequal weights are an abomination to the LORD,
>   and false scales are not good. (Proverbs 20:23 ESV)

This seems like fairly straightforward common sense on paper. However, unequal weights and false scales may be one of the practices I have seen play out most consistently in Christian and secular spaces. Many of my friends in the church have worked in real estate over the years. A friend who was a successful agent sold houses to people in the community as well as people in our local church. Many times, church friends with margin to pay a little more would negotiate the price of a house they were purchasing so low that it was clear the seller was going to lose significantly on the deal. In some cases, this is reasonable, and there could be a logical argument for it. However, the message this sent to the seller was that the Christian buyer did not care whether they benefitted from an exchange with them at all. The Christian buyer would go away and praise God for a deal they felt was blessed, while the non-Christian seller went away feeling cheated. This is a simple principle in Proverbs I don't ever think I have heard preached: Proverbs 3:27: "Do not withhold good from those to whom it is due when it is in your power to do it."

There is a key phrase in this verse: "whenever it is in your power to do it." In our Western mentality of inalienable rights and individual property rights, we get lured into thinking everything we earn belongs to us because, well, we earned it. However, this is not a kingdom principle. It is a cultural principle in the US. In 1 Corinthians 10:26, Paul is quoting Psalm 24:1 which says, "The earth is the LORD's, and all it contains, [t]he world, and those who live in it" (NASB). All that we have is God's, and all that we do and say is commanded to communicate his love and demonstrate his will. There is no better way to reflect the love of Jesus than to lay down our own, hard-earned resources for the blessing of others. Our right to what is ours was not a right that Jesus claimed for himself. He had earned the favor of God and the throne he sat on in heaven. He was perfection, yet he laid it down and freely gave us a righteousness that we did not deserve and definitely had not earned.

Perhaps the reward of blessings as wealth for the righteous is somewhat misunderstood, thus, it is important to keep reflecting on Proverbs 3:27b, "when it is in your power to do it." This does not mean that you buy products or property at a loss. However, I strongly believe that it means if you have a profit margin, you have a margin to be a blessing. If there is enough margin between your revenue (the price of the product) and cost (what you paid for the product plus cost of logistics), then there is a margin to be a blessing to others.

This has played out in corporate strategies over the years. For many years, Walmart had a reputation for being a bully when it came to buying. When Walmart first started to boom in the 1990s, companies rushed to get their products on Walmart shelves. Walmart underpaid its suppliers, and many of their suppliers declared bankruptcy because they could not cover the cost of the products they had sold to Walmart. Companies like Vlassic and Rubbermaid declared bankruptcy in order to write off debts.[16]

While Walmart did drive a lot of inefficiency out of the market with their tough-as-nails negotiating, over the years they realized that as a retailer, they need suppliers. Not only did they need suppliers, but they also needed loyal suppliers that would serve them well and find a win-win relationship in doing business with Walmart. Walmart shifted to a relationship management perspective with suppliers and does business very differently today. The lesson learned by Walmart has been learned in many industries through the

---

16. Charles Fishman, "The Wal-Mart You Don't Know," *Fast Company*, December 1, 2003, https://www.fastcompany.com/47593/wal-mart-you-dont-know.

maltreatment of both suppliers and customers. A mistreated customer will find the first opportunity possible to drop a supplier or product that does not meet their needs.

Finally, when discussing quality and value, price is a factor that should be addressed. It seems straightforward that you should only charge the customer what the product is actually worth. However, we see plenty of examples in the modern-day business of unethical pricing practices that depict the modern-day false balance. In recent years, we have seen retailers fall prey to false balances. Proverbs 11:1 states, "A false balance is an abomination to the LORD, but a just weight is his delight" (ESV). Whole Foods Market incorrectly weighed produce and got caught charging customers more for fresh-cut fruits than they were actually worth and 89 percent of their packaged foods were found to be mislabeled.[17] JCPenney, Kohl's, Macy's, and Sears were all sued for misleading pricing.[18] It is inherent in human nature to want to gain more for a product than what it is worth and to win a product for less than it is worth. However, Proverbs 20 makes it clear that both of these practices are not godly. That misleading pricing is not only determinantal to the individual, but it is also an abomination to God.

Jesus challenged the disciples and the Pharisees to live the kind of life where the quality of what they gave to others was not measured by the value of the other person to them. Jesus calls us to love others extravagantly in what we say *and* do.

Perhaps the ethics of Jesus are most clearly presented in a parable. After all, ethics are often best understood in the context of a difficult scenario. Interestingly, Jesus chose a controversial individual to demonstrate quality, an individual who probably would not have received the same quality service in return, in Luke 10:25–37. His parable of the good Samaritan demonstrates the quality of a service that is offered in love:

> Just then a lawyer stood up to test Jesus. "Teacher," he said, "what must I do to inherit eternal life?" He said to him, "What is written in the law? What do you read there?" He answered, "You shall love the Lord your God with all your heart, and with all your soul, and with all your strength, and with all your mind; and your neighbor as yourself." And he said to him, "You have given the right answer; do this, and you will live."

17. Chris Isadore, "Whole Foods Accused of Massive Overcharging," CNN, June 25, 2015, https://money.cnn.com/2015/06/25/news/companies/whole-foods-overcharging/.

18. Kathryn Vasel, "JCPenney, Kohl's, Macy's and Sears Sued over Misleading Prices," CNN, December 9, 2016, https://money.cnn.com/2016/12/09/pf/price-scheme-jcpenney-kohls-sears-macys/.

But wanting to justify himself, he asked Jesus, "And who is my neighbor?" Jesus replied, "A man was going down from Jerusalem to Jericho, and fell into the hands of robbers, who stripped him, beat him, and went away, leaving him half dead. Now by chance a priest was going down that road; and when he saw him, he passed by on the other side. So likewise a Levite, when he came to the place and saw him, passed by on the other side. But a Samaritan while traveling came near him; and when he saw him, he was moved with pity. He went to him and bandaged his wounds, having poured oil and wine on them. Then he put him on his own animal, brought him to an inn, and took care of him. The next day he took out two denarii, gave them to the innkeeper, and said, 'Take care of him; and when I come back, I will repay you whatever more you spend.' Which of these three, do you think, was a neighbor to the man who fell into the hands of the robbers?" He said, "The one who showed him mercy." Jesus said to him, "Go and do likewise."

The Samaritan could have done the minimum to alleviate his own conscience in his exchange with the Jew that was robbed, beaten, and left for dead on the side of the road. He expected zero payment for all he did for the Jewish man:

- He went to him.
- He bandaged his wounds, pouring on oil and wine.
- Then he put the man on his own donkey.
- He brought him to an inn.
- He took care of him.
- The next day he took out two denarii and gave them to the innkeeper. "Look after him," he said, "and when I return, I will reimburse you for any extra expense you may have."

The business argument I would anticipate is that you can't do business like this. You wouldn't make any money. However, I don't think the Samaritan went broke helping this man. It was within his power to help him. I don't think his shareholders would have been robbed of any profit in this scenario. I also believe that if he ever had any need in the future, this man he helped would be a loyal friend. However, I don't think the Samaritan helped the man for his own future security. This parable illustrates for us how we are to demonstrate love through quality deeds. This is a call to go above and beyond what is required to meet people's needs in order to demonstrate to the world how lavishly God loves us. With a kingdom mindset, we are not looking to overcome just the opportunism of win-lose transactions to create win-win exchanges. Kingdom mindset calls us to have a sacrifice-win mindset. Our sacrifice creates an opportunity for blessing and delight for someone else. In this way, we can answer Christ's call to discipleship. In all facets of life, we are called to pick up our cross, to embrace suffering, to prefer others, to truly mirror Christ's actions in all we do.

Any sacrifice incurred in delighting the customer is short lived in most companies. When resources are well stewarded (the budget is balanced and buying/spending is wise), delighted customers create inertia for firm growth for years to come. Providing a quality product drives customer value, and customer value that goes above and beyond customer expectations will result in customer loyalty. Business research has demonstrated this consistently over the last fifty-plus years.

Fifty-Plus Years of Quality Research

From 1950 to today, thousands of research projects have been conducted and articles have been written about Total Quality Management. Interestingly, the majority of the articles have focused on the healthcare industry. Below, you will find a breakdown of the fields of study that have explored TQM. Within the 3,500-plus business articles that are available on the Web of Science, the peak years of academic research into TQM are in the late 1990s and early 2000s. However, there continues to be a consistent contribution to knowledge about quality management over the years.

In 1993 and 1994 (perhaps at the peak of TQM research) both the *California Management Review* and the *Academy of Management Review* ran special issues on TQM.[19] Four journals focused in this area have been created including: *Total Quality Management & Business Excellence, International Journal of Lean Six Sigma*, and *Quality Progress*.[20] There continues to be research published in mainstream operations and business journals, such as the *Harvard Business Review* and the *Journal of Operations Management* in the past twenty years. When the search is broadened to include the concepts of lean, continuous improvement, six sigma, and the Toyota Production System, another 5,500-plus research articles appear.

---

19. *California Management Review*, Special Issue: TQM, vol. 35, no. 3 1993, https://journals.sage pub.com/loi/cmr; and *Academy of Management Review*, Special Issue: TQM, vol. 19, no. 3, 1994, https://journals.aom.org/toc/amr/19/3.

20. *Total Quality Management & Business Excellence*, https://www.tandfonline.com/loi/ctqm20; *International Journal of Lean Six Sigma*, https://www.emerald.com/insight/publication/issn/2040-4166; *Quality Progress*, https://asq.org/quality-progress.

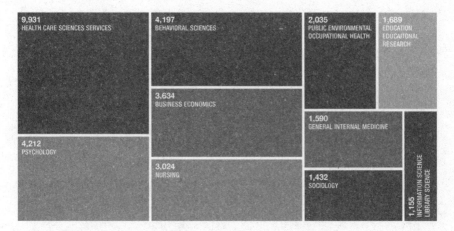

FIGURE 7.1: Sources of Total Quality Management Research from 1950–2020

While the popularity and practicality of lean management has perhaps peaked and begun to wane (leading journals report fewer lean-focused publications since 2017), the timelessness of a quality orientation has remained relevant. The quality orientation adopts the customer focus of the market orientation but delves deeper into the processes necessary to achieve customer-perceived quality. In her work on quality orientation conceptualization, Iris Mohr-Jackson defines quality orientation slightly differently to focus on the customer: "The organization-wide commitment to continuous improvement for delivery of customer-perceived quality and ultimately customer satisfaction."[21] The adoption of a quality orientation indicated that the leadership of the company recognizes the need to engage the customer in order to achieve long-term sustainable success.

In a study conducted in the late 1990s (published in 1998), Iris Mohr-Jackson at St. John's University in New York interviewed executives at fifty organizations, including nine consumer products, twenty-four industrial products, twelve services, and five retail and wholesale distribution companies to develop a comprehensive framework of total quality orientation.[22] Participating companies included some of the recognizable organizations below:

Marriott	Motorola
American Express	American Tobacco

21. Mohr-Jackson, "Conceptualizing Total Quality Orientation," 13–22, 19.

22. I. Mohr-Jackson, "Managing a Total Quality Orientation: Factors Affecting Customer Satisfaction," *Industrial Marketing Management* 27, no. 2 (1998): 109–25.

AT&T	Federal Express
Boeing	Target Stores
Cadillac Motor Company	Ford Motor Company
Colgate	Tetley Tea
Reynolds and Reynolds	Travelers
Sara Lee Hosiery	Hewlett-Packard
Shell Oil	Union Pacific
Corning	Honeywell
Sonoco Products	Xerox
Dunlop Tire	US Department of Agriculture
Southern Pacific	US Postal Service
3M	L.L. Bean
IBM	

Mohr-Jackson found the following practices to be antecedents to total quality orientation of a company:

- Senior management involvement
- Senior management consistency
- Participative management
- Proficiency of the process management
- Internal customer satisfaction (employee buy-in)
- Reliance on HR policies
- Empowerment
- Integration of total quality within the plan
- Reliance on meaningful data

Later research has built on the early conceptualization of quality orientation to explore the impact of quality strategies on revenue, efficiency, and customer satisfaction. In 2008, research published by Marinova et al. concluded that a quality orientation positively impacts financial-and customer-related outcomes.[23] Their research explored the impact of quality orientation at the frontline of nonprofit hospitals. All customer-facing frontline employees who were empowered and well-equipped to do their jobs had better per-unit revenue, better customer satisfaction, and a higher level of efficiency.

---

23. D. Marinova, J. Ye, and J. Singh, "Do Frontline Mechanisms Matter? Impact of Quality and Productivity Orientations on Unit Revenue, Efficiency, and Customer Satisfaction," *Journal of Marketing* 72, no. 2 (2008): 28–45.

Total Quality Management as a
Means to the End Goal of Wisdom

Management gurus Prahalad and Ramaswamy defined co-creation as "the joint creation of value by the company and the customer; allowing the customer to co-construct the service experience to suit their context."[24] The co-creation of quality products from a wisdom perspective can be defined as the act of engaging external parties, usually customer or suppliers, into a company's creative process to establish mutual value through high-quality product and service innovation that reflects a deep understanding of and love for customers.

We want what is best for our loved ones. Jesus challenges the disciples to not stop at loving their family and friends. Even evil people love their own family and friends. Jesus called the disciples to love their neighbors. A neighbor may be someone you love and want to help, but a neighbor may also be a stranger who wouldn't help you if the tables were turned. A neighbor may be someone who disagrees with your views and lifestyle. A neighbor may be someone who has a lot more or a lot less than you. Whatever the characteristics of a neighbor, we are called to love them all.

If we commit to loving our neighbors, the challenge is to demonstrate that by wanting what is best for them, even at a personal cost. It costs more upfront to implement continuous improvement in a manufacturing plant. It takes a lot more time in the short run to listen to employees and make changes to imperfect processes. But without investment, it is irrational to expect a return. Without sowing, it is impossible to reap a harvest.

The starting place and the end goal of wisdom is to love and honor God. We are called to give God our best and to give others the best we have. Quality is not just a Toyota philosophy; it is a kingdom mindset. We have a choice when we buy and sell products to do it at a standard of excellence that would make it work worthy of our calling.

Reflection Questions

1. Read and reflect on Proverbs 20 and Luke 10. How do the two passages compliment and explain each other?
2. Read Genesis 4:1–16 and describe how this passage could relate to our understanding of quality.
3. Describe an example of a company that gained a market advantage because of a higher-quality product.

24. Coimbatore K. Prahalad and Venkat Ramaswamy, "Co-Creation Experiences: The Next Practice in Value Creation," *Journal of Interactive Marketing* 18, no. 3 (2004): 5–14.

CHAPTER 8

SUPPLY CHAIN
ORIENTATION

To make cleanliness commonplace; to lessen work for women; to foster health and contribute to personal attractiveness, that life may be more enjoyable and rewarding for the people who use our products.

—William Hesketh Lever, 1890[1]

In 1885, William Hesketh Lever had a market orientation (a philosophy for understanding customers, the market, and corporate coordination) before its time. Working in his father's wholesale grocery business, he became aware of demand in the marketplace for soap. The challenge was selling it at an affordable price for the growing middle and working classes in England. Britain's squalid urban environments in the late 1800s were breeding grounds for typhoid, cholera, and smallpox—all diseases that basic hygiene and soap can help eliminate or reduce to some degree.[2]

To leverage the rising standards of living, Lever knew he needed to be able to mass-produce soap himself and to apply large-scale marketing methods to create visibility for his product. Three years after he rented a soap factory in Warrington, England, in 1885, Lever was able to purchase land and build a factory. His soap business was so successful that the town came to be named Port Sunlight after the Sunlight brand he created in the late 1880s. During the industrial revolution, Lever was unique in his creation of Port Sunlight. It offered generous wages and innovative benefits. While it wasn't a perfect model—it required compulsory participation in activities with many intrusive rules—the conditions, pay, hours, and benefits were all above average for the industry.

---

1. Unilever, "History of Unilever," http://www.historyofbranding.com/unilever/.
2. Christopher Barlett, "Unilever's Lifebuoy in India: Implementing the Sustainability Plan," *Harvard Business School Case Study*, March 8, 2017, https://store.hbr.org/case-studies/.

Soon after he established market share with Sunlight, he launched the Lifebuoy and Lux brands. His success grew so quickly that by the early 1900s, he was selling soap all over the world. However, while Lever had created global demand, he had supply problems. Raw materials for soap were in short supply. Lever began to vertically integrate his company upstream. He began buying plantations in the Solomon Islands and in the Congo to support demand for palm oil. Palm oil is a now-controversial raw material that has played a significant role in the development of many products over the last 100 years, including Lever's next product extension. In 1927, Lever Brothers diversified into another palm oil dependent product, adding margarine with the creation of the Viking brand. From early on in their corporate growth, the company now know as Unilever had a supply chain strategy that integrated raw materials supply (mainly palm oil) across product lines to streamline manufacturing and move product into the market.

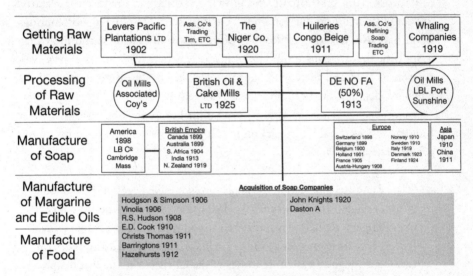

FIGURE 8.1: The Lever Organization 1927

Over a hundred years before Lever Brothers launched the Viking margarine brand, Dutch companies Jurgens and Van den Bergh competed in the butter industry before extending their product lines into margarine. Quickly the margarine giants all over Europe—Jurgens, Van den Bergh, Centra, and Schicht—signed a competition agreement in 1920. As the Lever Brother company launched the Viking margarine brand in 1927, the Margarine Union was formed between the leading butter/margarine companies. Just three years later, the company now called Unilever came into existence as the Margarine Union and Lever Brothers merged to reduce competition for the supply of fats and oils.

As the two European enterprises merged their markets on the European continent and in the UK, the impact of the merger was felt throughout the Lever plantations in Africa and around the world. Before the merger, Lever Brothers was the largest company in Britain. After the merger, Unilever became the first modern multinational company with operations and head-quarters in both the UK and the Netherlands, as well as an extended supply chain that reached from Europe to Africa and the Far East.

Unilever PLC was registered in the Netherlands in 1981 after years of having shares in both the UK and the Netherlands. Unilever has learned as it has grown. While William Lever had a unique philosophy of placing the welfare of his workers in the UK equal to his wealth, his philosophy of social impact did not extend beyond Europe to reach his African workers. Further, as Unilever has grown in a global footprint, it has worked somewhat retroactively to improve palm oil sourcing and growing standards to reduce the negative impact of palm oil production on the environment. Despite his shortcomings, Lever had an interesting philosophy of sociology and business and did things in his time that were uncommon. For instance, when William Lever was made a baron in 1917 and then a viscount in 1922, he combined his name with his wife's maiden name to become known as Leverhulme.[3]

In a speech given by Viscount Leverhulme before the Society of Chemical Industry at Liverpool University on July 10, 1924, he demonstrated his unique perspective on the world:

> Science and Religion cannot be made into scrambled eggs in the economy of life. Religion is not in conflict with science, nor is science in conflict with Religion. Religion must ever be the compass and chart through life's voyage, with its storms and passions. . . . It has been a bigoted attitude of the Church through at least 16 centuries of the Christian era . . . that has pro-duced a disastrously sterilizing effect on the benefits Science would have lavished with generous hand on mankind. It has been Science, in spite of all the persecution arising out of mistaken interpretation of the teachings of the Bible, that has been the vitalizing power in raising the condition of mankind to its present advances and the still higher level of comforts and elegancies of life the future should have in store for humankind. . . .
>
> Professors of religion and professors of science must learn to go arm in arm together through life to raise and elevate mankind higher and higher above the brute beast and nearer and nearer to the angels. . . .

---

3. "Leverhulme: Our History," https://leverhulme.net/our-history.

Religion, like Science, must progress by reason of the wise solution of new problems arising and requiring solution at each step forward made by mankind.[4]

While Viscount Leverhulme certainly introduced products that benefited humanity and had domestic policies that benefitted his workers, he did have blind spots in his practices in other parts of the world. Not meant to be a perfect case example, Unilever serves as an interesting exemplar of a company that grasped supply chain strategy and globalization far before it was ever taught in a business class. Over 120 *Harvard Business Review* articles and cases have been written about Unilever. Thirty-eight cases have been written on strategy and global business alone. With 400 brands sold in 190 countries, Unilever's supply chain reaches nearly every country on the globe. They have commercial operations and factories in more than 100 countries, making their vision to make sustainable living commonplace—a complex goal to achieve. According to Unilever reports, they have an annual buying program of nearly $40 billion, including agricultural raw materials, 51 percent of which are sustainably sourced. With the world's leading supply chain, Unilever has invested heavily in the efficiency and eco-production of its 306 factories.

Unilever has had a dynamic impact on the global economy and culture through its products and brands. At its inception, the goal was to improve hygiene, but over the years Unilever brands have had a much broader impact. In perhaps one of my favorite TED Talks[5] of all time, titled "Profit's Not Always the Point," Harish Manwani, global chief operating officer of Unilever, says that people and organizations need a purpose beyond profit.

Starting out in sales in India, his boss asked him, "Harish, why are you here?"

He responded, "To sell soap."

His boss then said, "No, you are here to save lives."

Unilever runs the largest handwashing program in the world with products that are changing the lives of more than half a billion people through a brand that is at the forefront of social change. Harish Manwani has gone on to join BlackRock as a senior operation partner. However, during his long tenure at Unilever, he grew to believe business growth should not only be consistent, competitive, and profitable, it also needs to be responsible. Responsible companies will bring social value by serving the communities that sustain them. Responsible

---

4. William Hesketh Lever, "Addressed at: 'The Messel Memorial Lecture', before the Society of Chemical Industry at the Annual Conference at Liverpool University, Liverpool," July 10, 1924, http://uni lever-archives.com/Record.aspx?src=CalmView.Catalog&id=GB1752.UNI%2FBD%2f2%2f1%2f1%2f19.

5. Harish Manwani, "Profit's Not Always the Point," TED Talk, https://www.ted.com/talks/harish _manwani_profit_s_not_always_the_point?utm_campaign=tedspread&utm_medium=referral&utm _source=tedcomshare.

companies do this by making money and doing good for people and the planet simultaneously. Unilever has contributed to global hygiene with its soap brands, has shifted perceptions of beauty with the Dove brand,[6] and delivered products that improve standards of living for the three billion people in the world who live in poverty at the bottom of the global economic pyramid.

In 2019, Gartner moved Unilever into the Supply Chain Masters category[7] after they were ranked in the top five global supply chain management companies for ten years consecutively. Joining Apple, Proctor & Gamble, Amazon, and McDonald's, Unilever has consistently attained top-five composite scores for the last ten years.

Perhaps nowhere in the world outside of England and the Netherlands does Unilever have a larger brand footprint than in Indonesia. As a byproduct of Dutch colonialism, the Dutch companies that later merged to become Unilever had operations and sourcing in Indonesia for a century before merging with Lever Brothers. To this day, Indonesia is the world's biggest producer of palm oil, a raw material that is globally scarce. Palm oil is the central ingredient in both soap and margarine; the scarcity of palm oil and other raw materials in Europe drove the companies to merge in the first place. The Lifebuoy and Sunlight brands are still front and center on the retail shelves in Indonesia, as well as many other Indonesian brands that Unilever has acquired over the years.

Over dinner at a trendy sushi restaurant in West Jakarta, I talked with a new friend who had started her career in the Unilever leadership development program in Indonesia. As a regional sales leader and market analyst, she was tasked with managing sales teams and boosting the sales of Unilever brands into the local retail markets in Sulawesi. Like many other workforces throughout Indonesia, the sales force in Sulawesi was paid weekly. Still an agrarian society where trading and hunting/gathering cover many daily needs, cash was primarily for nonessential items. She found that many of her employees spent a large percentage of their paychecks on cigarettes. Unilever has a thorough onboarding process that engrains its corporate mission and brand stories into the psyche of their leadership teams. Leadership training at Unilever sounds similar to officer training in the army. Long hours, hard tasks, and obstacles to be conquered are all a part of the journey to becoming part of the team. The socialization process at Unilever encourages employees to think outside of the box and to engage their local markets with not just data but also an understanding of the emotional connection and the story.

6. Dove Real Beauty, "Dove Campaign for Real Beauty," Dove US, 2013. See https://newsgeneration.com /2014/04/11/pr-case-study-dove-real-beauty/; and https://www.dove.com/us/en/stories/about-dove.html.

7. The Supply Chain Masters category is a categorization for companies who are consistently at the top of the list globally.

While my friend was trained in data analysis and accustomed to business presentations of spreadsheets and charts, she found that she was pressed to understand her team more deeply, to understand the local consumer better. She realized that the only person who seemed to have any motivational power over her sales team was their wives. Certainly unconventional in most US contexts, she hosted all her sales teams' wives for tea and discussed the opportunities Unilever held in store for their families if their husbands delivered slightly higher sales revenue. Within the quarter, her sales team hit the goals and exceeded them.

Successful supply chain management is not just about delivering inventory. As Unilever's 100-year-plus history demonstrates, successful supply chain management is about understanding demand by knowing the customer well. It is also about understanding suppliers and building relationships and partnerships with suppliers to make sure that the right supply of raw materials and finished goods are available to meet customer demand. Finally, it is about mobilizing and empowering people to build the trust necessary for relationships that facilitate financial exchange, information exchange, and action.

Supply Chain Orientation

Normally disciplines take 200 years to several centuries to evolve. In 40 to 50 short years, we've seen this discipline [logistics] evolve from physical distribution management, with a focus on outbound, to logistics, where we connected the dots further back in production and purchasing and out to second and third-tier vendors, and down to customers and customers' customers. And all the time that was happening, *the focus became more global; it became more integrated*, and it broadened the focus of this function.

—*Bud LaLonde, Ohio State University*[8]

The supply chain management field has grown exponentially in the last fifty-plus years. The supply chain management school of thought that I was trained in originally emerged out of marketing. When marketing first became a discipline 100 years earlier, the focus was on marketing distribution channels.

Products were mass-produced during the industrial revolution, and consumer options were initially limited. For instance, Ford made the model-T in one color, black, and people lined up to buy it. Marketing was focused on getting products to the market and less focused on advertising, which is what most

---

8. "Supply Chain Logistics Is the Name of the Game," *Materials Handling & Logistics*, October 14, 2009, https://www.mhlnews.com/transportation-distribution/article/22041842/supply-chain-logistics-is-the-name-of-the-game. Emphasis mine.

people think marketing is. As the industrial revolution progressed and competition proliferated, companies began broadening marketing to consumer awareness. With the advent of the radio, and later the television, mass marketing and advertising became more central to the broad understanding of marketing.

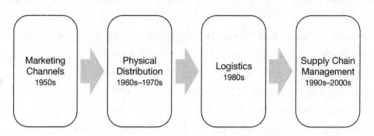

FIGURE 8.2: The Emergence of the Supply
Chain Management Concept[9]

Over the years, as the marketing discipline evolved to focus on consumer behavior and consumer psychology, marketing channels and physical distribution research shifted to logistics and then to supply chain management. Before Harvard professor Michael Porter dubbed the concept of the "value chain" in his influential book *Competitive Advantage*[10] in 1985, the "logistics legends" of the Big Ten land-grant schools Pennsylvania State University, Ohio State University, and Michigan State University were forging the academic field of logistics that would later become supply chain management.

In the early 1960s, three marketing channels professors, Dr. John J. Coyle (PSU), Dr. Bud LaLonde (OSU), and Dr. Don Bowersox (MSU), were among the first in the field to teach logistics courses, publish physical distribution research, and build what would become three of the top supply chain programs in the world. Supply chain management had evolved. Physical distribution was a single company's strategy for distributing products to the customer. Supply chain management encompassed the planning and management of all activities involved in sourcing, procurement, production, and logistics within and across three or more companies.[11]

9. Wroe Alderson, "Factors Governing the Development of Marketing Channels," *Marketing Channels for Manufactured Products*, ed. Richard M. Clewett (Homewood, IL: Irwin, 1954): 5–34; Donald J. Bowersox, "Physical Distribution Development, Current Status, and Potential," *Journal of Marketing* 33, no. 1 (1969): 63–70.

10. Michael E. Porter and Competitive Advantage, "Creating and Sustaining Superior Performance," *Competitive Advantage* 167 (1985): 167–206.

11. Adopted from the Council of Supply Chain Management Professionals (CSCMP), https://cscmp.org/CSCMP/Academia/SCM_Definitions_and_Glossary_of_Terms/CSCMP/Educate/SCM_Definitions_and_Glossary_of_Terms.aspx?hkey=60879588-f65f-4ab5-8c4b-6878815ef921.

By the time I arrived at the University of Tennessee in 2008 to pursue my PhD in logistics, my professors were the students of Coyle, LaLonde, and Bowersox. My first professor in the PhD program was Bowersox's protégé, Dr. Tom Mentzer. Tom Mentzer was a legend in his own right in the supply chain field and at the University of Tennessee. Throughout his career, Mentzer published more than 190 papers and articles and was recognized across the marketing and logistics academies as a leading thinker. Mentzer's school of thought was that supply chain management was at the intersection of supply and demand—that logistics and marketing should be integrated. While a student at the University of Tennessee, Knoxville, the supply chain faculty published the much-debated[12] *demand and supply integration framework of value creation*. Demand and supply integration is defined as "the balancing of demand and supply market information and business intelligence through integrated knowledge management processes to strategically manage demand and supply activities for the creation of superior customer value."[13]

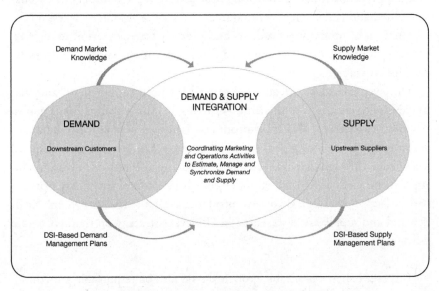

FIGURE 8.3: Demand and Supply Integration
Adopted from Stank et al.[14]

12. Much debated in an academic sense; less than 100 people alive are aware of the debate that took place at a Council of Supply Chain Management Professionals conference between Mentzer and a professor at Ohio State University a year before I arrived on the SCM academic scene.

13. Terry L. Esper, Alexander E. Ellinger, Theodore P. Stank, Daniel J. Flint, and Mark Moon, "Demand and Supply Integration: A Conceptual Framework of Value Creation through Knowledge Management," *Journal of the Academy of Marketing Science* 38, no. 1 (2010): 5–18, p. 7.

14. Theodore P. Stank, Terry L. Esper, T. Russell Crook, and Chad W. Autry, "Creating

Based on the faculty I worked with directly at UTK, my main focus in research became the exploration of social antecedents to demand and supply integration, cross-functional integration, and the potential environmental outcomes. While supply chain management encompasses multiple firms, demand and supply integration takes place initially within a single firm. At a strategic level, demand and supply integration is guided by the company's supply chain philosophy or orientation.

A supply chain orientation is defined as the recognition by a company of the systemic, strategic implications of the activities and processes involved in managing the various flows of products, information, and finances from raw material suppliers to the end-product retailer to the consumer and to end of product life.[15] A supply chain orientation that integrates demand and supply knowledge will likely include both social and environmental perspectives. On the social side, understanding suppliers' and customers' behavior and building trusting relationships will inform both demand and supply knowledge. Environmental initiatives are impacted by customer demand and the natural resources and service resources necessary for raw materials inputs into products and product transportation to market. Finally, all of this must be activated profitably for the supply chain to be sustainably viable.

Unilever provides a great case example for both supply chain and sustainability orientations of the firm. With 400 brands spanning home goods, personal care items, and food products, Unilever strategically balances consumer demand and global supply challenges. Unilever pursues demand knowledge through demand sensing (forecasting and market research) and supply knowledge through supplier coordination and inventory optimization (supply strategies) to have products available for customers. Both demand and supply are represented in Unilever's strategy on their corporate website:

> Unilever believes profitable growth should also be responsible growth. That approach lies at the heart of our business model, driven by sustainable living and the USLP. It guides our approach to how we do business and

---

Relevant Value through Demand and Supply Integration," *Journal of Business Logistics* 33, no. 2 (2012): 167–72.

15. Adapted from Mentzer et al., "Defining Supply Chain Management," and later defined by Min, Mentzer, and Ladd, "Market Orientation in Supply Chain Management."

how we meet the growing consumer demand for brands that act responsibly in a world of finite resources.

Our business model begins with consumer insight that informs brand innovation, often with partners in our supply chain, to create products we take to market supported by marketing and advertising across a range of distribution channels.[16]

The ultimate measures of supply chain performance are profitability and customer service. Without good customer service, it is difficult to remain profitable. Customer service is measured in retail and consumer packaged goods supply chains as on-shelf availability. The *seven rights* of logistics and supply chain goals are to have the *right* product, in the *right* place, at the *right* time, in the *right* condition, in the *right* quantity, for the *right* cost, for the *right* customer.[17] The work that I conducted after completing my dissertation took the supply chain orientation a step further by integrating an understanding of both the end-consumer and the shopper.

For some products, like dog food and diapers, the end-consumer is not the customer or the shopper who will physically purchase the product in the retail store. For a consumer packaged goods (CPG) company like Unilever, final delivery of the product through the supply chain requires not only knowledge of the end-consumer who will consume the product and the retail customer who buys the product initially from them, but also includes the shopper—the individual who will go to the store and purchase the product. The seven rights of logistics aim to meet the shopper at their place of need with the right product.

I have found that in large retail supply chains, multiple CPG companies will collaborate with the retail customer to integrate their internal demand and supply knowledge externally with each other. This is how we get grilling displays at Walmart or Target that include a grill, hotdogs from Oscar Meyer, buns from Wonder, and ketchup and mustard from Heinz all with a Walmart brand message.

---

16. "Our Strategy," Unilever USA, https://www.unileverusa.com/about/who-we-are/our-strategy/.

17. Martin Christopher, *Logistics & Supply Chain Management*, 5th ed. (London: Pearson Education Limited, 2011), 45.

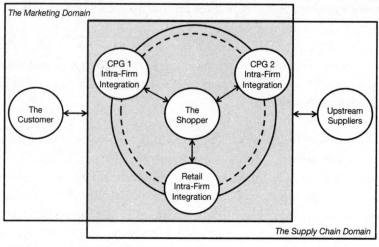

The shaded area represents the shopper marketing event, in which the CPG firms(s) and the Retailer experience both intra-firm as well as inter-firm integration for event execution.

—— Shopper Behavior Knowledge
------ Supply Chain System Knowledge

FIGURE 8.4: The Shopper Service Supply Chain Ecosystem[18]

I wouldn't have imagined how many ways there are to love people well through the simple act of delivering a product and meeting customer demand. The concept of having products available for the shopper is evident in Proverbs. Proverbs is clear that withholding products where there is need is wrong, while providing products helps to meet a need while also delivering profitability to a company.

The Wisdom of a Supply Chain Orientation

People curse the one who hoards grain,
     but they pray God's blessing on the one who is willing to sell.

—Proverbs 11:26 NIV

Chapter 7 on the quality orientation of the firm established that the Bible has a lot to say about how we engage with customers and suppliers. At first, I didn't think a supply chain philosophy existed in Scripture. Supply chain management has only been a discipline since the 1990s. However, as I explored Scripture, I kept finding examples of multiple individuals or companies collaborating to provide an end-consumer access to a product.

---

18. Adopted from Stolze, Mollenkopf, and Flint, "What Is the Right Supply Chain for Your Shopper?"

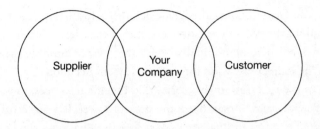

FIGURE 8.5: The Simple Supply Chain

Throughout Scripture, there are examples of God's attention to inventory and making products available to the world. Of course, wisdom personified as the Noble Woman in Proverbs 31:10–31 was the first place I came to terms with the fact that maybe the concepts written 3,000 years ago in Scripture could apply to the fields of logistics and supply chain management today. In Proverbs 31:10–31 alone, there are nearly half a dozen references to work that takes place within the supply chain:

v. 13   She *seeks* wool and flax and *works* with willing hands.

v. 14   She is like the ships of the merchant, she *brings* her food from far away.

v. 15   She rises while it is still night and *provides* food for her household and *tasks* for her servants.

v. 16   She considers a field and *buys* it; with the fruit of her hands she *plants* a vineyard.

v. 18   She perceives that her *merchandise is profitable.* Her lamp does not go out at night.

v. 21   She is *not afraid* for her household when it snows, for all her household are clothed in crimson.

v. 24   She *makes* linen garments and *sells* them; she *supplies* the merchant with sashes.

In action, she is buying raw materials (wool, flax, food, seed) and real estate (fields) and transforming the raw materials into products—food for employees, linen garments, sashes—then delivering the products to the marketplace profitably. In verse 21, she has a plan for seasonality, so her whole organization is prepared for winter seasons. Finally, in verse 20, she can open her hands to the poor and needy with the excess profitability and products.

Out of the five books of the Torah—Genesis, Exodus, Leviticus, Numbers, and Deuteronomy, also referred to as the Pentateuch—Exodus, Leviticus,

Numbers, and Deuteronomy all include detailed information about the inventory needed for the Ark of the Covenant, the tabernacle, and later, the temple. In 1 Kings 5, when Solomon finally begins the work of building the temple in Jerusalem, he sources the wood for the temple from Lebanon.

Of all of the Old Testament stories that include resources, raw materials, scarcity of supply, and human need, the story of Joseph is a powerful example. When Joseph ends up in Pharaoh's court wearing Pharaoh's signet ring with the charge of the whole land of Egypt in Genesis 41, it is because he was able to interpret Pharaoh's dreams about supply and demand. With the help of the Holy Spirit, Joseph understood Pharaoh's dreams as prophetic warnings of a coming famine. Joseph built what I would assume was the world's largest warehouse of the day and was able to store up enough supply of food that not only Egypt but also the surrounding areas were sustained. Genesis 41:57 says, "All the world came to Egypt to buy grain from Joseph, because the famine was sever everywhere." In a way, the whole world was saved.

Arguably, the first miracle Jesus ever conducted was to balance supply and demand. The supply of wine at the wedding of Cana had run out, and there was clearly demand for more wine among the wedding guests. In John 2, Jesus supplies more than enough quality wine to exceed the demand of the wedding guests. In fact, they are shocked by the high quality of the wine. Throughout the narratives in Scripture, supply chain management is demonstrated. However, a supply chain in action does not provide a sense of duty to the person of faith unless it is understood within the lens of wisdom.

Why is it wise to have a supply chain orientation? If found in the awe of God, how can a supply chain orientation further the ultimate goal of wisdom to love and honor God and others? Without a supply chain orientation, we are left blind to the impact of our firm within the network of firms it depends on to exist. Few companies exist without extended suppliers and customers. To do so, a company would have to be fully vertically integrated and local. For example, it is possible for a company that manufactures wooden blocks to own a forest. The wooden block company could cut down the trees and create lumber that they then transform to blocks and sell out of a local shop that they also own. But it is more likely that a company that manufactures wooden blocks will buy wood from a lumber yard (1) that bought trees from a forestry company (2). They would then pay a transportation provider (3) to transport the finished blocks to a public warehouse (4). From the public warehouse, the finished blocks may be delivered to retail customers (5) who will sell the blocks to the end-consumer (6). Even with one simple product, a company can easily impact the operations of six or more other companies.

We assume in this example that the only raw material in the product is wood and there is no packaging involved to protect the final product from damage on the retail shelf or in transport, which would add even more companies to the list.

If we are called to love God and to love our neighbor, we must understand who our neighbors are in business and how our work impacts our neighbors. Perhaps a supply chain orientation guided by wisdom would engage suppliers in vested relationships that ensure that the transactions between companies profit both parties. In past years, companies like Walmart learned the hard way that if suppliers are undercut and they are not profitable, they will go out of business and the supply of products the company needs to meet demand will no longer be available. Further, a supply chain orientation guided by wisdom would listen to customers to deliver the product to them in the right quantity, at the right location, and at the right price.

Economic models of competition lead us to believe that competition is driven by scarcity—that markets are healthy because of competition to gain access to the supply of scarce products or markets. Therefore, we can only win if we gain access to supply and customers at the expense of competition—other companies like ours. However, throughout Scripture, there is a recurrent model of the kingdom of God coming to provide more than enough.

During the exodus of Israel from Egypt to the promised land in the book of Exodus, there was always manna and quail left over.[19] Jesus provided more than enough fine wine to meet and exceed the needs of the wedding guests. When Jesus fed the five thousand, there were twelve baskets of bread leftover.[20] The supply chains of the Bible not only balanced supply and demand but had margin left over for those in need. I'll talk more about this in chapter 11 on comparative advantage, but if there is anything we can learn as Christians and people of faith from supply chain orientation research, it is that the most profitable supply chains are the world leaders in collaboration, in profit-sharing with suppliers, and delivering value to the end customer.

Of course, these examples all demonstrate a supernatural intervention of God in supply that is not a regular source of supply in most companies today (nor was it in ancient times either). However, the history of leaders like Joseph demonstrates that a relationship with God is not just about discernment in balancing spending with revenue; there is always potential for divine intervention in major and small ways. Joseph interpreted a dream that led him to

---

19. Exodus 16.
20. John 6:1–15.

discern the path for Egypt to supply enough grain to meet the demand for food during a coming famine. Whether natural or supernatural, Scripture provides evidence for the importance of inventory, supply, and our diligence to provide enough to meet our own needs, with margin left over to provide for the needs of others.

Supply Chain Orientation Research

Supply chain orientation research has tested and found evidence that supply chain oriented firms build and maintain trust, commitment, cooperation, and leadership support internally that is transferred to strategic relationships with supply chain partners. In a research study conducted by Tom Mentzer and Soonhong Min, the relationship between supply chain orientation and firm performance was significant across a sample of 442 companies.[21] Respondents to the survey were senior executives with visibility into at least one supply chain to which their company belonged, with direct supply chain responsibilities. The model they hypothesized is below in Figure 8.6 from the article they published in the *Journal of the Academy of Marketing Science* in 2007. They believed that market orientation (market intelligence) would guide a firm's internal supply chain orientation that would then positively impact the supply chain management with a positive boost to the firm's performance. The circles below market orientation, supply chain orientation, supply chain management, and firm performance represent the measures of each concept.

In their research, they did not find a direct impact of market orientation on firm performance. They also did not find that supply chain management impacted firm performance. However, they did find a direct impact of supply chain orientation on both supply chain management *and* firm performance. Based on this study, we can believe that a supply chain orientation has been found to positively impact firm performance measured through product availability, product and service offerings, timeliness, profitability, and revenue growth. Later research conducted at Michigan State University further demonstrated the relationship between supply chain orientation and balanced score-card performance outcomes, including customer satisfaction, financial growth, internal processes, and innovation.[22]

---

21. Min, Mentzer, and Ladd, "Market Orientation in Supply Chain Management."
22. G. T. M. Hult, D. J. Ketchen Jr., G. L. Adams, and J.A. Mena, "Supply Chain Orientation and Balance Scorecard Performance," *Journal of Managerial Issues* 20, no. 4 (2008): 526–44.

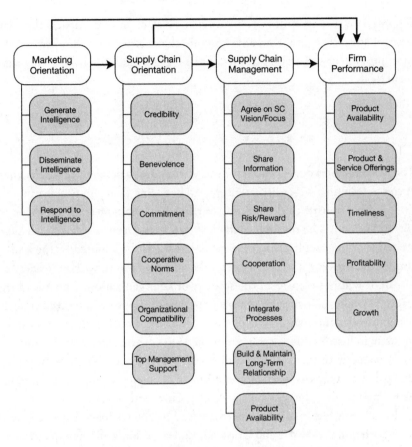

FIGURE 8.6: Proposed Impact of SC Orientation and SCM on Firm Performance[23]

A qualitative study conducted a few years later by Ayman Omar, Beth Davis-Sramek, and Brian Fugate explored the antecedents and the process through which firms adopt a supply chain orientation.[24] They found as firms move from traditional supply chains to best-in-class supply chain management, managers must (1) evolve their thinking from a firm-centric to a holistic supply chain view, and (2) execute synergistic interfirm interests through collaboration, moving from a win-lose to an and/both or win-win mentality.

More than 100 research studies have built on the early work of Min, Mentzer, and Ladd to establish the role of supply chain orientation in achieving

---

23. Adapted from Min, Mentzer, and Ladd, "Market Orientation in Supply Chain Management."

24. Ayman Omar, Beth Davis-Sramek, Brian S. Fugate, and John T. Mentzer, "Exploring the Complex Social Processes of Organizational Change: Supply Chain Orientation from a Manager's Perspective," *Journal of Business Logistics* 33, no. 1 (2012): 4–19.

supply chain sustainability[25] and customer satisfaction as it impacts the competitive advantage of a company.[26] Supply chain orientation has become the most prominent orientation studied in the logistics and supply chain management field.

Supply Chain Orientation as a Means to the End Goal of Wisdom

Today, companies don't function in silos; they are dependent on each other. A company with a wise orientation toward honoring God and people can only do so with a holistic understanding of the other companies it depends on to stay in business. The research conducted by Omar, Davis, and Fugate demonstrated that the supply chain orientation must first be adopted by the leadership of the firm for it to take effect. Like all orientations, without leadership buy-in, it will not transform the strategy of an organization. The role of the leader in helping a firm achieve a wise outcome cannot be emphasized enough. Servant leadership may be one of the most counterintuitive leadership styles in many industries. However, even in the logistics and supply chain industry, when tested with truck drivers and frontline employees, hierarchical leadership paled in comparison to the commitment of employees and the operational performance of employees who are led by a leader with a servant mindset.[27]

In my own research, I have been amazed by the feedback I have received from both blind reviewers and Christian audiences doubting the application of concepts like empowerment, compassion, and scriptural application in general toward the sustainability of a company. In a project I conducted in the supply chain of a large consumer packaged goods company in the US, I found that employees in the organization need to be empowered to have a supply chain orientation all the way to the front line. In order for a strategy to become a way of thinking, it needs to be adopted by leadership and the personnel at headquarters. For a strategy to be executed in the tactical day-to-day operations of a company, it needs to be diffused throughout the company's supply chain all

---

25. Akshay Jadhav, Stuart Orr, and Mohsin Malik, "The Role of Supply Chain Orientation in Achieving Supply Chain Sustainability," *International Journal of Production Economics* 217 (2019): 112–25; Jon F. Kirchoff, Wendy L. Tate, and Diane A. Mollenkopf, "The Impact of Strategic Organizational Orientations on Green Supply Chain Management and Firm Performance," *International Journal of Physical Distribution & Logistics Management* 46, no. 3 (2016): 269–92.

26. Alexander Ellinger, Hyunju Shin, William Magnus Northington, Frank G. Adams, Debra Hofman, and Kevin O'Marah, "The Influence of Supply Chain Management Competency on Customer Satisfaction and Shareholder Value," *Supply Chain Management: An International Journal* 17, no. 3 (2012), 249–62.

27. Overstreet, Hazen, Skipper, and Hanna, "Bridging the Gap between Strategy and Performance."

the way to the front line. The philosophy of a corporate leader remains merely the leader's philosophy if it is not adopted by the entire organization. Even the frontline truck driver or local salesperson needs to understand the balance of supply and demand if the organization is going to love and serve the customer (a retailer in my case) and the end-consumer well.

Sometimes our culture is obsessed with discipling and developing leaders. I have no problem with leadership development. I have grown to appreciate leadership development literature and tools in recent years. However, the mandate in Scripture is not to disciple only leaders; it is to disciple the whole world. Also, that mandate wasn't just left to the church leaders; it was diffused throughout the entire church. In ethics vocabulary, this would lead me to believe that we *all* have agency, we *all* have a responsibility to live out the Great Commission and the words of Christ in Acts 1:8 (ESV), "But you will receive power when the Holy Spirit has come upon you, and you will be my witnesses in Jerusalem and all Judea and Samaria, and to the ends of the earth." In business, there is no easier way to be a witness to the ends of the earth than in a supply chain management role.

In one of my very first entry-level jobs, I worked as a packaging buyer for a packaging importer. Every day, I worked with manufacturers and suppliers in Asia and Central America. I wasn't a corporate leader; I was just an entry-level employee building global relationships to get the job done. A supply chain orientation isn't about having the perfect routing algorithm to deliver a product by truck or knowing the economic order quantity for an inventory management system, although those things are important in achieving supply chain goals. A supply chain orientation is all about understanding resources: the supply of raw materials, works-in-process, and finished goods that are necessary to meet the demands and needs of humanity.

In Matthew 25, perhaps Jesus's longest teaching on wisdom, Jesus closes the story with a nod to those who comprehended supply chain orientation. The wise were those who understood the demands of their households and were wise enough to have enough supply to meet the needs of their immediate stakeholders with enough left over to share with stakeholders in the community. The sheep that inherit the kingdom of heaven are separated from the goats because they had enough food, enough water, enough space to extend hospitality, enough clothing to clothe a stranger, and enough time to visit the sick and the prisoners. I don't know how the idea emerged that poverty is a sign of sin and wealth is a sign of righteousness; this is not what Jesus is saying at all. The reason a supply chain orientation is central to our biblical call to love others, to disciple nations, and to spread the gospel is that it is the single philosophy of business that demands us to understand the needs of the world and the resources we have been entrusted with to meet those needs.

Jesus's ultimate goal was to pay the balance for our sins. During his perfect life on earth, he demonstrated for us how to walk in love and perfect righteousness. He taught his disciples and, through their writing, taught us how to live a life that honors and glorifies our Father in heaven. As he lived and taught, he not only healed the sick, he also supplied food to meet their needs. He supplied wine to meet their demand for merriment. He taught on money or mentioned money in eleven out of thirty-nine parables (roughly 15 percent of his teaching). He taught on the treatment of employees and the purpose of our excess supply to meet the demands of those in need. Wisdom personified in Proverbs 31 managed and ran a profitable supply chain that delivered quality goods to customers with a margin for the poor and to care for employees. It seems undeniable that an understanding of demand and supply is an important facet in demonstrating love.

Reflection Questions

1. Read and reflect on Proverbs 31:10–31.
   a. Draw the garment supply chain described in the text. Who were the suppliers? Who were the customers?
   b. What are the outcomes of the supply chain orientation of wisdom in this text?
2. Describe how a supply chain orientation can help a company love others well.
3. List other examples in Scripture that demonstrate the need to balance supply and demand.
4. Can you think of companies that have shifted their orientation and strategy to a supply chain orientation over the years? What do you think has driven the adoption of supply chain orientation recently?

CHAPTER 9

SUSTAINABILITY
ORIENTATION

My purpose at Telunas is to see movement happen, to see 5 generations and more than 100 villagers carrying forward the sustainable impact of Telunas beyond us.[1]

—*Pak Idaman, Director of Community Development*

On a hot, humid Indonesian afternoon, I sat with Pak[2] Idaman in a coffee shop in Batam near the ferry port connecting the Riau Islands. Pak Idaman shared about his journey across the archipelago of Sumatra from Nias Island to the Riau Islands. Despite an influx of money after the 2004 tsunami and 2005 earthquake, Nias Island remains one of the poorest districts in northwest Sumatra. Well below the national education average,[3] nearly 14 percent of adults never attend school, and for those who do, the student-to-teacher ratio is 70:1.[4]

Against these odds, Pak Idaman went to university, gaining fluency in English. This provided him with opportunities to travel and work all over Indonesia. Early in his career in hospitality, Pak Idaman found himself in the Riau Islands on the east coast of Sumatra. While there, he had a divine moment. He realized a calling to serve the people of the Riau Islands and see their economic and social opportunities develop. While his work took him to other areas around Indonesia, he felt that he was called to the Riau Islands, and at some point, he would return.

---

1. February 2020 interview with Pak Idaman.
2. Pak is an Indonesian term of respect for an adult male, like Mr. in English.
3. "In 2017, about 16% of young adults in Indonesia had attained a tertiary education, well below the G20 average of 38%." OECD 2019, https://www.oecd.org/education/education-at-a-glance/EAG2019_CN_IDN.pdf
4. OCHA, Relief Web, "Indonesia: Nias Island Public Expenditure Analysis," August 28, 2007, https://reliefweb.int/report/indonesia/indonesia-nias-island-public-expenditure-analysis.

Fast forward a decade from Pak Idaman's moment of calling to the Riau Islands. A small band of recent Wheaton graduates headed to Southeast Asia for adventure. In Indonesia, they befriended an expatriate with an export business. They asked him, "If you were our age, what would you do?" He said he would start a tourism business in the Sumatran Riau Islands near Singapore. He connected them with one of his employees, Pak Idaman, to serve as a guide. With a small rented boat, they explored the villages on the Riau Islands.

Intending to stay just an hour, Mike Schubert, Eric Baldwin, Pak Idaman, and company arrived at the small village on Sugi Island. Sugi villagers invited them to join a game of volleyball. They ended up playing volleyball late into the afternoon. As it grew late, the villagers invited them to stay for dinner and spend the night. Over dinner, they sat with a village elder. He told them that they were the first foreigners to visit the island. The group fell in love with the island, the people, and their hospitality. With just the beginnings of an idea, they returned to the US to build their plan for social impact. They realized that a nonprofit organization would not provide a sustainable impact. For the venture to work, it needed to generate revenue that could provide income for employees and opportunities for future expansion.

Three years later, they returned to realize their dream of creating a rustic resort on one of the Riau Islands. Armed with financial investors and Pak Idaman as a partner, Mike, Eric, and their families returned to the Riau Islands to begin building. They just needed a location with a beachfront and fresh water, since remote islands lacked public utilities or infrastructure. As fortune would have it, a village elder they befriended owned a stretch of beautiful beach at the edge of the jungle known as Telunas Beach.

Years ago, the Indonesian government had issued property grants to the citizens of the Riau Islands. Each head of household was given a land grant that partitioned off the island, leaving land for the government to claim for development. Villagers had little need for the pieces of paper issued to them. Most villagers live in houses built over the water that do not require land rights, and their livelihood is provided by fishing, hunting, and gathering food from the jungles. A shrewd man, the village elder began trading goats and chickens for people's land grants. Over time, he bought much of the island through bargaining and goat trade. He took the company to the edge of the jungle across the island, where they found streams of water and a pristine beach.

Few companies begin with a purpose beyond profit, but Telunas Beach Resort was founded for a larger purpose than profitability. Their corporate strategy was "purpose for people, prosperity, and the planet." As an organization, "Telunas is committed to bringing sustainable positive impact to co-workers, surrounding communities, ecosystems, and the local economy."[5] The first priority of the resort was to serve people and to positively impact local communities while providing value to resort customers. Today, Telunas employs 160 people from neighboring communities. The humility of the Telunas leadership allowed them to learn from their first few years of running a business in a remote area of the world without a history of employment.

People

In a fishing community, the fishermen go out and fish, sell the fish, and then live off of fish and fish sales until they run out of money. When the money and fish run out, they go back to their boats and catch more fish. In one of the most efficient cash-cash cycles I have ever witnessed, the fishing industry does not have business hours or paychecks. Employment at the resort required a new paradigm of thinking.

Pak Idaman approached community engagement with a five-year plan. He later realized that paradigm change is a longer-term investment. As they began to teach the staff English, the staff brought their families, and soon they were meeting regularly in the villages. The Keluarga Teladan (exemplary family program) grew out of employees' hunger for practical life skills training, like budgeting and differentiating between needs and wants. It involves mentoring and focuses on developing stronger family relationships and improving relationships between husbands and wives.

A native of a nearby island Pauh Island, Hanafi heard about the unique job opportunities at Telunas. Unlike the majority of the resorts around Indonesia who hire staff with hospitality training from Java, Telunas focused on employment opportunities in local villages. An intelligent and talented individual, Hanafi had no marketable skills aside from fishing and some construction when he joined the Telunas team. Trained by Pak Idaman, he was a fast learner and is now a talented craftsman. Hanafi hand built most of the furniture at Telunas. The opportunity transformed his life in more ways than one—while working and living on Sugi Island, Hanafi met his wife through a co-worker.

Hanafi transformed his life in the space Telunas gave him to work hard and learn. His passion in life has become training local workers to have marketable skills in carpentry. Most of the workers who come to work on the facilities crew have a background in fishing or ship maintenance. Hanafi focuses on their willingness to work and learn. He has seen the impact of Telunas on

---

5. See https://telunasresorts.com/our-impact/.

Sugi and surrounding islands. Unlike other resorts, the leadership of Telunas is accessible to the employees. Over the years of working for Telunas, Hanafi noted that the surrounding islands have become cleaner (we'll talk more about that later), English education has been provided in the communities for the first time, and economic opportunities have created better jobs locally so villagers don't have to commute to Batam to find employment. Overall, he has seen his lifestyle and opportunities improve and increase.

Prosperity

Early on, a leading school in Singapore began to bring student groups to Telunas Beach Resort for educational programs centered around community engagement and experiential learning. Soon many other international school programs followed. The international school programs provided Telunas with more consistent demand than the seasonal demand of college students. Telunas partnered with local villages to dig wells, pave roads, repair and paint buildings, and partner in English education programs as experiential learning projects.

By engaging with the communities around them, they began to see their employees embrace Telunas as an extended family. Telunas employees have proven to be gifted, talented, and innovative as they have applied the philosophy of Telunas in their villages. Trained in the LAYANI service principles, staff are empowered to find opportunities to drive change.[6] Like the facilities staff, most of the staff at Telunas have never been to a hotel or experienced the hospitality industry in any capacity. However, paired with heart, humility, and a hunger to learn, employees have created a dynamic environment that international school students from around Southeast Asia have come to love.

As Telunas grew in popularity with international schools, students began going home and asking their parents to take them back for a family vacation. Telunas began getting calls from families inquiring about vacation reservations. At that time, Telunas had minimal infrastructure—just dormitories, a classroom facility, and the main hall. Guests were willing to pay to stay in the dormitories for a week away on a secluded island with pristine beaches and a chance to unwind, and Telunas realized they had a new untapped market. In response to customer demand and with the extra money earned from family vacation visits, Telunas began building overwater villas that could house guests and their families for vacations.

---

6. L–*Luar Biasa Berkesan*, Leave an extraordinary impression; A–*Aman dan Selamat*, Make sure things are safe and sound; Y–*Yakin Selesai*, Finish tasks well; A–*Antisipasi Diri Yang Terbaik*, Anticipate guests needs; N–*Nayampakkan Diri Yang Terbaik*, Keep yourself professional; I–*Ikut Merawat*, Work together to keep things clean and orderly. From interview with Telunas Staff, March 2020.

To grow both markets (the international school programs and the family vacation rentals), they began to dream of expanding the resort to an exclusive private island experience. During a conversation with some guests, Mike and Eric were asked, "If you could do anything with this business, what would you do next?" Mike pointed at the island across the strait to a small private island and said, "I would buy that island."

It turned out that the guests were business coaches and investors. One of the men in the conversation said, "I'd loan you the money." With resources suddenly available, they started plans to expand to the business to the next island. Today, Telunas Private Island is a five-star experience frequented by families and corporate retreats.

As Telunas has invested in people, people have come along to invest in Telunas, buying into their purpose. Stewardship is multifaceted, though, and is not just limited to the people. Telunas leaders are conscious of their impact not just on the local community but also on the ecosystem. Building a resort in the remote islands of Indonesia requires a plan for the entire infrastructure of the resort, including water systems, electricity, supplies, and waste management.

Planet

As supervisor of guest relations, Ayu gets to see the whole world through the stories of Telunas guests. After growing up on Java, Ayu worked in pharmaceuticals until a series of life events redirected her path into hospitality. Ayu eventually came across Telunas, called to query about positions, sent her resume, and landed in customer engagement. Ayu noted that you cannot talk about Telunas without talking about impact. No other resort affects the islands like Telunas. Telunas has impacted the cleanliness of the villages. Of the many initiatives Telunas has launched to better steward the environment, waste management has had the biggest impact so far.

Thirty years ago, Sugi Village was entirely disconnected from the global economy. The local economy was based on hunting, fishing, and gathering. Living in huts on the water, a hole in the floor of a small back room served as both the bathroom and the trashcan as all organic waste was directly dropped into the ocean. Villagers ate off of banana leaves. Food was cooked over a fire with skewers and clay pots.

Consumer packaged goods (CPG) companies began expanding their business models to tap into the largest percent of the world population that lives below poverty level to raise standards of living and make additional profit. To price the products within the purchasing power of people who live on less than a dollar a day, CPG companies realized they needed to package products in smaller, more-affordable quantities. This introduced larger quantities of non-organic waste into village life. Remote villages in Indonesia do not have the infrastructure for a national electricity grid, plumbing, or waste management systems. Along with banana leaves, plastic water cups and single-use packaging are being disposed of in the ocean every day. With no garbage truck to pick up waste regularly, the current conveniently sweeps trash away.

Unless you are downstream. Islands downstream began to see trash collecting on the shores of the islands. Amplified by increased trash dumping by China (China is the number-one and Indonesia is the number-two plastics polluter of the ocean), the Riau Islands soon found their coastlines covered in trash. Before arriving at Telunas, Ayu had never owned a water bottle. Even in developed areas of Bali and Java, the water is not drinkable, and the single-use water cup industry is massive. All over Indonesia, you find plastic cups with thin plastic-film covers and a plastic straw encased in plastic. It's a lot of plastic. Telunas began giving all of their employees water bottles. Telunas created a water filtration system for the resort using the fresh water available nearby.

Telunas partnered with the communities to dig wells, providing better access to drinkable water. As employees realized the benefits of water bottles, they began implementing a reduce, reuse, recycle system in the villages as well. One of the employees even implemented a trash collection system in her village. She encouraged villagers to throw trash in bins instead of in the ocean so it can be sorted to be repurposed or disposed of in better ways. Her village is one of the cleanest in the Riau Islands.

Pak Idaman, Mike, and Eric have partnered with villages across the Riau Islands to see social and economic transformation. I am grateful I had the opportunity to travel with my kids across the diverse archipelago of Indonesia by taxi, plane, and boat to arrive at the unique location of Telunas Beach and Private Island Resorts. Telunas is a rare organization that exemplifies a sustainability orientation, with social impact as the end goal. Telunas has profitably expanded their social impact for nearly two decades.

Sustainability Orientation

As a firm philosophy, sustainability orientation builds on futurity or long-term orientation. A long-term orientation leads individuals to anticipate the consequences of their actions to plan goals strategically. Long-term oriented individuals will think of the benefits and prejudices their actions might produce on others and the environment.[7] A sustainability orientation is defined as "the overall proactive strategic stance of firms towards the integration of environmental and social concerns and practices into their strategic, tactical and operational activities."[8]

Over the past decades, the United Nations, the World Economic Forum, and leading financial thinkers have all stressed the need for more sustainable development.[9] As a Fulbright Scholar at the Universitas Pelitas Harapan outside of Jakarta, I had the opportunity to talk with several Indonesian delegates who were present at the 2020 World Economic Forum in Davos. The theme of 2020 was Stakeholders for a Cohesive and Sustainable World.[10] This is not a new trend—sustainability can no longer be considered a trendy buzz word. There has been a global acknowledgment of the importance of ESG (environmental, social, and governance) performance metrics for over a decade now. The 2030 sustainable development goals adopted by all members of the United Nations in 2015 guides global partnership.

1 no poverty	2 zero hunger	3 good health & well-being	4 quality education	5 gender equality	6 clean water & sanitation
7 afforable & clean energy	8 decent work & economic growth	9 industry, innovation, & infrastructure	10 reduced inequalities	11 sustainable cities & communities	12 responsible consumption & production
13 climate action	14 life below water	15 life on land	16 peace, justice, & strong institutions	17 partnerships for the goals	

FIGURE 9.1: 2015 UN Sustainable Development Goals for 2030

7. J. Q. Pinheiro, "Comprometimento Ambiental: Perspectiva Temporal e Sustentabilidade [Environmental Commitment: Time Perspective and Sustainability]," in *Temas Selectos de Psicologia Ambiental* [*Selected Themes of Environmental Psychology*], ed. J. Guevara and S. Mercado (Mexico City: UNAM, GRECO & Fundacio'n Unilibre, 2006), 463–81.

8. Colin C. J. Cheng, "Sustainability Orientation, Green Supplier Involvement, and Green Innovation Performance: Evidence from Diversifying Green Entrants," *Journal of Business Ethics* 161, no. 2 (2020): 393–414. Adapted from B. Roxas and A. Coetzer, "Institutional Environment, Managerial Attitudes and Environmental Sustainability Orientation of Small Firms," *Journal of Business Ethics* 111, no. 4 (2012): 461–76.

9. United Nations, https://sustainabledevelopment.un.org/?menu=1300; World Economic Forum, https://www.weforum.org/sustainability-world-economic-forum; BlackRock, https://www.blackrock.com/hk/en/insights/larry-fink-ceo-letter.

10. Oliver Cann, "Davos 2020: World Economic Forum Announces the Theme," October 17, 2019, https://www.weforum.org/agenda/2019/10/davos-2020-wef-world-economic-forum-theme/.

My work with Fortune 500 companies over the past decades also demonstrates that most supply chain captains (the largest company in the supply chain) have a sustainability strategy in place. As with other strategic orientations (long-term, stakeholder, or quality orientations), firms possessing a sustainability orientation recognize sustainability-oriented innovation opportunities and create the processes needed to take advantage of these opportunities.[11]

However, business research has explored sustainability through an instrumental logic.[12] Instrumental logic is a tradeoff logic that looks for scenarios where value can be maximized through balancing gains of one party in contrast to the losses of another party. Almost every research study utilizes a theory dominated by the impact of sustainability initiatives on profit as the predominate outcome variable and universal end goal. This continuously reinforces profit as the end goal for humanity's well-being as well as the firm's. A new ecologically dominant logic has been proposed to move beyond the current research that predominantly explores what unsustainable supply chains are doing to become more sustainable.[13] Current business research is focused on the reduction of harm rather than the increase of positive impact. Most research tries to balance the triple bottom line,[14] looking for win-win scenarios related to people, profit, and the planet. In reality, business is all about tradeoffs, and one of those three will be given precedence over the others.

Win-win is a recurrent theme in sustainability research. Porter's groundbreaking work in 1991 stated that "the conflict between environmental protection and economic competitiveness is a false dichotomy. It stems from a narrow view of the sources of prosperity and a static view of competition."[15] A new prioritization suggested by Griggs seems to align more closely with biblical principles of wealth and resources: "The global economy services society,

11. R. Adams, S. Jeanrenaud, J. Bessant, P. Overy, and D. Denyer, "Innovating for Sustainability: A Systematic Review of Body of Knowledge," Network for Business Sustainability, 2012, https://www.nbs.net/articles/systematic-review-innovating-for-sustainability.

12. Frank Montabon, Mark Pagell, and Zhaohui Wu, "Making Sustainability Sustainable," *Journal of Supply Chain Management* 52, no. 2 (2016): 11–27.

13. Montabonne, Pagell, and Wu, "Making Sustainability Sustainable."

14. Triple Bottom Line is an accounting framework that incorporates three dimensions of performance: social, environmental, and financial.

15. M. E. Porter, "America's Green Strategy," *Scientific American* 264, no. 4 (1991): 168; M. E. Porter and C. van der Linde, "Green and Competitive: Ending the Stalemate," *Harvard Business Review* 73, no. 5 (1995): 120–34.

which lies within Earth's life-support system."[16] But consider this: God created the natural environment first (environmental). Second, he placed people, men and women, together in that natural environment (social). Finally, he commissioned them to be fruitful and multiply their resources in the garden (economic). From the beginning of creation, we were created to worship and work together in the natural environment that God created as a reflection of his creativity in creating and building resources through fruitfulness and multiplication:

> So God created man in his own image, in the image of God he created him; male and female he created them. And God blessed them. And God said to them, "Be fruitful and multiply and fill the earth and subdue it, and have dominion over the fish of the sea and over the birds of the heavens and over every living thing that moves on the earth."[17]

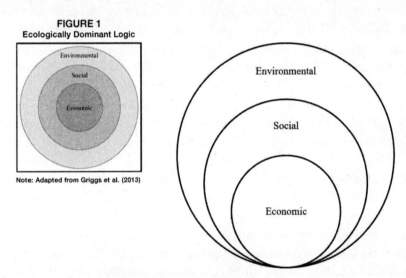

FIGURE 1
Ecologically Dominant Logic

Note: Adapted from Griggs et al. (2013)

FIGURE 9.2: Ecologically Dominant Logic
(Adapted from Griggs et al.)

Further, instead of a worldly equation of win-win, the wisdom equation is sacrifice-win. This is countercultural to worldly ethics, where win-win

---

16. D. Griggs, M. Stafford-Smith, O. Gaffney, J. Rockström, M. C. Öhman, P. Shyamsundar, I. Noble, "Policy: Sustainable Development Goals for People and Planet," *Nature* 495, no. 7441 (2013): 306, http://doi.org/10.1038/495305a.

17. Genesis 1:27–28 ESV.

outcomes would be ethically sufficient. Wisdom is predicated on the awe of God, building on the command in Deuteronomy 6 to love the Lord your God "with all your heart and with all your soul and with all your might." The word for *might* (Hebrew: *meod*) translates to resources. We are literally called to love God with our resources, with all that we have (including our money).

The sacrificial system is set up early in Genesis and described throughout Exodus, Numbers, Leviticus, and Deuteronomy. These books create a spiritual economy of a people who live together off the land and give the best of their resources to God, who then forgives them of their sins. The role of profit for them was to gain righteousness through physical sacrifices. The sacrifice of the Jews cost them their first fruits but won them righteousness and right relationship with God. Now in right relationship with God, Leviticus 19:17–18 takes it a step further and commands the Israelites to love their neighbors as they love themselves.

Jesus came and tipped the equation even more. He became the sacrifice so that we could become righteous. Jesus confirmed that we are still called to love the Lord with all of our hearts, souls, and resources, as this fulfills all of the law and the prophets. He also changed the Leviticus command when he said the following: "A new commandment I give to you, that you love one another: just as I have loved you, you also are to love one another. By this all people will know that you are my disciples, if you have love for one another."[18] Jesus called his disciples, and us, to choose sacrifice-win scenarios. Jesus didn't merely lay his life down for the disciples and his followers; his sacrifice was for the whole world.

This might lead some to conclude that the kingdom of heaven is now a social equation. Didn't Jesus die to redeem people? What does stewardship of the natural environment and environmental conservation have to do with this at all? Doesn't the New Testament focus on the spread of the gospel and people being baptized and made disciples? Yes, but not only those things. Paul talks about the longing of creation to be set free from the curse. Just as we have been redeemed and long for the fulfillment of God's kingdom on earth, creation also longs to be redeemed and to obtain freedom:

> For the creation waits with eager longing for the revealing of the children of God; for the creation was subjected to futility, not of its own will but by the will of the one who subjected it, in hope that the creation itself will be set free from its bondage to decay and will obtain the freedom of the glory of the children of God.[19]

---

18. John 13:34–35.
19. Romans 8:19–21.

The Wisdom of a Sustainability Orientation

"I, wisdom, was with the LORD when he began his work,
    long before he made anything else. . . .
I was like a child by his side.
I was delighted every day,
    enjoying his presence all the time,
enjoying the whole world,
    and delighted with all its people."
                    —*Proverbs 8:22, 30–31 NCV (emphasis mine)*

Wisdom Literature does not ignore our role in the fruitfulness of the natural environment. In Proverbs 31:10–31, wisdom personified as the Noble Women "considers a field and buys it; with the fruit of her hands she plants a vineyard."[20] The passage also states that she seeks wool and flax while working with diligent hands, indicating that while she likely has fields of flax and flocks of sheep, she has enough customer demand that she needs to outsource her flax and wool supply to have enough raw materials to make the products she sells in the marketplace. Her work is closely tied to the natural environment. The fruit of her fields enables her to buy more fields and to transform raw materials into the sashes she sells in the marketplace. The economic returns or profit is then sown back into her family, her employees, and her community. Proverbs 31:10–31 captures the fruitfulness of Wisdom in the natural environment, economic, and social spheres. In this passage, she is praised for her fear of the Lord as she buys, sells, plants, tends, cares for others, and laughs at the future.

Chapter 5 on long-term orientation explored the role of covenants in establishing a long-term perspective as the promises of God focused on future generations. A theme unfolds throughout the entire Bible, following the story of God's covenant with Abraham to the new covenant established in Jesus. The Pentateuch established God's covenant, the historical narratives described Israel's obedience and disobedience to the covenant, the prophets called people back to a proper relationship to the covenant, and Wisdom Literature expands the theme of obedience to God's covenant.

While it is not a part of the Wisdom Literature, all of the ancient Near East had an account of the consequences of humanity's disobedience to the gods, and flood narratives taught on the consequences of disobedience and

20. Proverbs 31:16.

unrighteousness. Across Mesopotamia, there were four main flood narratives: the Sumerian account, the Atrahasis Epic, the Gilgamesh Epic, and the account in Berossus.[21] Most flood narratives highlight the importance of obedience to the gods and the gods' preservation of the natural environment despite the destruction of evil humanity. Most do not include the covenant between God and people as in the biblical flood narrative. The consequences of evil for humanity play out in Genesis 6:5–8 (NIV):

> The LORD saw how great the wickedness of the human race had become on the earth, and that every inclination of the thoughts of the human heart was only evil all the time. The LORD regretted that he had made human beings on the earth, and his heart was deeply troubled. So the LORD said, "I will wipe from the face of the earth the human race I have created—and with them the animals, the birds and the creatures that move along the ground—for I regret that I have made them." But Noah found favor in the eyes of the LORD.

As the flood ends, the Genesis account records a promise from God that there will never be another worldwide flood.[22] Steven Bouma-Prediger notes that this promise is not only to Noah and humanity but also to all the creatures in the ark. Even the ugliest and unimportant species were preserved on the ark, providing one of the first biblical theologies from which we derive a principle of sustainability. We should understand from this passage that all creatures are to be cared for and their ability for multiplication preserved. Genesis 6:18–19 reflects this:

> "But I will establish my covenant with you; and you shall come into the ark, you, your sons, your wife, and your sons' wives with you. And of every living thing, of all flesh, you shall bring two of every kind into the ark, to keep them alive with you . . ."

After the floodwaters subsided, God makes a covenant to never again destroy creation. Six times it is reiterated that God's promise is to all of creation in Genesis 9:12–17. The extension of the promise to humanity and creation is clear for future generations:

---

21. Katharine J. Dell and Paul M. Joyce, eds., *Biblical Interpretation and Method: Essays in Honour of John Barton* (Oxford: Oxford University Press, 2013), 74–88.

22. Genesis 9:11. See also Day, "Comparative Ancient Near Eastern Study," 80.

"This is the sign of *the covenant that I make between me and you and every living creature* that is with you, *for all future generations*: I have set my bow in the clouds, and it shall be a sign of the covenant between *me and the earth*. When I bring clouds over the earth and the bow is seen in the clouds, I will remember my covenant that is *between me and you and every living creature of all flesh*; and the waters shall never again become a flood to destroy all flesh. When the bow is in the clouds, I will see it and remember the everlasting covenant *between God and every living creature* of all flesh that is on the earth." God said to Noah, "This is the sign of the covenant that I *have established between me and all flesh that is on the earth.*" (emphases mine)

Then, in Genesis 9, God recommissions Noah, humanity, and all of creation to be fruitful and multiply, to increase greatly on the earth, and to multiply. Like humanity, creation is also called to be fruitful. Thus, we have a moral obligation to use the fruit of creation in a way that is sustainable so both humanity and creation can fulfill God's call to fruitfulness. The book of Proverbs captures our interaction with the natural environment and describes how we can aid it in fruitfulness. Concepts of reaping, sowing, and planting all point to multiplication in creation: "They sowed fields and planted vineyards that yielded a fruitful harvest; he blessed them, and their numbers greatly increased, and he did not let their herds diminish" (Ps. 107:37–38 NIV).

Sustainability Research

Sustainable SCM is broadly defined as the cooperative management of material, information, and capital flows among supply chain companies with a focus on the triple bottom line (TBL) derived from understanding customer and stakeholder requirements and perceptions.[23] Triple bottom line is the accounting term that captures the economic bottom line, the social bottom line, and the environmental bottom line of the firm. Rather than the bottom line just capturing cost, the triple bottom line captures all of the positive and negative impacts of a firm across profit, people, and the planet.

Within the sustainable supply chain literature, social SCM is defined as "product or process-related aspects of operations that affect human safety, welfare, and community development."[24] Environmental SCM is "integrating

---

23. Stefan Seuring and Martin Müller, "From a Literature Review to a Conceptual Framework for Sustainable Supply Chain Management," *Journal of Cleaner Production* 16, no. 15 (2008): 1699–1710.

24. Robert D. Klassen and Ann Vereecke, "Social Issues in Supply Chains: Capabilities Link

environmental thinking into supply chain management, including product design, material sourcing and selection, manufacturing processes, delivery of the final product to the consumer, and end-of-life management of the product after its useful life."[25] Finally, economic sustainability in SCM is defined as the "effort to enhance total (firm) value while reducing supply chain cost associated with the manner in which the firm conducts its business."[26]

Managers today still tend to focus singularly on the economic dimension of TBL, although the inclusion of the environmental and social dimensions may yield even greater overall benefits for firms.[27] For example, environmental initiatives can reduce a firm's carbon footprint, fuel consumption, and transportation miles,[28] while social initiatives can increase revenue, mitigate risks, and improve operational performance.[29] The inclusion of social and environmental goals incorporates strategies that have slowly gained importance as managers seek competitive advantage.[30]

In 2008, I landed my first academic research project with a $20 billion railroad company. Mostly based on my extrovert-driven knack for being in the right place at the right time, I was able to connect with the chief operations officer (COO) of the company who was a University of Tennessee alum. Applied research projects fit somewhere in the space of addressing a corporate problem while testing a theoretical hypothesis. I was already working in the environmental sustainability space and was hoping to test some questions around the value of environmental initiatives. We were still building the business case for sustainability back then, which boiled down to exploring whether it was profitable. At the same time, the railroad is the most environmentally efficient mode of transportation on land, and the railroad company wanted to explore the value of that to their customers.

Responsibility, Risk (Opportunity), and Performance," *International Journal of Production Economics* 140, no. 1 (2012): 103–15, p. 103.

25. Samir K. Srivastava, "Green Supply-Chain Management: A State-Of-The-Art Literature Review," *International Journal of Management Reviews* 9, no. 1 (2007): 53–80, p. 54.

26. David J. Closs, Cheri Speier, and Nathan Meacham, "Sustainability to Support End-To-End Value Chains: The Role of Supply Chain Management," *Journal of the Academy of Marketing Science* 39, no. 1 (2011): 101–16, p. 107.

27. John Elkington, "Years Ago I Coined the Phrase 'Triple Bottom Line.' Here's Why It's Time to Rethink It." *Harvard Business Review* 25 (2018), https://hbr.org/2018/06/25-years-ago-i-coined-the -phrase-triple-bottom-line-heres-why-im-giving-up-on-it.

28. Susan Golicic, Courtney Boerstler, and Lisa Ellram. "'Greening' the Transportation in Your Supply Chain," *MIT Sloan Management Review* 51, no. 2 (2010): 47.

29. Wendy L. Tate, Lisa M. Ellram, and Jon F. Kirchoff. "Corporate Social Responsibility Reports: A Thematic Analysis Related to Supply Chain Management," *Journal of Supply Chain Management* 46, no. 1 (2010): 19–44.

30. A. Galvas and J. Mish, "Resources and Capabilities of Triple Bottom Line Firms: Going Over Old or Breaking New Ground?" *Journal of Business Ethics* 127, no. 3 (2015): 623–42.

That year I worked with the chief marketing officer (CMO) and his team to set up interviews with their top forty customers. I spent hours on the phone and in face-to-face interviews with the key decision makers of each company exploring the value they received from their most important logistics service provider. Now, this was over a decade ago, so context matters for my findings. We were coming out of eight years of a Republican, Bush presidency and moving into a Democratic, Obama presidency. As we moved into a new political climate, I had the opportunity to explore the scope of value creation between organizations in the physical supply chain and the support chain such as logistics service providers (LSPs), to create win-win outcomes that, in a supply chain context, enhance economic performance and address broader stakeholder concerns.

I built on past research focusing on sustainable supply chain management (SSCM), which asserts the importance of interorganizational relationships between profit-driven businesses to address environmental or social issues and meet stakeholder expectations.[31] I specifically examined value creation in interorganizational relationships between LSPs and profit-driven businesses (in this study, railroad customers).

Although it is often assumed that service providers have a minimal environmental impact, logistics companies are charged with executing a company's logistics activities, including transportation. To put their potential impact in perspective, 26 percent of the total greenhouse gas (GHG) emissions in the US come from the transportation sector.[32] Traditionally, the LSP-customer relationship was efficiency-driven and cost-focused. Increasingly, however, LSPs can play a significant strategic role when they aid in reducing their customers' environmental footprint in terms of carbon emissions, waste management, and reverse-logistics activities.[33]

I used a means-end lens to understand the railroad company's customer perspectives. The means-end value hierarchy (MEVH) offers a novel framework to understand the type and process of value creation from the perspective

31. D. A. Mollenkopf, H. J. Stolze, W. Tate, and M. Ueltschy, "Green, Lean, and Global Supply Chains," *International Journal of Physical Distribution and Logistics Management* 40, no. 1-2 (2010), 14-41; C. Giminez V. Sierra, and J. Rodon, "Sustainable Operations: Their Impact on the Triple Bottom Line," *International Journal Production Economics* 140 (2012): 149–59; Aßländer, Roloff, and Nayir, "Suppliers as Stewards?"

32. Gang He, Zhenling Cui, Hao Ying, Huifang Zheng, Zhaohui Wang, and Fusuo Zhang, "Managing the Trade-Offs Among Yield Increase, Water Resources Inputs and Greenhouse Gas Emissions in Irrigated Wheat Production Systems," *Journal of Cleaner Production* 164 (2017): 567–74.

33. Guowei Hua, T. C. E. Cheng, and Shouyang Wang, "Managing Carbon Footprints in Inventory Management," *International Journal of Production Economics* 132, no. 2 (2011): 178–85.; Claudia Colicchia, Gino Marchet, Marco Melacini, and Sara Perotti, "Building Environmental Sustainability: Empirical Evidence from Logistics Service Providers," *Journal of Cleaner Production* 59 (2013): 197–209.

of the customer. Customer value is the "centrally held, enduring core beliefs, desired end-states, or higher-order goals of the individual customer or customer organization that guides behavior."[34] The MEVH was established to understand a customer's desired end state, whereby products and services are the means by which end states are pursued.[35] In all of my interviews, I laddered from the explicit attributes of the transportation service provided to the more intrinsic goals that those attributes helped to achieve. The customer sample provided by the railroad company included seventeen retailers and manufacturers that were both consumer goods and industrial companies. I spoke with around twenty-four transportation managers.

The results of the analysis led to two distinctly different end states, which precipitated the need for developing two aggregated hierarchies. One hierarchy is driven by the desire for customers to achieve *sustainability leadership* (one desired end state focused on sustainable outcomes). These customers had a clear sustainability orientation. The other hierarchy is driven by customers' desires to achieve *revenue/market share leadership* (a second desired end state focused on more traditional economic goals). Those customers had a profit orientation, or more generously, a market orientation. To capture the essence of the distinct dimensions of customer value and to highlight the overlaps, the figure below offers a summarized interpretation of the two value hierarchies.

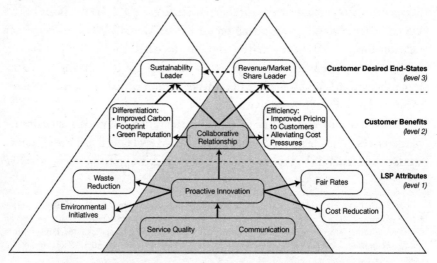

FIGURE 9.3: Railroad Customer Means-End Hierarchy

34. D. J. Flint, R. B. Woodruff, and S. F. Gardial, "Customer Value Change in Industrial Marketing Relationships," *Industrial Marketing Management* 26, no. 2 (1997): 163–75, p. 170.

35. Gutman, "A Means-End Chain Model Based on Consumer Categorization Processes."

Consistent with the sustainable development literature on collaboration, my data revealed that interorganizational relationships are important *because* they are an integral part of the value-creation process. For exemplar firms, relationship connections were deepened when value creation aligned with sustainable outcomes. I found additional insights indicating that additional value creation can be generated in interorganizational relationships in the context of a sustainability orientation. In research across several business disciplines, SSCM reflects the strategic actions that businesses are taking to assume extended environmental and social responsibility for their products both upstream and downstream.[36] My research began to provide evidence that a sustainability orientation was the ultimate state of a true market leader, not necessarily revenue or market share.

Sustainability Orientation as a Means to the End Goal of Wisdom

In the work I conducted with the railroad company, I realized that a sustainability orientation was tied to a firm's end goal to be a leader and to have a positive impact on their industry profitably. Over a decade ago, some of the largest companies in the world saw sustainability as their comparative advantage. Further, it became clear that it was possible to become a market leader without the largest market share. Participants (using pseudonyms) in my research stated:

Tom: "Well, from a sustainability standpoint, we're trying to be a leader out there on the retail side. So it's really good for the bottom line from both a profit and from saving money because every time you do that you start to save money. We don't ask anybody to do anything that's going to cost money. It's going to always flow to the bottom line, and it's good just for us to be saying that we want to be a leader in sustainability."

---

36. Magnus Boström, Anna Maria Jönsson, Stewart Lockie, Arthur P. J. Mol, and Peter Oosterveer, "Sustainable and Responsible Supply Chain Governance: Challenges and Opportunities," *Journal of Cleaner Production* 107 (2015): 1–7; David Eriksson and Göran Svensson, "The Process of Responsibility, Decoupling Point, and Disengagement of Moral and Social Responsibility in Supply Chains: Empirical Findings and Prescriptive Thoughts," *Journal of Business Ethics* 134, no. 2 (2016): 281–98; Craig R. Carter and Dale S. Rogers, "A Framework of Sustainable Supply Chain Management: Moving toward New Theory," *International Journal of Physical Distribution & Logistics Management* 39, no. 5 (2008): 360–87, https://doi.org/10.1108/09600030810882816.

Tabitha: "However, we do also recognize being one of the largest consumer products companies in the world, that when we choose to focus on sustainability, it would definitely influence the industry and the solutions that we're going to use to try to achieve those goals."

Whether their motivation was economic or for the impact on future generations, companies have continued to realize the business case for a sustainability orientation. However, for most of the companies in my sample, their motivation was purely utilitarian. Like the Yili Group, the journey toward a sustainability orientation was driven by market demand and not by a pre-existing philosophy of the firm leadership. I would categorize this as a worldly mindset. When a company has a wisdom orientation, they look more like Telunas. Telunas was founded with a long-term view of impacting people and the ecosystem around their business from the very beginning.

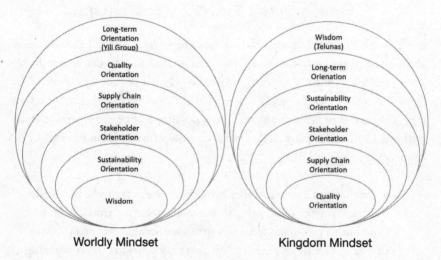

FIGURE 9.4: Worldly Mindset vs. Kingdom Mindset

While it is possible to think of sustainability as the end goal, that is still a worldly mindset. The world may or may not acquire wisdom in their pursuit of sustainability. A kingdom mindset starts with wisdom. Wisdom isn't the end goal; it is the foundational paradigm of thinking. Divine wisdom requires awe and fear of God at the outset. Within the kingdom mindset, sustainability is still a means to our end goal as people of faith. When you consider that the wisdom orientation of the firm is the set of beliefs that prioritizes a love for God (faith) and others as the end goal, this love-centered philosophy will direct organization strategies toward balancing the sustainability of economic health, social equity, and environmental resilience to achieve the goal of loving God and others well.

Reflection Questions

1. With the rise of B-corps, can you think of other examples of companies like Telunas that are incorporated for a purpose larger than profit? What does their strategy focus on?
2. Can you find other examples in Scripture where it seems like care for people and creation are interwoven? Why do you think God cares about both?
3. Why do you think it may be important for some companies with a purpose beyond profit to be for-profit and not an NGO or nonprofit organization?

CHAPTER 10

REPUTATION

Her husband is known in the city gates,
    taking his seat among the elders of the land.

—Proverbs 31:23

Give her a share in the fruit of her hands,
    and let her works praise her in the city gates.

—Proverbs 31:31

When good things happen, we probably get more than our fair share. And when unfortunate things happen, we probably get more than our fair share. The good news is, people care.

—Brian Niccol, CEO of Chipotle[1]

What is the end result of a population who believes the data and information they receive is mostly fake news? The last thirty years have reshaped the availability of information and consumers' access to corporate information. With the growth, development, and global adoption of the internet, consumers around the world now have access to more information and data than ever before. The problem with the explosion of data and information availability is that we have not necessarily had the same explosion in values, wisdom, and ethics to go with it. To complicate things, Pew Research has established that 67 percent of US adults gather their news from social media sources, and 43 percent of US adults get their news from Facebook.[2] As we learned in the 2016 US election cycle, not all of the news on Facebook, or any social media source, is accurate data or information. We now live in a world where consumers have

---

1. Katy Steinmetz, "Chipotle's Second Act," *Time*, 193 (4/5), 2019, 88–91.
2. Pew Resaerch.org, "Demographics of Social Media Users and Adoption in the United States," Pew Research Center (2018), https://www.pewresearch.org/internet/fact-sheet/social-media/.

more access to news than ever before with seemingly less wisdom to discern its validity.

This poses a huge challenge to companies. Their reputations are at the mercy of what people believe about them, true or not. They are faced with a world that has more ability to blatantly share stories about their successes and failures. Not many companies have lived and survived the roller coaster of good and bad news and corporate failures with the sustained financial success and positive reputation of Chipotle Mexican Grill.

Fast-casual dining emerged in the 1990s to challenge both the unhealthy offerings of fast food (quality) and the expense of sit-down restaurants (price). My very first place of employment was one of the first fast-casual dining restaurants called St. Louis Bread Company. Nationally known as Panera Bread Company, they offered baked goods, sandwiches, salads, and soups with open preparation of food in full view of the customer and no table service. Panera was established in Kirkwood, Missouri, in 1987 and has led the US's fast-casual restaurant segment for decades. Chipotle Mexican Grill was established by Steve Ells in Denver, Colorado, just a few years later in 1993. Ells was a classically trained chef who picked up on the growth of demand by consumers for healthier convenient dining options. Within a month of opening, his store was selling more than 1,000 burritos each day. Early on, Ells was quoted in a 2011 *Business Insider* article saying:

> When I created Chipotle in 1993, I had a very simple idea: Offer a simple menu of great food prepared fresh each day, using many of the same cooking techniques as gourmet restaurants. Then serve the food quickly, in a cool atmosphere. It was food that I wanted and thought others would like too. We've never strayed from that original idea. The critics raved and customers began lining up at my tiny burrito joint. Since then, we've opened a few more.[3]

McDonald's bought minority shares in Chipotle in 1998 and basically owned the company by 1999 when they purchased majority shares. McDonald's later spun the business off in the stock market in 2006. In 2011, the press was *loving* Chipotle. They were the new, healthy alternative to Taco Bell and Don Pablos. In 2001, Chipotle launched a "Food with Integrity" campaign. They committed to sourcing the best ingredients raised with respect for the animals,

---

3. Kal Gullapalli, "How Chipotle became the Gold Standard of Mexican Fast-Food," *Business Insider*, January 21, 2011, https://www.businessinsider.com/chipotle-the-new-gold-standard-2011-1.

the environment, and farmers. The buying power of McDonald's certainly helped them to negotiate low prices for high-quality produce and meats. With just sixty-four main ingredients, they led the way in identifying GMOs on their menus until they were fully eliminated in 2015. Between 1999 to 2014, Chipotle grew by 550 percent.[4]

Unlike McDonald's, Chipotle did not adopt a franchise model. Chipotle chose to keep ownership and tight control of the quality and simplicity of their menus as they expanded. With a simple menu of burritos, burrito bowls, tacos, and chips, Chipotle served fresh food and meats. The meats sold at Chipotle are 100 percent naturally raised. In 2011, Chipotle was dominating the Mexican casual dining market. In 2014, Chipotle was number two in the fast-casual dining segment behind Panera Bread.

In 2015, as Chipotle stock reached an all-time high, Chipotle began to face a series of food safety missteps. Perhaps due to lack of employee training or oversight, Chipotle had a series of unfortunate food poisoning outbreaks. The US Department of Agriculture closely monitors food safety through the Hazard Analysis and Critical Control Point System (HACCP). Most large-scale food producers incorporate the HACCP principles into their food handling operations and supplier requirements to reduce the risk of food contaminants that cause *E. coli*, salmonella, norovirus, and other food poisonings. In 2015, Chipotle had food poisoning outbreaks in all three categories:

Salmonella	Aug. 2015	60 people sick at 28 restaurants in Minnesota and Wisconsin
E. coli	Oct. 2015	22 customers sick in Oregon and Washington
Norovirus	Aug. 2015	82 people and 17 employees sick at Simi Valley, CA
	Dec. 2015	500 customers sick in Boston

Chipotle hired a food safety research firm and began working to improve the food safety procedures at its restaurants. In early 2016, Chipotle closed all of its stores with problems in food sourcing and preparation practices. In April of 2016, Chipotle took its first-ever quarterly loss. Throughout the crisis, Chipotle ran ads when food-safety issues surfaced both alerting the public and apologizing. Upon reopening, Chipotle increased advertising and free food promotions. In 2017, another outbreak prompted the company to put all

---

4. Roberto A. Ferman, "The Chipotle Effect: Why America Is Obsessed with Fast Casual Food," *Washington Post*, February 2, 2015, https://www.washingtonpost.com/news/wonk/wp/2015/the-chipotle -effect-why-america-is-obsessed-with-fast-casual-food.

70,000 employees through a food-safety training program, and by the end of the year, founder Steve Ells announced that he would step down as CEO.

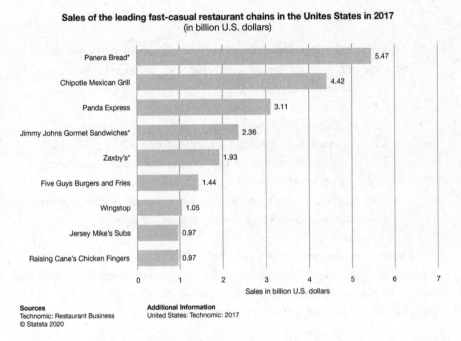

Sales of the leading fast-casual restaurant chains in the Unites States in 2017
(in billion U.S. dollars)

FIGURE 10.1: Sales of Leading US
Fast-Casual Restaurant Chains[5]

Despite the tumultuous bad press from 2015 to 2017, Chipotle managed to maintain the number-two spot in the fast-casual restaurant segment. It seems shocking that after the two years leading up to 2017, Chipotle could still maintain the second largest revenue in the industry. However, reputation is not just about image. Reputation is about matching image to reality. Chipotle promoted an image of integrity, the quality of being honest and having strong moral principles. When Chipotle screwed up, even though they lost money in 2016, they were honest about the problems and worked hard to fix them. Chipotle's image matched the reality of their behavior. Where firms run into trouble is when their image does not match their behavior. (We'll come back to this later in the chapter.)

After 2017, the leadership of Chipotle was demanding a more dramatic

5. "Sales of the Leading Fast-Casual Restaurant Chains in the United States in 2017 (in Billion U.S. Dollars)" [Graph], Statista, September 20, 2018, https://www-statista-com.ezproxy.wheaton.edu /statistics/299350/leading-fast-casual-restaurant-segments-by-their-largest-selling-chains-us/.

change. Founder Ells stepped down and past Taco Bell CEO Brian Niccol was hired to lead Chipotle forward with five strategies. While they don't perfectly align with the five strategies or orientations of a wisdom-based orientation, several of them do.

We are a brand with a demonstrated purpose of cultivating a better world. Our mission is to win today while creating a bright future by focusing on five key fundamental strategies:

- Making the brand more visible and loved;
- Creating innovation utilizing a stage-gate process;
- Leveraging our digital-make line to expand access and convenience;
- Engaging with customers through our loyalty program;
- And running successful restaurants with a strong culture that provides great food, hospitality, throughput, and economics.[6]

The number-one strategy of Chipotle is to make its brand more visible and loved. This could also be referred to as building brand reputation and brand loyalty in marketing terminology. Of the wisdom orientations, we see all the orientations are present indirectly in some form:

- sustainability: cultivating a better world
- quality: great food and hospitality
- stakeholder engagement: customer loyalty programs (and farmer engagement)
- supply chain: throughput (balancing inventory, managing supply and demand)
- long-term: creating a bright future

Chipotle's reputation is based on integrity. A reputation is defined by Merriam-Webster as the "overall quality or character as seen or judged by people in general."[7] Even though Chipotle had quality problems, they maintained their character by being honest about both the good and bad things they were doing as an organization. In retrospect, Chipotle leaders said they wished they would have been less harsh about what their competition was

---

6. Chipotle Mexican Grill Inc., "2019 Annual Report," https://ir.chipotle.com/annual-reports.

7. "Reputation," *Merriam-Webster's* (online), https://www.merriam-webster.com/dictionary/reputation.

doing wrong. In a 2019 *Time* article, Niccol was quoted saying, "We spent too much time talking about other people doing wrong and not enough time talking about what we were doing to change food culture."[8]

Over the years, as I have conducted sustainability research with companies both small and large, I have found that many corporate leaders are hesitant to talk about the good they are doing to change culture. The challenge comes from perceptions of green marketing or "greenwashing" that became prevalent in the 1960s. In 1992, an article by J. J. Davis explored the ethics of environmental marketing.[9] Davis argued that many firms position their products to address the needs of environmentally conscious consumers with claims that are confusing, misleading, and even illegal. However, this is a narrow view of marketing to only include environmental advertising or the promotion piece of marketing. If encompassing customer knowledge and all four Ps of marketing, true environmental marketing would include the following:

- **Customer/Stakeholder:** understanding and exploring multiple stakeholders needs (including customers, suppliers, employees, and community members)
- **Product:** green product development (also known as design for the environment)
- **Price:** fair pricing strategies that enable suppliers to achieve environmental standards
- **Place:** a plan for distribution into the market that reduces carbon emissions of transportation and packaging
- **Promotion:** appropriate advertising to inform the customer of the companies' actions and product benefits

Chipotle learned the hard way that building a reputation isn't just about pointing out what others are doing wrong in comparison to their business practices. Reputation is dependent on good and bad information about the initiatives they are executing to improve culture and well-being. When you visit their website today, you learn the following things about Chipotle's values as they still strive to have integrity:

---

8. Katy Steinmetz, "Inside Chipotle's Plan to Make You Love It Again," *Time*, January 24, 2019, https://time.com/longform/chipotle-plan-to-make-you-love-it-again/.

9. J. J. Davis, "Ethics and Environmental Marketing," *Journal of Business Ethics* 11, no. 2 (1992): 81–87.

Reputation as a Resource
of the Firm

Business research has demonstrated that a good reputation is one of the primary drivers of sustained financial performance. Organizational reputation is defined in the academic business literature as *the stakeholders' cumulative judgments of a firm.*[10] From a stakeholder view, there is both an internal reputation held by employees and shareholders and an external reputation that is held by external stakeholders such as suppliers, customers, and the community. Further, a corporate reputation is built through perceptions about the company's business and social practices:[11]

Business Reputation	Social Reputation
Investment Value in the **Long Run** Use of Corporate **Assets/Efficiency** **Innovation** Level Corporal Governance & **Managerial Quality** **Product & Service Quality** Capability to Attract, Develop, & Retain Talented **People**	Community and **Social** **Responsibility** **Financial Strength**

TABLE 10.1: Business and Social Reputation

As previously stated, we live in a world where consumers have more access to data and information than ever before, which increases the need for wisdom to discern its validity. Reputation is directly tied to the stakeholder's knowledge about a company. This means that consumers, suppliers, customers, employees, and other stakeholders are going to be faced with a lot of data and information about an organization that will shape what they think they know and understand about the company's practices. They will know when companies make mistakes. This is why wisdom, discernment, and understanding are crucial for our role as business leaders *and* consumers as we make decisions about how to invest, where to innovate, and how to assess true quality to drive our individual and corporate reputations.

---

10. C. Fombrun and M. Shanley, "What's in a Name? Reputation Building and Corporate Strategy," *Academy of Management Journal* 33 (1990): 233–58, p. 235.

11. Gregorio Martin de Castro, Jose Emilio Navas Lopez, and Pedro Lopez Saez, "Business and Social Reputation: Exploring the Concept and Main Dimensions of Corporate Reputation," *Journal of Business Ethics* 63 (2006): 361–70, doi: 10.1007/s10551-005-3244-z.

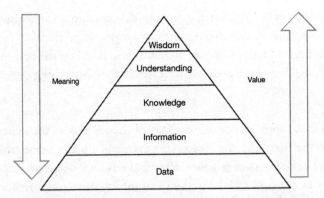

FIGURE 10.2: Transformation of Data to Wisdom

Strategies are built on corporate identity, and corporate identity is reinforced by reputation. In 2010, a team of marketing and business ethics researchers[12] laid out the path to a sustainability orientation of the firm. They integrated the concepts of market orientation and stakeholder orientation with a resource-advantage lens. They suggest that social and financial performance that will drive the corporate reputation of the firm are based on the DNA of the firm. They use the biological concept of DNA to define the ideology and dynamic capabilities of the firm. Their model is based on engagement with key stakeholders. If we combine Crittenden et al.'s model of sustainability with Castro et al.'s model of corporate reputation, we derive the following description of sustainability and reputation to predict positive outcomes for the firm:

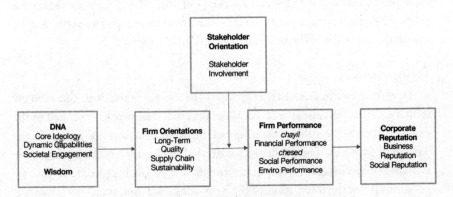

FIGURE 10.3: Orientation, Sustainability, and Business Reputation

12. V. Crittenden, William F. Crittenden, Linda K. Ferrell, O. C. Ferrell, and Christopher C. Pinney, "Market-Oriented Sustainability: A Conceptual Framework and Propositions," *Journal of the Academy of Marketing Science* 39, no. 1 (2011): 71–85.

Crittenden et al. propose that sustainable performance begins with the DNA of the firm. Sustainable performance captures profitability (economic), environmental, and social impact. Reputation is based on the perceptions and the reality of what a firm does and how well it does those things.

DNA

The DNA captures the core ideology of the leadership, the dynamic capabilities of the firm, and the societal engagement. I believe that this DNA is captured in the layers of wisdom. Practical wisdom, *phronesis*, captures the capability of the firm to take in data and information and transform it into knowledge and understanding that is useful for discerning the wisest strategies and orientations, whereas divine wisdom, *sophia*, captures the firm's ideology that is positioned to honor God and others.

Firm Orientations

Throughout this book, I have used the terms orientation and strategy somewhat interchangeably. However, they aren't quite synonymous. An orientation is a corporate strategy that is based on the ideology of the organizations' leadership. An orientation is arguably the optimal strategy. Anyone can develop a strategy based on conjecture, but it takes wisdom to develop a strategy based on ideology (or philosophy) because this requires the leadership to have a sense of identity and purpose before approaching strategic planning. The ideology or philosophy that drives corporate orientations from a wisdom perspective is rooted in the desire to love and serve God and others, thus a stakeholder orientation (that captures the strategy of the firm to engage and serve people) will shape how each of the wisdom orientations is applied.

Performance

I have continually stressed that profit can be a virtue of the firm. The Hebrew term *chayil* that describes the *Noble* Woman is most frequently translated to the word *wealth*. She is capable of creating wealth, profit, and financial returns in the passage in Proverbs. The challenge I addressed in chapter 2 is that most people stop there when measuring corporate outcomes. The missing piece for most corporations is not the integration of their environmental and social performance. The ability of an individual to create resources that are invested for the "greater good" seems to reflect the important Hebrew concept of *chesed,* which means "mercy, kindness, and steadfast love." When *chesed* and *chayil* are outcomes of firm performance, the reputation of the firm is solidified by establishing both the business reputation of the firm as well as the social reputation of the firm.

Corporate Reputation

Corporate reputation legitimizes a firm for sustained performance. The reputation of an organization is always tied to its leadership. Further, reputation is directly impacted by all stakeholder perspectives. The reputation of the firm is the sum of the way the firm and its leadership is viewed by employees, customers, suppliers, shareholders, and the surrounding community. Without a stakeholder perspective, a firm will not perform to meet the needs of multiple stakeholders and will not be viewed favorably by those stakeholders. Reputation data has been collected and published annually by *Newsweek*, KLD (Kinder, Lindenberg, Domini, and Company), *Fortune*, and the Reputation Institute to establish measurable reputation data that is used by investors and consumers in assessing companies. What all of these groups establish every year is that firms have unique reputations. Sometimes those reputations match the reality of their business practices, and sometimes they do not.

Companies with the best reputations are trusted, esteemed, admired, and respected and have an overall "good feeling."[13] Research has demonstrated that a firm's reputation regarding its financial stability, environmental initiatives, and social engagement will contribute to sustained financial benefits and firm performance that are important for a comparative advantage.[14] While firms will not always have positive news, how they manage that news will shape consumer trust, respect, and admiration. Reputation is not about attaining perfection; it is better managed through transparency, integrity, honesty, and demonstrating steps toward better outcomes and impact.

The Reputation of Wisdom

Two concepts in the Wisdom Literature define reputation at the individual level. These are the Hebrew concepts of being praiseworthy (*halal*) and being known (*yada*). As Christians, we are called to be known and to make God known. We do this as Jesus's witnesses in both our words and our deeds. James, a New Testament book of wisdom, notes that faith without deeds is dead, that our claims about faith are dead without action.[15] In Proverbs 31:10–31, both words and deeds are present, as the Noble Woman is a woman of action in her business, but teaches *chesed*—mercy, kindness, and steadfast love—with

---

13. L. J. Ponzi, C. J. Fombrun, and N. A. Gardberg, "RepTrak™ Pulse: Conceptualizing and Validating a Short-Form Measure of Corporate Reputation," *Corporate Reputation Review* 14 (2011): 15–35.

14. Yijing Wang and Guido Berens, "The Impact of Four Types of Corporate Social Performance on Reputation and Financial Performance," *Journal of Business Ethics* 131, no. 2 (2015): 337–59.

15. James 2:14–26.

wisdom. I believe that nothing captures the gospel narrative we are called to make known to the world more succinctly than a message of mercy, kindness, and steadfast love. The gospel is the good news of God's steadfast love for us. This love is made perfect through Jesus's mercy when he chooses to die on the cross to cancel out our sins so that mercy would triumph over justice. We need to be praiseworthy in our actions. With the help of the Holy Spirit, we help others transform their information about this world into knowledge and understanding so that they can *know* who God is and his heart for them.

Known	Proverbs 31:23	"Her husband is known in the city gates."
Praise	Proverbs 31:28	"Her husband too, and he praises her."
	Proverbs 31:30	"A woman who fears the Lord is to be praised."

In Proverbs 31, the Noble Woman's direct stakeholders reinforce her reputation in verse 28, "Her children rise up and call her happy; her husband too, and he praises her." In fact, her husband's reputation is enhanced because he is connected to her in verse 23. Her reputation goes beyond her direct stakeholders to include all who come and go in the marketplace through the city gates—"Let her works praise her in the city gates" (v. 31b).

The entire book of Ecclesiastes is about the elusiveness of what we know. It opens in chapter 1 with this statement: "I . . . applied my mind to seek and to search out by wisdom all that is done under heaven; it is an unhappy business that God has given to human beings to be busy with. I saw all the deeds that are done under the sun; and see, all is vanity and a chasing after wind."[16] Each chapter of Ecclesiastes addresses what we lack in knowledge, the difficulty of knowing what is good, but the recognition that in the end, we do know that God's actions endure forever.[17]

The Tale of Two Reputations

Perhaps the best illustration of the reputation of the wise versus the fool in the Gospels is the story of Zacchaeus in Luke 19. Jesus had a reputation for teaching and performing miracles. His reputation was so great that some perceived him to be a prophet like Elijah or even Moses. The story opens with Jesus passing through Jericho. His reputation has preceded him, and a man named Zacchaeus desires to see him because of his reputation.

---

16. Ecclesiastes 1:12–14.
17. Ecclesiastes 3:14.

Zacchaeus has a reputation of his own. He is a chief tax collector with great wealth. As a chief tax collector, he would have been employed by Herod and perhaps the Sadducees to force the Israelites to pay taxes to Rome. Clearly, he also took extra payment for himself. He would have been seen as an extortionist and a sinner in the eyes of the crowd. They know who he is.

Luke describes Zacchaeus as a short man. Because he is small in stature, he climbs a sycamore tree so that he can see Jesus pass by. However, Jesus also sees Zacchaeus. Jesus stops and talks to him and invites himself over to Zacchaeus's house for lunch. The crowd knew who Zacchaeus was, and they grumbled about Jesus seeking to be the guest of such a great sinner.

However, throughout lunch, Zacchaeus stands and declares that he will give half of his goods to the poor and that he will return any money he got through fraud. At which point, Jesus said, "Today salvation has come to this house because he too is a son of Abraham. For the Son of Man came to seek out and to save the lost."[18] After he leaves Zacchaeus's house, he tells the crowds the parable of the ten minas—about the master who went to a far country to receive a kingdom. He tells this parable to clarify the kingdom of God because they supposed that the kingdom of God would appear immediately with his arrival:

"A nobleman went to a distant country to get royal power for himself and then return. He summoned ten of his slaves, and gave them ten pounds, and said to them, 'Do business with these until I come back.' But the citizens of his country hated him and sent a delegation after him, saying, 'We do not want this man to rule over us.' When he returned, having received royal power, he ordered these slaves, to whom he had given the money, to be summoned so that he might find out what they had gained by trading. The first came forward and said, 'Lord, your pound has made ten more pounds.' He said to him, 'Well done, good slave! Because you have been trustworthy in a very small thing, take charge of ten cities.' Then the second came, saying, 'Lord, your pound has made five pounds.' He said to him, 'And you, rule over five cities.' Then the other came, saying, 'Lord, here is your pound. I wrapped it up in a piece of cloth, for I was afraid of you, because you are a harsh man; you take what you did not deposit, and reap what you did not sow.' He said to him, 'I will judge you by your own words, you wicked slave! You knew, did you, that I was a harsh man, taking what I did not deposit and reaping what I did not sow? Why then did you not put my

18. Luke 19:9–10.

money into the bank? Then when I returned, I could have collected it with interest.' He said to the bystanders, 'Take the pound from him and give it to the one who has ten pounds.' (And they said to him, 'Lord, he has ten pounds!') 'I tell you, to all those who have, more will be given; but from those who have nothing, even what they have will be taken away. But as for these enemies of mine who did not want me to be king over them—bring them here and slaughter them in my presence.'"[19]

In this parable, it is clear that we need to know our master who has gone away but has already established his kingdom for us to carry out. We also need to conduct ourselves by doing deeds that are praiseworthy. I have heard many people state that their hope in life is to live worthy of this master's praise: "Well done good and faithful servant!"

The Already, Not Yet Kingdom

We learn from the lessons of Chipotle and Zacchaeus that the most important thing a witness brings to the table is credibility. The first thing the defending and opposing counsel do in a trial is to establish or discount the reputation of the witness as to whether or not they are truthful and credible. Zacchaeus and Chipotle both knew they had messed up and had a negative reputation to overcome. Both owned their mistakes and took action to correct them. Actions are an important part of being a witness. Zacchaeus's testimony was powerful because his actions demonstrated his change of heart and gave credibility to the salvation that had come to his house. Sometimes we think our witness is about our righteousness, but Zacchaeus was a witness to his community of how Jesus had come to seek and save the lost. His reputation for being a lost sinner saved provided a living and active witness to Jesus's reputation and identity.

Our reputation matters as Christians. We are witnesses for Christ, and as his representatives on earth, our actions and behavior do matter. This is where virtue ethics (our character) is best when matched with duty ethics (our action). An ancient heretic called Pelagius offered a terrible solution that many Christians today still believe: that we can be righteous in our own strength. Pelagius believed that people are in the same condition as Adam and Eve, not broken by sin.[20] He was an advocate for free will and asceticism that would have lined up well with virtue ethics. He believed that we are all capable of

---

19. Luke 19:12–27.
20. Beth Felker Jones, *Practicing Christian Doctrine: An Introduction to Thinking and Living Theologically* (Grand Rapids: Baker Academic, 2014).

virtue without any divine help. Rather than recognizing people are broken by sin, he believed that we have free will to choose to be more virtuous.

Augustine confronted Pelagius, saying that to deny the brokenness of our fallen world and the concept of sin was like telling a person in a deep pit to climb out without any way of doing so.[21] Only with salvation, only if we know the master is kind and merciful and we receive his mercy, can we be effective in his kingdom. The servants in Luke 19 who invested their money understood their master's gift of grace and were able to go on and perform good works and loving acts to serve their master. The servant who did not understand the master's gift was terrified of his inability to invest and feared the master's anger. He did not understand the master's heart or that the money from the master was a gift, and he was rendered incapable of praiseworthy good works and loving acts.

Zacchaeus's reputation was awful. The power of his witness was exactly because of his awful reputation. He was lost, and when he was saved his witness wasn't to his righteousness, but the character and grace of Jesus—that he could be transformed because of Jesus.

I learned this the hard way. I grew up with lessons about how to be virtuous, but I was in a Pelagian conundrum. If my reputation was about my good deeds and accomplishments, it was doomed to be broken over and over. However, if my reputation was rooted in recognizing that I am imperfect, but Christ in me is perfect, then I could truly walk in an integrity I was never capable of before. Yes, integrity involves having strong moral principles, but it is mostly about the quality of being honest. In ethics literature, integrity is regarded as the honesty and truthfulness or accuracy of one's actions. Integrity is the key to a powerful reputation. It is the state of knowing who the master is and the ability to quickly repent and recognize wrongdoings and mistakes to move toward good works, positive impact, and loving acts. This is important for us in our individual lives as well as how we do business.

Reputation Research

I've said multiple times now that with increased visibility and access to firm information, often through social media outlets, bad news has never been more rampant. News about poor supply chain practices (child labor, unfair/below-market wages, environmental abuse) affects consumers' perceptions and alters their confidence in the products made by a firm. This means that the issue

---

21. Jones, *Practicing Christian Doctrine*.

is not only one of moral or ethical judgment, but one pertaining to the reputation of the company, to product performance, and to consumer confidence. Based on research I have conducted over the last three years, my colleagues and I lay out specific steps that firms can take to apply this knowledge and limit the potential damage to their reputation by taking specific steps to mitigate the effects of getting it wrong and making mistakes—which are guaranteed to happen. The ongoing *spillover effect studies* I have conducted with friends at the University of Northern Kentucky and East Carolina University explore how news about supply chain operations related to sustainability impact consumer perceptions and corporate reputation.[22]

The Impact of Bad News Is Broader Than Sales

The *spillover effect studies* explore the impact of both positive and negative news related to the economic, environmental, and social triple bottom line (TBL) on consumer product quality perceptions.

Participants read a Facebook news post about the positive or negative TBL operations of a fictitious company. Of the positive news stories, only favorable economic news, such as increased returns on investment for stakeholders, raised consumer perceptions of product quality. Positive environmental and social news did not have a similar effect. Seemingly, consumers now hold firms responsible for sustainability, so good news about environmental initiatives and social programs did not significantly improve consumer perceptions of the brand and product quality, but are expected norms. However, negative news about economic, environmental, and socially-focused operations in the supply chain significantly decreased consumer perceptions of product quality and influenced purchase intentions.

It Doesn't Matter If the News Is a Little Troubling or Catastrophic

While consumers may find it troubling that a firm does not recycle, it is shocking if a firm is knowingly dumping toxic waste. Most people would assume that as bad news gets worse, consumer responses should grow more dramatic. The *spillover effect studies* tested the impact of varying intensities of news from very bad (near bankruptcy, waste dumping, and child labor) to moderately bad (5 percent decrease in profit, no energy conservation

---

22. Bridget Satinover Nichols, Hannah Stolze, and Jon F. Kirchoff, "Spillover Effects of Supply Chain News on Consumers' Perceptions of Product Quality: An Examination within the Triple Bottom Line," *Journal of Operations Management* 65, no. 6 (2019): 536–59; Bridget Satinover Nichols, Hannah Stolze, and Jon Kirchoff, "Are You Prepared for Bad Press about One of Your Suppliers?," *Harvard Business Review*, July 10, 2020. Accessed at https://hbr.org/2020/07/are-you-prepared-for-bad-press-abo ut-one-of-your-suppliers.

certification, and no pay raises) on both quality perceptions and consumers' willingness to buy.

The results indicate that consumers' reactions to all negative news are equally condemning, whether the news is more or less severe in nature. It did not matter *how* bad the news was, *all* bad news decreased consumers' perceptions of product quality regardless of the intensity or type of news. The results were slightly different for consumers' willingness to buy—as news grew worse about environmental and social actions of a company, the less willing consumers were to buy.

Something Will Go Wrong and Consumers Will Hear

Finally, it is guaranteed that something will go wrong somewhere in the supply chain and the negative news will eventually reach consumers. Today there are many risks and opportunities for operational failures, including some risks global supply chain managers may not even be aware of. When negative news does emerge, firms need to be prepared to reinforce positive consumer perceptions about their brands and product quality. This is increasingly important for TBL sustainability tied to economic, environmental, or social failures.

When the *spillover effect studies* tested the impact of recovery news on consumer perceptions and willingness to buy, it found *all* recovery actions of a company, whether small or large, increased both the perception of quality and the willingness of consumers to buy the company's product in the future. Social and environmental recovery efforts had a more dramatic effect than economic initiatives, but news of recovery efforts across all three types of TBL initiatives can drastically reduce the negative spillover effects of bad news and improve consumer perceptions.

Today, consumer interest and involvement extend beyond the brand itself to include a company's operations, stakeholder management, employee relations, community involvement, and other areas not directly related to the actual product. Positive news reinforces consumers' desires to identify with a brand but seems to serve as a baseline and will meet consumer expectations without necessarily increasing quality perceptions or purchase intention. On the other hand, negative news regarding any economic or environmental failure will decrease perceptions of quality and purchase intentions beyond the immediate direct impact on sales. Thus, firms need to be prepared to reinforce positive consumer perceptions about their corporate sustainability initiatives by demonstrating how they have mitigated the failure and taken action to recover. Fortunately, all recovery efforts can undo all wrongs and even win deeper consumer loyalty.

Reputation as a Means to the End Goal

From a biblical kingdom perspective, we should think about reputation as witness and testimony. What is our witness in the world? Are we credible witnesses of a Master or Savior who is merciful and steadfast in his love? Do we try to demonstrate our righteousness or his righteousness as we are justified by his work on the cross and are continually sanctified as he continues his work in us?

I'm not saying that we haven't been made righteous. We are in a world where Jesus's kingdom has come and is here. However, it is not fully realized. When Jesus returns, the kingdom of God will be established in its fullness. While sin has been defeated for those who recognize the work of the cross and repent to receive salvation, upon Jesus's return, sin will be fully defeated. We have been made righteous as believers, but we live in a world that is fallen. We still face the temptations of sin. I don't know if we can live a perfectly righteous life or not, but I do know that when we receive salvation, our sins—past, present, and future—are forgiven. I know that when I mess up and sin, God continues to forgive me. I know that as a believer I walk in grace and I need the work of the cross to be righteous because I cannot attain righteousness without Jesus.

Our reputation is based on our witness to having been forgiven. Part of loving others is forgiving others. When we realize that our reputation is not really about who we are but is about who Christ is in us, then our reputation can truly become a means to the end goal of loving God and loving others well. When Peter asked Jesus how often he should forgive a brother who sinned against him, Jesus answered, "I do not say to you seven times, but seventy-seven times."[23] Jesus went to tell another story about a master who forgave his servant of what his servant owed him. In this lesson on the kingdom of heaven, Jesus encourages us to forgive our brothers and sisters from our hearts.[24] We need the integrity to be honest about who we want to be while also giving an accurate assessment of our actions. With integrity, a positive reputation can be maintained even when negative things happen.

When it comes to reputation, we need to know that we will mess up from time to time and that is okay. Our reputation is not based on our perfection, but on our ability to repent and change. The more we are capable of forgiving others for their debts and mistakes that impact us, the more likely others will be to forgive us. In the Lord's Prayer, Jesus teaches the disciples to pray, "forgive us our debts, as we have also forgiven our debtors."[25] Our reputation is not

---

23. Matthew 18:22 ESV.
24. Matthew 18:23–35.
25. Matthew 6:12.

tied to perfection, but to our honesty about who we want to be and how well we are doing in achieving that goal. In this way, companies can market their goal of being sustainable and all of the actions they are taking to attain that goal. As long as they are honest about it when they don't attain their goals and correct their mistakes, the consumer will forgive them, and their reputation will remain intact.

Reflection Questions

1. Name a company that you think has a great reputation. What makes this company's reputation good?
2. What should our reputations as Christian businesspeople be?
3. What are the characteristics of the reputation of an organization led by Christians with purpose beyond profit?

CHAPTER 11

COMPARATIVE
ADVANTAGE

Blessed are those who find wisdom,
    those who gain understanding,
for she is more profitable than silver
    and yields better returns than gold.
She is more precious than rubies;
    nothing you desire can compare with her.

—Proverbs 3:13–15 NIV

Trader Joe's is for overeducated and underpaid people, for all the
classical musicians, museum curators, journalists—that's why
we've always had good press, frankly!

—Joe Coulombe, founder of Trader Joe's[1]

In 2012, when I took my first academic job at Florida State University, on the top of my criteria for places to live was access to a Trader Joe's store. From 2008 to 2012 we lived in Knoxville, Tennessee, a land devoid of Trader Joe's! During those four years in Trader Joe's exile, we stocked up on our favorite Trader Joe's items every time we visited friends in Chicago, saw family in St. Louis, or just passed a Trader Joe's as we drove through Cincinnati. My husband and I can tell you the location of every Trader Joe's on highways 70, 64, 40, 65, and 75 between Knoxville and St. Louis or Chicago. They carried a specific coffee that we loved that we could only find at Trader Joe's. They also had unique canned Cuban black beans; many whole-grain items like pasta, cereal, and quinoa; and a specific enchilada sauce that passed my husband's Mexican heritage standards.

---

1. Patt Morrison, "Joe's Joe: Joe Coulombe," *Los Angeles Times*, May 7, 2011, https://www.latimes.com/opinion/la-xpm-2011-may-07-la-oe-morrison-joe-coulombe-043011-story.html.

Between 2012 and 2013, Trader Joe's openings across the country drew crowds of excited customers and hopeful candidates for employment. At the same time, big box retailers watched the rising success of Trader Joe's and began opening small-format stores. Walmart planned to open over 100 small-format neighborhood stores in 2013. As we now look back on this time, we know that Trader Joe's was able to maintain its advantage in the retail industry, continuing growth as the Walmart neighborhood stores failed and closed down and Amazon continued to push into the grocery business with the purchase of Whole Foods. In 2013, a Harvard Business Case was published on Trader Joe's under the topic of comparative advantage.[2] Years later, a search on comparative-advantage cases on the *Harvard Business Review* website delivers hundreds of cases with Trader Joe's as the number-one case example.

As a native Midwesterner, I was surprised to realize that Trader Joe's was first opened in 1967 in California. When founder Joe Coulombe looked at the retail industry in the late 1960s, he realized that there was an increasing population of educated individuals because of the G. I. Bill. With ten years of experience running a convenience store chain in California, Joe wanted to deliver something different to this newly educated population. Joe's target market segment was the overeducated and underpaid: the classical musicians, museum curators, and journalists in the Los Angeles area. Joe focused on private label products with the Trader Joe's brand on almost everything sold in the store (aside from wine and beer). This allowed him to buy in bulk and to avoid shelving fees (known as slotting fees) charged by large retail chains to big brands. He passed along the savings to his customers by providing quality products at the best everyday prices.[3]

Purchased by Theo Albrecht, the CEO of German grocery chain Aldi, in 1979, Trader Joe's has remained a lifestyle feature with a cult-like customer following that weathered the 2008 recession and the rise of Amazon. Trader Joe's remains in the top ten ranked supermarkets by American consumers since 2012. With a unique and varied product selection, Trader Joe's claims that 80 percent of its customers have attended college, and they open new stores in college towns or urban hubs.[4] Trader Joe's has historically paid its employees better than market rate and offered generous benefits. Over the years, Trader Joe's crewmembers have tended to be creative, college-educated young people who graduated without the hard skills necessary for technical jobs. Stores were staffed with history, theater, and music majors who enjoyed the creative environment Trader Joe's offered.

---

2. D. L. Ager and M. A. Roberto, "Trader Joe's," *Harvard Business School Case* 714–419, September 2013 (revised April 2014.), https://store.hbr.org/product/trader-joe-s/714419.

3. Trader Joe's, "Our Story," https://www.traderjoes.com/our-story.

4. Ager and Roberto, "Trader Joe's."

Trader Joe's and Aldi have grown and maintained American consumer favor over the years as trendsetters in the retail industry.[5] With smaller floorplans than most big-box chain grocery stores and lower prices than Whole Foods, both Trader Joe's and Aldi have led the charge in low-cost, healthy food options (no additives and lots of organic offerings) with generic labels.

Trader Joe's and Aldi have two interesting advantages over their retail counterparts. First, they both have loyal, even fanatical, customer and employee fan clubs. In 2019, Trader Joe's was rated America's Best Large Employer in a survey conducted by Statista & Forbes.[6] The majority of the brands sold in both stores are 80 percent generic store brands (Trader Joe's) or genericized brands (Aldi). When a customer shops at Trader Joe's, the only brand they encounter is the brand of the store. This builds a huge relational advantage compared to the top four grocery retailers—Walmart, Kroger, Safeway, and Supervalu—that mainly sell manufacturer brands such as Frito-Lay, Dove, Quaker Oats, Coca-Cola, Kraft, and Pepsi. These brand-name products can be bought at any of the top four retail grocery stores, while Trader Joe's classic products like Speculoos Cookie Butter, Charles Shaw Wine (Two-Buck Chuck), and Trader Ming's Mandarin Orange Chicken can only be found at Trader Joe's. Because of their unique generic brand product assortment, Trader Joe's also has strong relationships with their suppliers.

Second, Trader Joe's and Aldi have a unique organization strategy and culture that is un-replicated by any other retail chain and allows for a low-cost high-quality product brand. Whole Foods seems to come the closest to the Trader Joe's product strategy with their organic and whole-food products. However, Whole Foods—which some people have derisively called "Whole Paycheck"—doesn't come close to competing in the cost/value category. A 2019 *Business Insider* article by Soshy Ciment compared the shopping experience at Trader Joe's to Whole Foods and found that Trader Joe's offered the better grocery-shopping experience, stating that Trader Joe's "low prices and endearing nautical charm made it the better option overall."[7]

Trader Joe's may be ranked number twelve in revenue, but at $7.6 billion in 2012 and a projected $9.458 billion in 2020, they have consistently operated with

5. Brad Tuttle, "How Two German-Owned Sister Supermarket Brands Became Hot Trendsetters in the U.S.," *Time*, July 29, 2013, https://business.time.com/2013/07/29/how-two-german-owned-sister -supermarket-brands-became-hot-trendsetters-in-the-u-s/.

6. Niall McCarthy, "America's Best Large Employers in 2019," digital image, April 18, 2019, https:// www-statista-com.ezproxy.wheaton.edu/chart/17726/top-10-us-employers-as-rated-by-employees-in-2019/.

7. Shoshy Ciment, "We Shopped at Both Whole Foods and Trader Joe's, and the Amazon-Owned Chain Was Disappointing in Comparison," *Business Insider*, August 2019, https://www.businessinsider .com/whole-foods-or-trader-joes-best-healthy-grocery-store-2019-8.

a lean strategy that allowed them a cash advantage that allows them to adjust to the market. Trader Joe's has maintained the margin to continue to grow even when political, legal, and consumer trends shift. In 1975, the fair trade law that was originally intended to protect small business from the buying power of very large chains was repealed. This allowed big-box giants like Walmart to bulk buy and promote everyday low prices, but left smaller retailers like Trader Joe's at a huge buying disadvantage. Joel Coulombe said this in the *LA Times* in 2011:

> In fact, people thought we'd go bankrupt when fair trade was repealed. I didn't, because I had paid off all debt in 1975. Trader Joe's never had one penny of debt [after that] and that was one of the reasons we were able to make so many deals—we could wire cash. When fair trade went out, man, we took that and we ran with it, and within 90 days we were making more money than ever before.[8]

More recently, during the 2020 COVID-19 pandemic, Trader Joe's saw record sales as American consumers rushed grocery stores. While eighteen Trader Joe's stores closed for COVID-19, they continued to pay crew members for their scheduled shifts while decontaminating stores.[9]

Trader Joe's mission statement is to "give customers the best food and beverage values that they can find anywhere and to provide them with the information required for informed buying decisions. We provide these with a dedication to the highest quality of customer satisfaction delivered with a sense of warmth, friendliness, fun, individual pride, and company spirit."

In 2001, Trader Joe's came under pressure from activist group Greenpeace to drop GMOs (genetically modified organisms). After a controversy around unapproved genetically engineered corn found in the food supply, Trader Joe's partnered with consumer advocacy groups and within a year converted to non-GMO ingredients in all private-label products (around 70 percent of the selection in the store in 2001).[10]

Trader Joe's has come under fire for lack of transparency because they closely guard the identities of their suppliers and for not labeling their products as non-GMO. Trader Joe's response to consumer complaints is as follows:

---

8. Morrison, "Joe's Joe: Joe Coulombe."

9. Betty Gold, "18 Trader Joe's Stores Are Closing Temporarily Due to Possible COVID-19 Contamination," *Real Simple*, April 15, 2020, https://www.realsimple.com/food-recipes/shopping -storing/food/trader-joes-covid-closings.

10. "Trader Joe's Bans GMOs from Private-label Products," *Progressive Grocer*, November 15, 2001, https://progressivegrocer.com/trader-joes-bans-gmos-private-label-products.

We have yet to take the approach of labeling products as non-GMO because there are no clear guidelines from the US governmental agencies covering food and beverage labeling. Instead of waiting for such guidelines to be put into effect, and based upon customer feedback, we took a more holistic approach and made the no GMO ingredients position part of what the Trader Joe's label encompasses.[11]

From its inception, Trader Joe's has maintained all of the wisdom-based strategic orientations. They have sustained their commitment to being a good neighbor for over fifty years. They prioritize the community they are in and the sustainability and quality of their products and operations. In 2019, Trader Joe's donated nearly $384 million dollars of food and beverages to those in need and recycled over 450 million pounds of packaging materials.

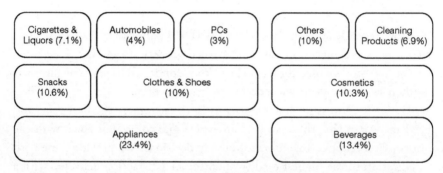

TABLE 11.1: Trader Joe's Wisdom-Based Strategic Orientations

Trader Joe's has seemingly maintained an advantage in a highly competitive market by investing in the long-term and committing to being a good neighbor.[12]

Comparative Advantage of the Firm

As I began my undergraduate studies in International Political Economics and Mandarin, the world was facing increasing rates of change in technology and globalization. Walmart was expanding to become the largest retailer in the world, and sourcing/manufacturing was quickly moving to China to meet the everyday low-cost demands. The dot-com boom had captured the imaginations of investors, and the bubble was about to burst.

11. Trader Joe's, FAQs, https://www.traderjoes.com/faqs/general-information?categoryid=2.

12. Trader Joe's, "Sustainability and Your Neighborhood Grocery Store," January 1, 2018, https://www.traderjoes.com/Announcement/Index/sustainability-and-your-neighborhood-grocery-store.

When I entered Carthage College, I had just finished boot camp in the US Army. I went on to spend the next year divided between college and training as a psychological operations (PSYOPs) cultural analyst. The Split Ops program for enlisted soldiers allowed me to pursue military training in the summers while serving as a reserve soldier on weekends during the school year.

In the late 1990s, PSYOPs was focused on rebuilding US relations in Bosnia and Herzegovina. By the time I shifted my military occupational specialty from PSYOPS to ordnance, we were on the brink of 9/11 and war in the Middle East. As a cultural analyst, I studied the psychological differences between cultures. It all boiled down to motivation. A goal of psychological operations was to motivate "the other side" to opt out of war and to build up global perceptions of the US. I needed to understand how people were motivated in order to persuade them to ally with the US instead of fighting. The government defines the purpose of PSYOPs a little differently—to shape the global security environment and achieve US national security goals.[13]

Around that time, I was introduced to the Ricardian theory of comparative advantage.[14] Ricardian macro-economic theory is not a fun read. It contains mathematical formulas that capture all of the variables that differentiate nations, demonstrating which countries are better off engaging in one industry over another (for example, it is better for Canada to sell lumber and maple syrup, while Indonesia should focus on palm oil and spices). Despite its tedious nature, in 1817 the Ricardian theory of comparative advantage began to explain why countries engage in international trade. It was one of the first frameworks for free trade. In a nutshell, comparative advantage is the ability of one nation to more efficiently or cheaply produce a product than another nation. I recognize that Ricardo's theory wasn't perfect. However, his greatest contribution was the concept of the comparative advantage of a nation.

In the mid-1990s, business strategy researchers began to explore the concept of comparative advantage of firms instead of at the national level. By the early 1990s, firms had already begun to grow so large that their revenue (annual sales) exceeded the GDP of many countries. Texas Tech strategy theorists Shelby Hunt and Robert Morgan began to explore the role of a comparative advantage for a company by adapting Ricardo's theory of the comparative advantage of nations to the comparative advantage of the firm.[15] Competitive

13. US Army, Careers & Jobs: Psychological Operations.

14. David Ricardo, *On the Principles of Political Economy and Taxation* (London: John Murray, 1817).

15. Shelby D. Hunt and Robert M. Morgan, "The Comparative Advantage Theory of Competition," *Journal of Marketing* 59, no. 2 (1995): 1–15.

and comparative advantages of the firm became the focus of business strategy research in the 1990s, and theories of competition multiplied.[16] The article Hunt and Morgan published is one of the most impactful articles guiding marketing and supply chain research to date. They shifted the traditional neo-classical economic mindset that defined free-market capitalism to explore the resources that help companies achieve an advantage over their competition in a less-than-perfect market.

Hunt and Morgan introduced comparative advantage as the ability of a firm (company) to make a specific product more efficiently (lower cost) and effectively (higher quality/value) than another company.[17] The comparative-advantage theory of the firm focuses on the unique resources of the firm, allowing them to attain profitability with a differential advantage relative to other firms. For example, Trader Joe's didn't have the largest market share in the retail industry, nor do they have the highest revenue or financial performance, but they maintained consistent growth in a subsegment of the small-format retail industry due to a differential advantage based on their unique relationships with customers, employees, and suppliers, and their capability (knowledge) to deliver quality products to their customers at low cost. Later called the resource-advantage theory, comparative advantage captures the firm's unique capabilities to understand and engage stakeholders, build collaborative supply chain relationships, and utilize human, natural, and economic resources to innovative and efficiently deliver a quality product to the customer.

This is not meant to be a thorough analysis of comparative-advantage theory. If you love business theory, I recommend you read Hunt and Morgan's work for yourself. At a high level, it is important to be aware of it because it began to shift some of the traditional economic mindsets away from perfect competition and "pure capitalism" as the best environment for a firm to thrive. The "pure capitalism" and perfect-competition mindset had two particularly challenging fundamental axioms (foundational beliefs) that put the marketplace at odds with Christianity. With the separation of church and state in the US, the following two premises limited the positive impact Christians could have in the marketplace:

- Humans are motivated by self-interest.
  - Self-interest can be captured as greed or an individual's desire to have wealth at the expense of others.

---

16. Michael E. Porter, "The Competitive Advantage of Nations," *Harvard Business Review* 68, no. 2 (1990): 73–93.

17. Hunt and Morgan, "The Comparative Advantage Theory of Competition."

- o Neoclassical economic theory proposes that self-interest will perfectly motivate. People will realize that it is in their best self-interest to not cheat or swindle other people due to longer-term costs. Therefore, the marketplace will force people to do the "right thing" out of self-interest.
- The sole purpose of the firm is to maximize profit.
  - o The Milton Friedman (neoclassical economist)/Edward Freeman (ethicist) debate inspired stakeholder theory. Friedman argued superior performance was equal to profit and shareholder value maximization, while Freeman argued that superior performance was maximizing value for all stakeholders (not just shareholders).

The economic crash in 2008 turned out to be based on the corruption of the financial industry, bringing to light the inability of the market to correct self-interest and profit maximization through competition. The market did not force the financial industry to "do the right thing," and a single-minded focus on profit maximization without any constraints brought the financial industry to its knees.

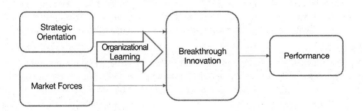

TABLE 11.2: Neoclassical Theory vs. Resource Advantage Theory[18]

The shift in motivation and the purpose or objective of the firm made resource-advantage theory a better model through which to explore how firms compete to create a comparative advantage. Perhaps the greatest contribution of the theory of comparative advantage is the inclusion of multiple resources of the firm that can lead to an advantage. Neoclassical economic theory focuses on capital, land, and labor—all tangible, measurable resources that are great for mathematical modeling. However, in reality, firms compete based on a number of intangible resources that include supply chain relationships, organizational knowledge, and organizational strategies.

---

18. Hunt and Morgan, "The Comparative Advantage Theory of Competition," 3; Hunt and Davis, "Grounding Supply Chain Management in Resource-Advantage Theory."

Resource Advantage Theory	Trader Joe's Example	Wisdom View
Demand Heterogenous *Customers are different.*	Unique segment (over-educated, underpaid) wanted a different retail experience.	The wise recognize that God has uniquely gifted us (1 Cor. 12:12–27)
Customer Information Imperfect and Costly *Some firms invest in big data and have more info.*	Spends time/money engaging customers to understand.	It takes wisdom and discernment to understand others (1 Kings 3).
Human Motivation Constrained Self-Interest *Allows for morality to be a factor.*	Motivated to meet the unmet needs of a market segment both profitably and with positive impact.	The wise are motivated by love of God and others (Matt. 22:36–40).
Firm's Objective Superior Performance	Use TBL, not just financial performance.	The wise are called to achieve fruitfulness (profit) to meet needs of others (Matt. 25).
Firm's Information Imperfect and Costly *Firms invest in R&D to have different information.*	Trader Joe's keeps supplier information proprietary to gain savings.	The wise know and prophecy in part, as the kingdom has come but isn't fully revealed in the earth (1 Cor. 13:9–12).
Resources Financial, Physical, Legal, Human, Organizational, Informational, and Relational	Trader Joe's has a unique organizational capability to sell a high-quality product at a low price.	All resources are a gift from God. Understanding and knowledge lead to the wisdom necessary to steward resources (Matt. 25).
Resources Characteristics Heterogeneous, Imperfectly Mobile *Companies have access to resources others don't— difficult to replicate and transfer.*	Wal-Mart and Whole Foods couldn't replicate Trader Joe's lower-cost neighborhood stores.	The wise are uniquely gifted with resources and capabilities that are difficult for others to replicate (1 Pet. 4:10).
Role of Leadership Recognize, Create, Implement, and Modify Orientations/Strategies	Joe's role was to determine market opportunities and strategy.	The role of the wise leader is to serve others (Matt. 20:26).
Role of Environment Influence Conduct and Performance *There are industry norms, some firms are outliers.*	Trader Joe's was an outlier —small floor plans and highly paid employees.	The role of the wise is to set a standard of excellence that challenges the status quo (Matt 28:19).
Competition Comparative Advantage *Differentiation with unique product at low cost/ high value.*	Trader Joe's does not have the largest market share, but has a differentiated strategy that allows continued growth.	The wise have an advantage —superior performance is attained through care for those in need (Matt. 25).

TABLE 11.3: Trader Joe's Comparative Advantages

Trader Joe's was an early exemplar of a company that managed to grow profitably with a strategy around quality products at low prices. Trader Joe's had unique relational resources. They had strong relationships with customers and employees. They also had access to unique information resources regarding high-quality, low-cost products that allowed them to maintain a comparative advantage over other small format grocery stores in the 1990s to 2010s as they grew. Table 11.3 demonstrates the comparative advantage of Trader Joe's and how this theory can be applied to achieving the goal of wisdom—to love and honor God and others:

Chayil, Wisdom, and Comparative Advantage

"The right hand of the LORD does *valiantly*;
    the right hand of the LORD is exalted;
    the right hand of the LORD does *valiantly*!"
    (Ps. 118:15–16, emphases mine)

A *valiant* woman who can find?
    She is far more precious than jewels. (Prov. 31:10)[19]

She dresses herself with *strength*
    and makes her arms strong. (Prov. 31:17 ESV)

Strength and dignity are her clothing,
    and she laughs at the time to come. (Prov. 31:25)

Many women have done *valiantly*,
    but you *surpass them all*. (Prov. 31:29 NET)

Proverbs 31:10–31 demonstrates competition in warlike terminology. Not only is the woman in the passage valiant (*chayil*), she is also strong and surpasses, exceeds, and is superior to all other valiant women. The title of the passage, *eset chayil*, is a term that can be translated many ways. It is typically translated in English Bibles as the Noble Wife. However, according to Al Wolters, it is more accurately translated as the Valiant Woman or the Mighty

---

19. *Chayil* is only translated to "valiant" in the Douay-Rheims Bible, in Wolter's exposition, and in the *Theology of Work Bible Commentary*: https://www.theologyofwork.org/old-testament/proverbs/what -do-the-proverbs-have-to-do-with-work/the-valiant-woman-proverbs-3110-31.

Woman of Valor.[20] The counterpart to *eset chayil* is *gibbor chayil*, the title given to the mighty men of valor; a term used to describe David's mighty men.[21] The term for *chayil* shows up twice in Proverbs 31:10–31, at the beginning of verse 10 and near the end of verse 29. In verse 29, the term *excellently* here is literally *as a chayil*, a term that regularly means to do valiantly in a military context. Like the heroic poetry that celebrated the exploits of David and his mighty men in battle and the song of Deborah in Judges, the song of the valiant woman displays wisdom in action. The passage is a portrait of excellence in business as an aspect of what it means to be wise.

Beyond the two occurrences of *chayil*, strength emerges as a pattern. In verses 17 and 25 Wisdom is clothed with strength and makes herself strong. The central images in the passage refer to her arms and her hands. At first glance, the two central verses seem to reflect domestic work and charity:

> She stretches out her hands to the distaff
> and her hands hold the spindle. (v. 19)

> She opens her hand to the poor
> and reaches out her hands to the needy. (v. 20)

Wolters argues that the phrase in verse 19 is an aggressive action.[22] It uses similar terminology as Jael grasping the tent peg when she kills Sisera in the story of Deborah in the book of Judges. Common to heroic poetry, the language here is warlike and violent. The image of a women holding two tools in her hands in the ancient Near East was not necessarily a picture of the domestic tasks of knitting and making yarn. It is likely that it would have brought to mind Ishtar, the Mesopotamian goddess of love and war who held tools (a rod and ring of leadership) or weapons of war in her hands. Ishtar was closely associated with vengeance, justice, and maintenance of cosmic order. Interestingly, she also represented a spouse and mother.

The term *chayil* is important in understanding the role of valor (nobility, strength, might, efficiency, wealth, and force) when wisdom is in action. Thus far, I haven't paid as much attention to *chesed* as I have to *chayil*, the competitive nature of wisdom. In short, the concept of *chesed* is translated into several terms, including "steadfast love," "loving kindness," and "mercy." In Proverbs 31:26 when the Woman of Valor opens her mouth with wisdom, the teaching of

---

20. Wolters, "Proverbs xxxi 10–31 as Heroic Hymn."
21. 1 Chronicles 5:24.
22. Wolters, "Proverbs xxxi 10–31 as Heroic Hymn."

chesed is on her tongue. This teaching is translated in most Bibles to "kindness." However, *chesed* is translated to "steadfast love" throughout Psalms and the Wisdom Literature ("The steadfast love of the Lord never ceases" in Lam. 3:22). Finally, the concept of *chesed* is one of three actions the Lord requires of us in Micah 6:8: to do justice, to love mercy (*chesed*), and to walk humbly with God.

The book of Ruth provides an in-depth example of wisdom and both *chayil* and *chesed* in action. My Old Testament professor at Wheaton College, Daniel Block, first alerted me to the importance of the book of Ruth in understanding the concepts of *chayil* and *chesed*. In the Ben Asher family of ancient biblical manuscripts, the book of Ruth is sandwiched between Proverbs and Qoheleth (Ecclesiastes).[23] This location places the story of Ruth immediately after the alphabetic celebration of the woman of valor in Proverbs 31:10–31. The location demonstrates the importance of Ruth as another example of wisdom in a narrative story.

As I mentioned earlier in this book, expression of *eset chayil* (woman of nobility) only occurs in Proverbs 31:10 and Ruth 3:11. This suggests that the book of Ruth demonstrates a supreme example of the valor and nobility described by the term *chayil*. The term *gibbor chayil*, which is used to describe King David and his mighty men in 1 Chronicles 11, is used to describe Boaz in Ruth 2:1. In case you aren't familiar with the book of Ruth, the story goes as follows.

Chapter 1
- Famine hits and Elimelech, Naomi, and their two sons move from Bethlehem to Moab.
- Elimelech and their two sons die.
- Naomi is left with her two daughters-in-law; Ruth insists on going with Naomi to Bethlehem.
- Naomi changes her name to Mara (bitter).

Chapter 2
- Ruth—who is described as *eset chayil*, a valiant woman—meets Boaz, Noami's kinsman gleaning crops in Bethlehem.
- Boaz is referred to three times as a kinsman redeemer and as *gibbor chayil*, a man mighty of strength.

Chapter 3
- Naomi encourages Ruth to approach Boaz as a potential kinsman redeemer, *go'el*.

---

23. Daniel I. Block, *Ruth: A Discourse Analysis of the Hebrew Bible*, Zondervan Exegetical Commentary on the Old Testament (Grand Rapids: Zondervan Academic, 2015).

- Ruth asks Boaz to be her kinsman redeemer.
- Boaz responds in kindness and mercy to bless Ruth for her kindness to Naomi. He says that he will seek a redeemer, as she is truly an *eset chayil*!

Chapter 4

- Boaz marries Ruth to restore Naomi back to pleasantness, restoring Elimelech's lineage.
- Their son Obed becomes the father of Jesse, the father of David.
- David becomes King David, king of Israel.

In this short book, the will of God is enacted through day-to-day business. Boaz, with his wealth and fields, has the resources to provide a large enough harvest to have margins for the poor, the immigrants, and the needy in the community. The noble characters of Boaz and Ruth secure blessing and praise for multiple generations. They bless the generation before them as Naomi is celebrated. The generations to follow are also blessed as their great-grandchild David establishes Israel's royal lineage.

Like Boaz and Ruth, the language describing the Noble Woman in Proverbs 31:10, 19 indicates that she has resources and skills that are unique in her day. She is clearly a rarity and flourishes with strength. Her unique resources that provide an opportunity for profitability would be categorized in management literature as a comparative advantage, and as the Scripture states, she "surpass[es] them all" (v. 29). Thus, wisdom is inimitable—difficult to replicate and hard to find. In the marketplace, wisdom provides skills and methods that lead to financial success. An awe of God enables us to find this divine wisdom that leads to blessing, redemption, and restoration of not just one, but multiple generations.

Comparative Advantage Research and Business Strategy

In 1995, Texas Tech professors Morgan and Hunt received the Maynard Award for the theory of comparative advantage for the firm. More than 3,000 articles have tested, cited, and built on their theory of comparative advantage, and their article on comparative advantage was recognized as the leading *Journal of Marketing* article on theory.

Building on Ricardo's theory of comparative advantage for nations, Hunt and Morgan's work highlighted the importance of intangible resources. Capabilities, orientations, and strategy became central resources to create a market advantage for the firm. Neoclassical economic theory focused on the tangible and measurable land (you can count acres), labor (you can take a census of your workforce), and money (you can count money). On the other hand, the resource advantage theory recognized the role of intangible capabilities as well as the tangible assets in gaining a marketplace advantage.

In highly competitive markets, it is extremely difficult for firms to differentiate themselves. Firms that target new and unserved emerging markets can introduced unique innovations that may provide opportunities for growth. Trader Joe's is a great example of this in the US market. They could not compete based on the neoclassical definition of competition and performance based on their access to land, labor, and financial capital. Instead, Trader Joe's created a unique strategy that allowed them to target an unserved market (the overeducated and underpaid) with a unique retail service that other companies found difficult to imitate.

In 2010, my friends Donna Davis and Susan Golicic explored the impact of a strategic orientation as a firm resource that drives information flows to help firms attain relational and informational advantages in their supply chains relative to their competition.[24] They explored market orientation as a competence of the firm that increases the use of information technologies to gain effective access to markets and efficiencies to improve bottom-line measures. The outcome of the market orientation is a comparative advantage when the firm is able to produce a market offering that is perceived by the customers to have superior value (quality) at a lower cost.[25] Davis and Golicic noted in the article that some resource advantages are more sought after than others. Information and relational advantages are among the most sought-after resources because they are more difficult to imitate and cannot be directly purchased.

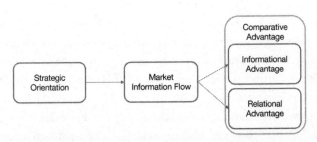

FIGURE 11.3: The Role of Orientations in Driving Information Flow and Comparative Advantage

24. Donna F. Davis and Susan L. Golicic, "Gaining Comparative Advantage in Supply Chain Relationships: The Mediating Role of Market-Oriented IT Competence," *Journal of the Academy of Marketing Science* 38, no. 1 (2010): 56–70.

25. Hunt and Morgan, "The Comparative Advantage Theory of Competition," 7.

Davis and Golicic tested this model with data from logistics service firms. Participants included carriers (trucking and railroad companies, transportation providers), warehousing firms, and other third-party providers that move goods. They ultimately collected data from managers at 673 US-based logistics companies. They found across their sample that a strategic market orientation helped the companies develop relationships and have access to unique information in their distinct supply chains. While a market orientation explores relationships and information regarding customers and competition, a supply chain orientation would have an even stronger impact on market information flow and relational advantage as it engages suppliers as well as customers and competition. A stakeholder orientation takes this another step further by including employees and the local community in the sample.

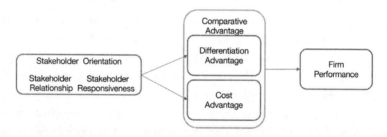

FIGURE 11.4: The Role of Stakeholder Orientation in Driving a Comparative Advantage

In 2016, business professors Alexander Kull, Jeannette Mena, and Daniel Korschun integrated stakeholder theory and the concept of stakeholder orientation with the resource-based view of the firm.[26] They proposed that comparative advantage is the outcome for firms with the unique resource of a stakeholder orientation, and that firms with a strong stakeholder orientation will have a better differentiation advantage and cost advantage that will lead to sustained performance. When combined with the concept of a comparative advantage, a stakeholder orientation can help us understand the expected outcomes of a company that strategically focuses on the needs of others in order to provide a unique resource in the marketplace.

---

26. Alexander J. Kull, Jeannette A. Mena, and Daniel Korschun, "A Resource-Based View of Stakeholder Marketing," *Journal of Business Research* 69, no. 12 (2016): 5553–60.

Comparative Advantage as a
Means to the End Goal

Now, I realize that my model of the wisdom-based view of the firm is now massive! But, if we put all of these concepts together, this is what we get:

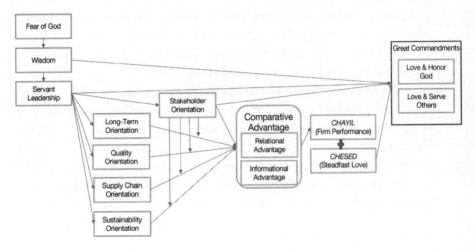

FIGURE 11.5: Wisdom-Based Model of the Firm

Proverbs 31:10–31 is full of action as the Noble Woman works as the chief executive servant leader to:

- buy raw materials and sell (supply chain management) a quality product fit for royalty in the colors of purple and scarlet (quality orientation),
- with a plan for profit, people, and the planet (sustainability orientation),
- and joy for the future (long-term orientation).

She does all of this while caring for multiple stakeholders, including setting tasks for her employees, profiting her husband, providing for the poor, delivering value to her customers, and meeting the needs of the next generation as her children rise up and call her blessed. She is both relationally advantaged through her network of stakeholders and informationally advantaged as she teaches others. The result of her work wins her the description of *chayil*, while her works are *chesed*.

In the corporate world, the *chayil* firm represents the wealth, strength, valiance in battle, and ableness (or capableness → capabilities) of an organization that has faced competition with efficiency and force. Only if paired with *chesed*, loving-kindness and mercy, can individuals in an organization achieve the end goal of loving God and others. The comparative advantage of Trader Joe's was that it was able to provide quality products at a lower cost than its competition, but a comparative advantage alone does not attain the great commandments to love God and others.

I chose to focus on a comparative advantage rather than a competitive advantage, even though the warrior metaphor in Proverbs 31:10–31 would certainly provide a great competitive story. This is because we are not called to compete in the world with a pure competition mindset.

Neoclassical economics introduces a world where scarcity drives competition and the actors in that world are motivated by self-interest as they win or lose access to the supply of products they need to meet customer demand. However, a wisdom-based view of economics introduces a world where the natural world conforms to a supernatural God and creator. There is no scarcity in the kingdom of heaven, only opportunities to create something new or an opportunity to see a miracle. In the beginning there was no heaven or earth or sea or land or garden or animals or people in it, yet God created it all out of nothing.

God is not confined to natural resources. When it appears that a natural resource is becoming scarce, it is an opportunity to innovate and create a new way of making a product or meeting a need. Jesus's first miracle was a miracle of demonstrating the resources of the kingdom of heaven in response to natural scarcity. He was at a wedding in Cana and the wine had run out. He transformed water into wine, providing high-quality wine that the steward and wedding party marveled at. When faced with the hunger of a crowd of 5,000, he utilized scarce resources by multiplying five loaves and a few fish to feed them all. We don't see multiplication miracles every day in the marketplace, but we certainly see the fruitfulness of organizations who don't succumb to scarcity but have an orientation to serve others well through new and creative ways.

A neoclassical competitive advantage view also introduces a win-lose mindset. In a competition there are winners and losers. However, in the kingdom of heaven, we are all called to be part of an ecosystem where we each play a unique role. Instead of losing when someone else gains access to a resource, the entire system is actually healthier. Redemption is all about sacrifice, or losing so others can win. Turning the win-lose mindset on its head, Jesus establishes a culture where he, as the king, dies for all of his people so they can live life more abundantly. Jesus gave up life and seemingly lost so we could all gain access to God. Of course, he had the ultimate victory and now sits at the right hand of

God in a place of honor for eternity. Why should we expect any less? When we lose or sacrifice so that someone else can gain access to blessing and resources, we seem to think that we will lose out or that it doesn't make "good business sense." Somehow, over the centuries of separation of church and state in the US and in Western culture generally, a mindset has snuck into Christian business practice that has put profitability and short-term gains ahead of the long-term blessing that comes with short-term sacrifice and losses.

Hunt and Morgan originally suggest that a comparative advantage leads to superior firm performance, which is a competitive advantage in the marketplace. However, what if a comparative advantage is not about achieving a competitive advantage so that one company can win at the expense of others? What if a comparative advantage, when defined within the context of wisdom, is about having an advantage compared to others so that others can be blessed?

The ability of the Noble Woman in Proverbs 31:10–31 to profit and bless her stakeholders allows her the margin to care for those that are poor and needy. Compared to others, she surpasses them all. This is not so she can amass wealth, but so she can have margin to provide for others. Boaz has this same margin as he conducts his business in a way that allows the poor and needy to benefit from his success.

I believe that wisdom leads to a comparative advantage, not a competitive advantage. We do not have more because we have won access to a scarce resource at the expense of the losers. If we have more compared to others, it is not because we are better or more righteous than them. Whatever we have, whether we have more or less, it is because we are servants who have been entrusted with the resources of heaven while our master is away.[27] We are called to multiply those resources. We are called to multiply the resources God has entrusted to us whether it is tangible wealth and economic capital or intangible capabilities such as knowledge or an ability to love others like Jesus loved us.

In my model, wisdom and servanthood have arrows that can lead directly to loving God and loving others. Business is only one means through which we can lead and multiply the resources entrusted to us by God. There are many other means to the end goal of loving God and others. Other means include education and teaching or leading in the church to disciple and serve others as they conduct their works of service and ministry by going into all of the world and making disciples of all nations, baptizing them in the names of the Father, Son, and Holy Spirit and teaching them to obey everything Jesus commanded.[28]

---

27. Mathew 25.
28. Matthew 28:19–20a.

If we are going to teach others to obey everything Jesus commanded us, we need to first live it ourselves. Fortunately, Jesus summed up all his teachings in two commandments:

- Love God with all your heart, mind, and resources.[29]
- Love one another, as I have loved you.[30]

It is no surprise that the most valuable intangible resource of a firm is its relationships. Inimitable relationships are characterized by patience, kindness, lack of envy, and honor. Healthy relationships cannot have two self-seeking members, but both members of the relationship should rejoice in each other's successes, protecting each other, trusting each other, hoping for the best outcome for each other, and persevering. In essence, the greatest resources of a firm, the most valuable capability your company can have in attaining profitability and the margins necessary to grow and serve people well is love! Perhaps you recognized the language of 1 Corinthians 13 as I described the love that characterizes a healthy relationship. The capability to build relationships based on win-win or even sacrifice-win economics, trust, and the goal to serve others well will be difficult to imitate in the marketplace. But it drives customer and supplier loyalty and long-term profitability even if it demands short-term losses. If the end goal is eternal, then a comparative advantage is all about attaining margin to love, serve, and provide for others just like Jesus did for us.

Reflection Questions

1. In what ways has God uniquely gifted you compared to others?
   a. In what ways has God gifted you with tangible resources?
   b. In what ways has God gifted you with intangible resources?
2. How can your unique individual comparative advantage position you to love God and others?
3. Find examples of short-term losses made by companies that have led to long term advantages and gain in the market.

---

29. Deuteronomy 6:5.
30. John 15:12.

CHAPTER 12

KINGDOM
IMPACT

Can a virtuous mouse and the wealthy elephant live happily ever after? Small, iconoclastic companies' social images have been rooted in values and practices that contrast dramatically with those of conventional big companies like those purchasing or seeking to purchase them (emphasis mine).[1]

Over the past fifty years, business researchers have demonstrated that companies can do well by doing good. Thousands of articles have examined companies across a myriad of industries around the world and have provided decades of evidence confirming the benefits of doing the right thing. In this book, I have cited over 300 academic research projects, studies, and articles that have scientifically tested and provided evidence that each of the orientations of wisdom will not only increase profitability but will also reduce the negative impacts of a firm while enhancing positive impacts. The case-study examples are not perfect companies, but they provide unique exemplars of each of the wisdom orientations.

Historically, most business research stops at profitability as the ultimate outcome because that is what neoclassical journal reviewers have demanded. Academics have held themselves to a reductionist mindset of profitability as the best outcome of the business, thanks in part to Milton Friedman, father of Western capitalistic economic thinking. But the articles I've cited in this book begin to demonstrate that shareholders are not the only individuals businesses should be serving.

---

1. James E. Austin and Herman B. "Dutch" Leonard, "Can the Virtuous Mouse and the Wealthy Elephant Live Happily Ever After?" *California Management Review* 51, no. 1 (2008): 77–102.

Finally, a shift has taken place in the ivory towers of the academy to acknowledge that businesses should discern the impact on all stakeholders in business decision making. However, the academic world could still stand to learn how to better communicate their findings to leaders in the marketplace. Often, business research is left on the shelf as unreadable while increasing evidence is collected to demonstrate the power of morality in the market-place. Further, theologians at Princeton University have demonstrated that the integration of faith and work has become a bonafide social movement,[2] as have conscious capitalism and the B-corp movement. Corporate leaders of all different faiths have found that faith is a better path to business performance than making their shareholders happy.

In this chapter, I will provide one last example of a company that truly embraces all the orientations of wisdom. What do Tom's of Maine, Ben & Jerry's, The Body Shop, Honest Tea, and Stonyfield Farm all have in common? They were all social enterprises, organizations founded with a strong mission beyond profit, that were later acquired by leading multinational/global com-panies. The question remains to be answered for many investors and critics of the conscious capitalism, purpose beyond profit, and social entrepreneurship movements: Can companies do well by doing good? A few examples such as Patagonia, The Container Store, and New Belgium Brewing demonstrate that companies can truly gain market scale while balancing purpose and profit. Other examples like ServiceMaster and Whole Foods demonstrate the chal-lenges in aligning strategies when purpose-driven organizations are acquired by larger organizations.

Companies that seem to be able to scale their organizations with a pur-pose beyond profit have multiple strategies in place to attain their end goals.[3] Christian business leaders pursue the end goal of serving others and honoring God through stakeholder-, quality-, long-term-, supply chain-, and sustainability-oriented strategies while secular organizations without faith-based leadership similarly push toward serving others with an outcome focused on societal well-being. Throughout this book, the stories and narratives I have told about corporate strategies all start with recognizing multiple needs in the marketplace:

---

2. Miller, *God at Work*.

3. Michael Porter, "The Case for Letting Business Solve Social Problems," TED Talk 2013, https://www.ted.com/talks/michael_porter_the_case_for_letting_business_solve_social_problems?utm_campaign=tedspread&utm_medium=referral&utm_source=tedcomshare.

ServiceMaster	Moth extermination/labor dignity	Quality cleaning services
Container Store	Better retail labor conditions	Quality storage options
Yili Group	Long-term quality control strategy	Safe/quality dairy options
Giving Keys	Employment for homeless	Inspiring pay-it-forward product
Admont Abbey	Economic development	Education and construction services
I Have a Bean	Employment for ex-cons	Quality coffee bean options
Unilever	Need for hygiene	Global coordination of soap supply
Telunas	Social/Economic development	Quality eco-tourism experiences
Chipotle	Healthier fast food	Quality food with integrity
Trader Joe's	High-end, low-cost grocery	Quality retail grocery option

Some of the companies addressed the need directly with a product. Others addressed needs by creating jobs through the production of a quality product that is in demand in the market. In their stories, the founders and leaders of these organizations all had a personal "aha!" moment where they saw a need and took on the responsibility to address that need with a profitable solution. These companies were founded through both personal needs and recognition of the needs of others. All are great examples of actively loving our neighbors well. My final example is of a company that was founded to create a quality product not available on the market that offered a better quality of life for the customer while also caring for the planet and the community.

Tom Chappell, co-founder of Tom's of Maine, graduated from Trinity College in 1966 with a degree in English. He started his career at Aetna. He quickly discovered that not only was he a talented salesperson, he outperformed his entire class of recruits. He also found that he did not enjoy the constraining environment of the large corporate structure. Subsequently, he moved to Maine to help his father start a company producing cleaning solutions for textile and tanning factories.[4]

When Tom and Kate Chappell moved to Maine in 1968, they were not necessarily looking to start a personal care product company. They had access to great natural foods in Maine but found that they could not find personal

---

4. Andy Isaacson, "Why the Tom's of Maine Founder Thinks He Can Create the Next Patagonia," *Inc. Magazine*, April 2017, https://www.inc.com/magazine/201704/andy-isaacson/the-very-long-road.html.

care products with the same quality ingredients. They began creating their own.[5] They realized there was a huge need in the marketplace for organic personal care products and began to build a personal care product manufacturing company. In 1975, they introduced the first natural toothpaste into the US market. As the Chappells grew the company, they built on the belief that the business could be run with capitalist and moralist perspectives.

In 1991, after twenty-one years in business, Chappell took a step back to pursue a theology degree from Harvard Divinity School. In 1993, he published a book called *The Soul of a Business: Managing Profit and the Common Good*. In 1996, *The New York Times Magazine* ran an article about Tom Chappell called "God and Toothpaste."[6] The article told the story of how Tom had charted a new course in business by actively integrating his faith. The article quotes the book in saying:

> The ultimate goal of a business is not profit. Profit is merely a means toward the ultimate aim of affirming the health and dignity of human beings and their families, affirming aspirations of the community and affirming the health of the environment—the common good.[7]

The Tom's of Maine business model demonstrated to larger corporations that a small family-owned business could grow its market share. Tom's of Maine showed that happier, well-treated, well-paid employees are more productive, and that staying ahead of environmental regulations reduces fines and attracts consumers. While companies like Starbucks, Whole Foods, and Ben & Jerry's were all offering evidence that socially responsible entrepreneurship was a viable business growth strategy, Tom Chappell explored more eternal questions: "What is my role in relationship to God? And what do I do with my business?"[8]

Tom became an avid fan of deontological thinkers focused on the ethics of duty. He studied and adopted the philosophies of deontologists like Immanuel Kant, Martin Buber, and Jonathan Edwards. All of these thinkers believed that virtue needed to be activated. In *The New York Times Magazine* article, Tom stated:

---

5. Tom's of Maine, "The Backstory," https://www.tomsofmaine.com/the-backstory.

6. Doug S. Barasch, "God and Toothpaste," *New York Times Magazine*, December 22, 1996, p.27, https://www.nytimes.com/1996/12/22/magazine/god-and-toothpaste.html.

7. T. Chappell, *The Soul of a Business: Managing for Profit and the Consumer Good* (New York: Bantam, 1994), 202.

8. Barasch, "God and Toothpaste."

My responsibility is to use my gifts in service to God's work. I am ministering—and I am doing it in the marketplace, not in the church because I understand the marketplace better than the church.[9]

Tom worked with his board to create a mission statement that included the goal to be a profitable and successful company while acting in a socially and environmentally responsible manner. This mission cost them money in the short term as they committed to focus on long-term outcomes. For example, in 1992, Tom realized that a new deodorant formula magnified human odor in half its customers, conking out in the middle of the afternoon. Even though deodorant accounted for 25 percent of their business, they recalled all the deodorants, losing nearly half a million dollars, to reformulate the deodorant to work as promised. The deodorant wasn't harming anyone, but it didn't deliver the quality promised. While many companies would have just sold through the subpar inventory and apologized as they fixed the problem, Tom's recalled the product.

Over the years, Tom's of Maine grew to become a $100 million company. In 2006, Tom's of Maine was bought by Colgate. As a global leader in oral care products, Colgate gained credibility from the Tom's of Maine brand of natural products. Tom's of Maine gained cost reductions and top-line growth opportunities through the scale of Colgate's supply chain buying power and advertising reach. Colgate offered access to mainstream marketing channels, experience, and capital to scale the Tom's brand market share. Tom's of Maine brought a unique social product innovation to Colgate, which had struggled to tap into the natural product industry. Tom Chappell is quoted in a *California Management Review* article saying:

> The interest in naturals was growing faster than we were able to grow. We knew it was going to be a long time for us to get to critical mass, and we ultimately didn't have the resources. . . . Tom's of Maine is an admirable company up there in Maine doing these wonderful things, in everybody's mind, it's still fringe. Colgate has provided legitimacy to everything that we do, overnight.[10]

Both Tom's of Maine and Colgate gained legitimacy through each other's corporate reputations. Colgate had a brand familiarity that Tom's of Maine

---

9. Barasch, "God and Toothpaste."
10. Austin and Leonard, "Virtuous Mouse," 85.

didn't have. Colgate VP Dennis Hickey noted that the Tom's of Maine consumer base was better educated with a higher income. Colgate sought the credibility and relationship Tom's of Maine had with the natural-products-focused consumer base. The learning and agile innovativeness of Tom's of Maine provided insights and expertise in social-value creation Colgate didn't have in-house. Upon purchase, Colgate preserved Tom's of Maine's unique culture as a special business unit focused on the naturals segment. Both Colgate and Tom's of Maine looked for values alignment in the acquisition—Colgate was very caring and values sensitive for a large company, and the two firms were able to partner to continue toward common values and goals. Colgate agreed to continue the Tom's of Maine commitment to allocate 10 percent of pretax profit for charitable giving.

Tom Chappell presents one example of how a Christian leader can profitably grow a business with purpose. From the very beginning, Tom was committed to focusing on social values and the environment to gain customer satisfaction and manage the bottom line. He published another book in 1999, *Managing Upside Down*,[11] which further demonstrates the impact of leadership in shaping a values-driving company that has a comparative advantage based on the shared values of stakeholders. The Tom's of Maine stewardship model is a process that guides the sourcing of all of their products through natural, sustainable, and responsible practices.[12] Their standards for responsible business practices continue to engage multiple stakeholders with a supply-chain view to:

- Delivering value to consumers
- Sufficient research conducted to show safety and efficacy
- Purposeful in system of ingredients, with complete transparency about the purpose and source of the ingredient
- Sourced from suppliers that respect human and labor rights
- Honesty in all claims made for ingredients, packaging and products
- Conform to the requirements of regulatory authorities and other professional organizations with which we partner[13]

11. T. Chappell, *Managing Upside Down* (New York: William Marrow, 1999).

12. Tom's of Maine, "Our Stewardship Model," https://www.tomsofmaine.com/our-promise/stewardship-model.

13. Tom's of Maine, "Our Stewardship Model."

Wisdom-Based Strategic Orientations
Quality Orientation - Tom's of Maine offered high quality, all-natural products.
Sustainability Orientation - People) Tom's of Maine focused on treating employees and customers well to benefit the community, embracing a full stakeholder perspective. Profit) Tom's of Maine mission is to be profitable AND succesful while acting socially and enviornmentally responsibly. Planet) Tom's of Maine made it a mission to connect their audience with nature.
Stakeholder Orientation - Tom's of Maine actively pursued relationships with co-workers/employess, suppliers, owners, enviornment, community, government, and customers to build value and give back.
Supply Chain Orientation - Tom's of Maine had a be clear, pay promptly perspective with suppliers and a customer oreintation around innovation and quality.
Long-Term Orientation - Tom's of Maine committed to purusing the common good through "common good capitalism" and creating an organization of co-creation to benefit society and solve common problems.

TABLE 12.1: Tom's of Maine Wisdom-Based
Strategic Orientations

In terms of social impact, Tom's of Maine is seen as one of the leaders in establishing a mission-driven business. Tom Chappell provided evidence that business could be transformational. Instead of discovering a call to traditional ministry in the church as a theology student at Harvard Divinity School, he found a call to ministry within his business. He didn't just engage social and environmental change, he sought to create a better world by exchanging faith, experiences, and hope.

Scaling Value and Purpose

The biggest challenge for nonprofits and the NGO model of helping people is scalability. In his 2013 TED Talk on the case for letting business solve social problems, Michael Porter stated,

> There's simply not enough money to deal with any of these problems at scale using the current model [nonprofit/government model]. There's not enough tax revenue, there's not enough philanthropic donations to deal with these problems the way we're dealing with them now.[14]

---

14. Porter, "The Case for Letting Business Solve Social Problems."

Aside from World Vision, few organizations have achieved scalability as nonprofits, and many social problems persist. This may be due to the fact that nonprofits are dependent on the profitability of other organizations for donations and gifts, whereas for-profit organizations like Tom's of Maine create value for the end-customer by providing a quality product that drives profitable revenue growth, enabling them to give directly back to the community. Rather than driving consumerism (increased consumption and materialism) in consumers, Tom's of Maine strives to drive quality of life. This concept of creating products and services that increase the well-being of the end-customer directly has begun to capture the imaginations of academic researchers. Over the years, many of my friends have moved into this field, looking for further evidence of the good organizations can achieve.

The transformative consumer research movement has challenged consumer researchers to focus on empirical studies[15] that demonstrate the potential for businesses to enhance the well-being of all stakeholders, including consumers, employees, communities, and social ecosystems.[16] This movement occurred in direct response to the 1980s–1990s era of faith in capitalism. Corporations and people became engrossed with profit and the pleasures of consumption as opposed to quality of life. However, as large and highly profitable corporations like Enron and Tyco were destroyed by rogue executives, evidence has continued to emerge around the downsides of unfettered capitalism, such as the real estate industry collapse in 2008 and the Wells Fargo payout to settle criminal charges for falsifying customer accounts from 2002 to 2016.[17] This paradox between the potential good of capitalism and the potential opportunism in capitalism creates the discomfort between the worlds I live in every day. In the religious world, business is sometimes seen as a lesser calling, less holy than traditional full-time church ministry. In the liberal academic contexts, capitalism is sometimes seen as utilitarian profit maximization that robs the world of the true quality of life. The potential good of profit, wealth, and resources is lost in the debate about the potential harm of opportunism, self-interest, and greed.

---

15. Empirical research is research based on observation or experience rather than purely theoretical.

16. M. Rosenbaum, C. Corus, A. Ostrom, L. Anderson, R. Fisk, A. Gallan, M. Giraldo, M. Mende, M. Mulder, S. Rayburn, K. Shirahada, and J. Williams, "Conceptualisation and Aspirations of Transformative Service Research," *Journal of Research for Consumers* 19 (2011): 1–6; D. G. Mick, "Meaning and Mattering through Transformative Consumer Research," *Advances in Consumer Research*, http://www7511.ssldomain.com/acrwebsite/assets/PDFs/2005%20ACR%20Presidential%20 Address%20on%20TCR.pdf.

17. Emily Flitter, "The Price of Wells Fargo's Fake Accounts Scandal Grows by $3 Billion," *New York Times*, February 21, 2020, https://www.nytimes.com/2020/02/21/business/wells-fargo-settlement.html.

The debates have intensified about capitalism versus materialism, religion, consumption, immigration, discrimination, economic growth, and environmental sustainability. This is a worldly approach to the debate. The root problem is not capitalism; the problem is a broken world full of people in need of redemption and restoration. In this broken world, we have the opportunities to be entrusted with resources we can choose to put toward our self-interests or the well-being of others. Well-being is defined by Mick et al. as the "state of flourishing that involves health, happiness, and prosperity" across the dimensions of physical, emotional, spiritual, economic, environmental, and political.[18] The transformative consumer research movement has extended to explore the transformative potential for services industries. My colleagues and I have extended this further as we have begun to explore transformation in supply chain ecosystems.

Traditional research approaches adopt a neoclassical view of business outcomes and focus on measures such as profit maximization and customer satisfaction. However, transformative consumer, services, and supply chain ecosystem research focus on the role that business can play in affecting individual and collective well-being.[19] Aligned with the UN Development goals, well-being outcomes have included research topics around poverty alleviation, sustainability, health, food, service research, and many other topics. Transformative consumer research (TCR) has four envisionments (i.e., prophetic pillars):

1. *Practical Wisdom*

    Accumulation of knowledge does not drive change; practical wisdom is required to consider the well-being of others and the survival of the planet. Knowledge advancements have contributed weapons of mass destruction and marketing strategies that take advantage of human biases. Wisdom is necessary to utilize knowledge in a value-adding, life-giving manner, as opposed to an opportunistic manner.

2. *Alternative Communication Strategies*

    In the past, academic researchers have mainly communicated among themselves without translating findings to industry and practice. Thus

---

18. Mick et al., eds., *Transformative Consumer Research for Personal and Collective Well-Being*, 6.

19. Rosenbaum et al., "Conceptualisation and Aspirations of Transformative Service Research"; Mollenkopf, Ozanne, and Stolze, "A Transformative Supply Chain Response to COVID-19," *Journal of Services Management* (2020), https://doi.org/10.1108/JOSM-05-2020-0143.

practice has been broadly disconnected from the data and evidence supporting doing well by doing good, a purpose beyond profit, and the potential for transformation of well-being.

3. *Social-Change Agents*

Business is only one venue or sphere through which change can be driven. Well-being requires voices from other fields, such as religion, education, healthcare, and the natural sciences.

4. *Theoretical Contributions*

New paradigms and frameworks need to be introduced for us to move beyond neoclassical and our cultural norms of thinking to think more broadly and longer-term about our impact in the future.

The secular academy is calling for science to be inspired by practical wisdom. Aristotle's notion of *phronesis*, practical wisdom, has become a critical driver of business solutions that are well reasoned and capable of action regarding the well-being of humanity. The Academy for Consumer Research has called for practical wisdom to be a bedrock of transformative consumer research.[20]

This book addresses all four of these tenets at the intersection of business practices and Scripture as it explores the business strategies that bring about meaningful impact. First and foremost, wisdom is the foundation of transformation in the public square. In the Wisdom Literature in Scripture, Wisdom is in the streets calling out to the foolish. She implores the foolish consumer to be wiser, she gathers the fools to her table, and the teaching of kindness and wisdom is on her lips. Without wisdom, the impact of advances in knowledge is not considered. The foolish act out of their own interest, but the wise act out of a fear of the Lord and love for neighbor.

We can all foster and develop practical wisdom, but our goal should ultimately be divine wisdom. Fortunately, if we need wisdom, we can ask God and he freely gives it to us so that we can grow in our knowledge of him.

If you need wisdom, ask our generous God, and he will give it to you. He will not rebuke you for asking.[21]

---

20. D. Mick, Simone Pettigrew, C. Pechmann, and J. Ozanne, "Origins, Qualities, and Envisionments of Transformative Consumer Research," in *Transformative Consumer Research for Personal and Collective Well-Being* (New York: Routledge, 2011), 16.

21. James 1:5 NLT.

As we grow in spiritual wisdom and our knowledge of God, this book attempts to demonstrate that we also adopt a new paradigm of thinking (theory) and a new way of communicating that knowledge to our neighbors (communication strategies). The philosophies and ideologies we adopt will shape the culture that we bring to our homes, to our workplaces, to the companies we may lead, to the communities we impact, and ultimately to the nations. Finally, we all become change agents as we realize our own opportunity to be wise and discerning in whatever work we have in front of us. As Christians, we are called to the common good, to take into account the needs of others and the welfare of the entire human family.

Attention to the common good and well-being requires social innovation. Innovation is the result of new knowledge as it pertains to the invention and implementation of new products, practices, or techniques that further organizational goals. Social innovation is driven by wisdom. Social innovation has been defined by the Stanford School of Business as "any novel and useful solution to a social need or problem, that is better than existing approaches (more effective, efficient, sustainable or just) and for which the value created benefits society as a whole rather than private individuals."[22] There is increasing recognition in social innovation and transformation literature that wisdom is the critical motivation for ethical solutions.

A strategic wisdom orientation of a firm that prioritizes God and others should drive social innovations and transformative outcomes that benefit society and humanity at large. Defined as the set of beliefs that prioritizes a love for God (faith) and others as the end goal, this love-centered philosophy will direct organization strategies toward:

- understanding the needs of **stakeholders**,
- viewing time holistically in the **long-term**, valuing the past and the future,
- co-creating **quality** products,
- recognizing and strategically managing the various flows of products through the **supply chain**,
- and finally, balancing **sustainability** of economic health, social equity, and environmental resilience.

---

22. James A. Phills, Kriss Deiglmeier, and Dale T. Miller, "Rediscovering Social Innovation," *Stanford Social Innovation Review* 6, no. 4 (2008): 34–43.

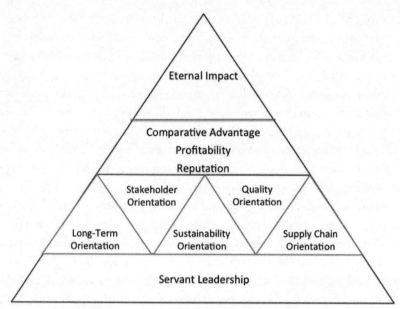

FIGURE 12.1: Proverbs 31:10–31 Means-End Hierarchy

Wisdom is the penultimate resource that motivates the human ability to achieve good ends. Wise leaders understand that the ultimate goal of reflecting Christ in this world is to see redemption and restoration of the whole earth. In John 3:16, it doesn't just say that God loved all of humanity. It says, "For God so loved the *world* that He gave His only Son, that whoever believes in Him should not perish but have eternal life" (NIV). The Greek word *kosmos* means the world, the earth, the whole ecosystem, the whole universe.

Secular schools of thought see wisdom as a critical driver of ethical business that doesn't make profitability the end goal. A kingdom mindset similarly doesn't make profitability the end goal. The transformative research and social innovation literatures all look at the well-being of humanity and the natural environment as the end goal. Meanwhile, the marketplace seems to continue to care most about profitability and competitive advantage. Without effective communication, profitability and competitive advantage will continue to be end goals for many. This is an opportunity for moral communities to demonstrate that the end goals for many are the resources to achieve the highest goal of eternal, kingdom impact. Profit is an important outcome of a firm's orientations and leadership, but the end goal of wisdom is greater than profitability. Profitability is a means through which companies exist, but the end goal of wisdom is to honor God and people, to impact the world for the kingdom of heaven.

The Role of Wisdom in Advancing the Kingdom

Businesses provide many products that meet the needs of the end consumer. In Proverbs, Wisdom also meets her guests' most basic needs as she lays a table with fine meats and wine. She invites all who want to leave their simple ways to join her at her table, to live, to walk in the way of insight. It is easy to think business is just about exchanging products and services with a consumer. However, business, like Wisdom's table, provides a place where people gather to have their needs met and to potentially find something even more transformative.

Romans 14:17 states that the kingdom of God is not a matter of eating and drinking, even though Jesus transformed water into wine, fed the 5,000, and hosted the Last Supper. The kingdom comes when we walk in righteousness, peace, and joy in the Holy Spirit. Wisdom demonstrates this for us in the marketplace. If we define righteousness as a morally right person or in right relationship with God, then Wisdom demonstrates how to walk in right relationship with God through a foundation of awe. Fear of God—the awe of God—is her most praiseworthy characteristic in verse 30 of Proverbs 31:10–31. We see she walks in peace as she has no fear for her household when it snows in verse 21, and we see her joy as she laughs at the days to come in verse 25.

N. T. Wright indicates the following three things about the kingdom of God:

1. The kingdom was inaugurated by Jesus in his life and on the cross.
2. The kingdom is radically redefined in relation to Jesus's entire agenda of suffering.
3. The kingdom Jesus inaugurated is emphatically *for* this world.[23]

A long-term orientation leads to kingdom impact if the goal is to love God and others. The longer-term vantage point in setting goals and objectives for the firm will most certainly lead to a positive kingdom impact on stakeholders and achieve kingdom purposes. The disciples truly believed that the kingdom of God would be fully inaugurated upon Jesus's resurrection from the cross. When they questioned the timing of the fulfillment of the kingdom in Acts, Jesus responded:

"It's not your business to know about times and dates," he replied. "The father has placed all that under his own direct authority. What will happen, though, is that you will receive power when the holy spirit comes upon you. Then *you will be my witnesses* in Jerusalem, in all Judea and Samaria, and to the very ends of the earth." (Acts 1:7–8 NTE, emphasis mine)

23. Wright, *How God Became King.*

The awe of God is the beginning of wisdom. It is through wisdom that we come to know and love God more deeply. Jesus teaches the disciples that the greatest commandments are to love God and to love others. He disciples his followers to live like him and to take up their crosses daily, to love others as he has loved them. Upon his ascension, he commissions his disciples to,

> Go therefore and make disciples of all nations, baptizing them in the name of the Father and of the Son and of the Holy Spirit, and *teaching them to obey everything that I have commanded you.* And remember I am with you always, to the end of the age. (Matt. 28:19–20)

Perhaps I am biased as an academic and a teacher, but when I read this passage I think, *Aha! We need to teach disciples of all nations to love God and to love others as he loved us! We need to teach business students to lay their lives down like Jesus laid his life down for us, offering all that we have, all our resources.* When we embrace the nature of Christ, we embrace the power and wisdom of God:

> But to those called by God to salvation, both Jews and Gentiles, Christ is the power of God and the wisdom of God. (1 Cor. 1:24 NLT)

Scripture tells us the following things about wisdom:[24]

- Wisdom is more precious than jewels; nothing you desire can compare with her.
- Wisdom will protect you. Love her, and she will guard you.
- If you prize wisdom, she will make you great. Embrace her, and she will honor you.
- Wisdom will multiply your days and add years to your life. If you become wise, you will be the one to benefit. If you scorn wisdom, you will be the one to suffer.
- To acquire wisdom is to love yourself; people who cherish understanding will prosper.
- If you need wisdom, ask our generous God, and he will give it to you. He will not rebuke you for asking.
- God, the glorious Father of our Lord Jesus Christ, gives spiritual wisdom and insight so that you might grow in your knowledge of God.

---

24. Proverbs 3:15; 4:6, 8; 9:11–12; 19:8; James 1:5; Ephesians 1:16–17.

Wisdom clearly is a valuable resource to all who attain her. Honor, greatness, and life come from wisdom.

The Impact of the Kingdom of Heaven on the Marketplace

In each chapter of this book, I have attempted to demonstrate that Scripture has a *lot* to say about business and the marketplace. I have provided evidence that many of the business principles in the Wisdom Literature are best practices in many industries today and are based on years of academic research. Some of that research has been communicated in easier-to-digest articles like those in the *Harvard Business Review* and *Sloan Management*, but many of them remain dense mathematical manuscripts that provide evidence across thousands of companies around the world profitably pursuing wise strategies that provide benefits to the common good.

Business is just one means of using our resources to love God and serve others. Many wise people fear and love God and are wise with the resources he has entrusted to them. If entrusted with leadership in an organization, business research has demonstrated that servant leadership is one method of leadership that drives employee productivity, operational efficiency, and relational and informational advantages. Servant leadership sets the relational culture that should inspire the awareness of others.

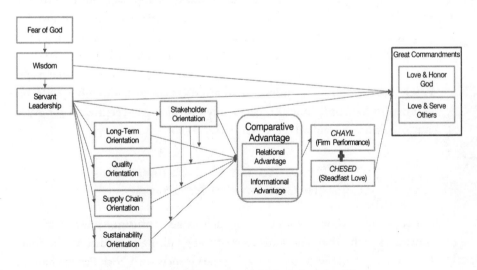

FIGURE 12.2: Wisdom-Based Model of the Firm

In the past, I thought the role of business was to fund the kingdom or that business was a side business, like Paul's tent making, to support the livelihood of someone while they did the real work of the church. However, in recent years I have become convinced that God calls some of us to business to extend his kingdom by bringing strategies to the table that can enable us to achieve purpose beyond profitability. We can create wealth with the goal of sharing with the poor and needy. We can build relationships and bring joy and life to people by leading them well in our organizations, whether they are employees, customers, or suppliers. We have an audience with whom we can share information and teaching with both kindness and wisdom.

As wise leaders who build resources and opportunities for others, we have a unique reputation of *chayil* and *chesed* that reflects wealth, strength, nobility, and vigilance, as well as mercy, kindness, and steadfast love. As servants and stewards, we can be witnesses of Jesus's servanthood and stewards of his creation as our work becomes worship and our good deeds reflect his creative work. We have an amazing opportunity to work as God worked as we steward creation and to serve as Jesus served when he made all things news. When Jesus instructed his disciples on leadership, he taught them in Matthew 23:11, saying, "The greatest among you will be your servant."

I currently run the Wheaton Center for Faith & Innovation. Over the first year and a half of founding and launching an academic research center with the mission of integrating theology and business research to pursue innovative solutions for business, I have encountered over a hundred Christian leaders and CEOs who are seeking God to have a meaningful impact in the marketplace. COVID-19 has driven home the need to not only approach business from a place of prayer, but to also approach every day with a God-inspired love for people. Kingdom impact may start with something simple, like praying for a co-worker, but it can escalate with a global sustainable supply chain strategy to steward customer, suppliers, and the environment well. One new friend and CEO who exemplifies a wisdom-based mindset has not only embraced foster children in his family but also personally provided gift-certificates for every employee who was laid off due to COVID-19 shutdowns.

The Culture of the Kingdom of God as the End Goal

For the longest time, I found the Gospels to be confusing. They seemed to contradict each other, and Jesus seemed to be talking in riddles all the time. However, the semester I spent studying the Gospels with Nick Perrin changed my view of them altogether. He presented the narratives of Jesus's life as the biographies captured by his closest friends and his followers, chronicling the impact his messages had on them. Rather than seeing them as a riddle, I became swept away in Jesus's three years of ministry as if alongside his disciples.

Jesus called ordinary people. They weren't priests in the tribe of Levi or future kings in the tribe of Judah. They were ordinary fishermen. Most of them were uneducated; they weren't Pharisees, trained in the Old Testament law. They weren't the privileged elite. There is no evidence that any of them were related to the Sadducees. They ran businesses. They caught fish and presumably sold the fish at the local market.

With this new perspective, I found in Jesus's words and teaching a sense of friendship and familiarity I hadn't recognized there before. As I read his words about servanthood, love, and suffering, I began to see another way of engaging in the world as a Christian. Christ came to earth to defeat the brokenness of the world on the cross and to become king of the kingdom of heaven. The disciples expected him to take the throne of David in Jerusalem. When Jesus rode into the city on the donkey straight into the temple, it would have been like the parade of a king returning from battle. However, rather than making a sacrifice to God in thanks for the battle he had won as David did, Jesus became the sacrifice so that the ultimate battle against sin and death could be won once and for all.

When we talk about the kingdom that Jesus taught about and established, N. T. Wright points out that Christians have multiple reactions to the kingdom Jesus established but we don't yet fully live in:[25]

Reaction 1: This Doesn't Matter		Reaction 2: The Church Must Put Its Own House in Order
We're going to heaven and we'll leave this old world behind.		The church should be a beacon of light without engaging in the world.
Kingdom NOW		
Reaction 3: Adopt Right-Wing Conservativism		Reaction 4: Adopt Left-Wing Conservativism
The government should support free trade, abolish abortion, the church will take care of the poor and needy, not government—adopts Fox News worldview.		Concern for the poor and the needy is the higher moral ground, and the church should set the moral standard.

TABLE 12.1: Perceptions of the Kingdom
of Heaven by N. T. Wright[26]

25. Wright, *How God Became King*, 246.
26. Wright, *How God Became King*, 246.

None of these reactions actually capture the mission of the Gospels and Acts to establish the kingdom of heaven here and now. They all capture our interpretation of the kingdom of heaven from our Western context and perspective (especially when it comes to political parties). Jesus came because God loved this whole *kosmos*, his whole creation. We know he came so that we would not perish, but gain eternal life. However, we sometimes fall into the trap of thinking that Jesus came to save us from this world and not *for* this world. Jesus came to bring us eternal life that starts *now*, not after we die and go to heaven.

Instead of a king on the throne of Israel, Jesus became the suffering servant that Isaiah prophesied would come to redeem God's people.[27] Jesus's death and resurrection were *the* events that dealt the death blow to sin and sickness and dark forces to establish God's new kingdom of powerful, creative, and restorative love, arriving on earth as in heaven.[28] If we see the kingdom of God as already established but not fully realized until Jesus's return, then we can also realize that we were not only saved *from* sin and death, but we were also saved *for* life. This reality is the revelation of righteousness (Christ has made us righteous), peace (he did it for us, so we don't need to walk in fear) and joy (pleasure and happiness in the Holy Spirit) so that we can attain what Aristotle may never have attained: the good life. When we use our resources to love and serve others, we establish for ourselves and our community selflessness that allows peace and joy to reign. In this way, business can become a tool through which we can have kingdom impact by loving and serving every person God brings across our paths just as Christ loved and served us!

As I finished writing this book, I had the opportunity to spend a little time with Bill Pollard, former CEO of ServiceMaster. During Pollard's years at Wheaton College, Ken Hansen, Ken Wessner (former CEOs of ServiceMaster), and Billy Graham were all engaged at the college in various capacities. All three men served as sources of inspiration and discipleship to Pollard as he moved from his position at Wheaton to work at ServiceMaster, eventually leading the company to over $6 billion in revenue and 100,000 employees. As he reflected on his impact at ServiceMaster, he acknowledged the tension between profit and people, saying,

> The biggest impact I had in business is where it took me in engagement with others in this world that God so loves. At a public company, you engage

---

27. Isaiah 40–55.
28. Wright, *How God Became King*, 246.

with all kinds of different people—shareholders, stockbrokers, customers. You engage a lot of different customers when your revenue is over $6 billion dollars. It provided opportunities for me to share what I believed, to answer the questions "Where did you get the name ServiceMaster?" It came from a group of men who had a commitment to Jesus, and I do too. Service to the master, who is God.

We sought to reflect the master's way of doing things, and we wanted people to know that there is a master, there is a God, and there is a story. This reached people across countries. The marketplace provided the opportunity to engage the breadth of the world that God so loved.[29]

Regardless of the sphere we are called to, whether it is in the marketplace, government, or full-time work in the church, as Christians we want to steward whatever people and responsibilities we are entrusted with in excellence so we have the opportunity to answer questions from others regarding our purpose and motivation in life. While Pollard achieved worldly success in growing a company with 20 percent growth year after year, he noted that the biggest challenge was asking for forgiveness when he lost his sensitivity to the people around him due to quarterly pressures. The kingdom of heaven comes today, and now we walk in righteousness (fulfilling all the law), peace (without anxiety for tomorrow), and joy (taking pleasure and delight in God as he delights in us). We attain this righteousness by walking in wisdom, which begins with the awe of God that inspires our love for him and for others.

Reflection Questions

1. How does your attitude toward money impact your ability to love others well?
2. What are three ways you can bring the kingdom of heaven in your business practically? How do righteousness, peace, and joy come into play in your work?
3. What is the importance of wisdom for achieving the goal of good and faithful servant?

---

29. C. William Pollard, personal conversation with the author, used by permission.

EXEGETICAL
SOURCES

This book does not attempt to do primary exegesis. Rather, it draws from biblical scholars' work to provide a summary of these exegetical works.

Apple, Raymond. "The Two Wise Women of Proverbs 31," *Jewish Bible Quarterly* 39, no. 3 (2011): 175–80.

Block, Daniel. *Ruth*, Exegetical Commentary on the Old Testament 8. Grand Rapids: Zondervan, 2015.

Brown, Jeannine K. *Scripture as Communication: Introducing Biblical Hermeneutics*. Grand Rapids: Baker Academic, 2007.

Classen, L. Juliana, "The Woman of Substance and Human Flourishing: Proverbs 31:10–31 and Martha Nussbaum's Capabilities Approach," *Journal of Feminist Studies in Religion* 32, no. 1 (2016): 5–19.

Crenshaw, James L. *Old Testament Wisdom: An Introduction*. 3rd ed. Louisville: John Knox, 2010.

Goh, Samuel T. S. "Ruth as Superior Woman of חיל? A Comparison between Ruth and the 'Capable' Woman in Proverbs 31:10–31," *Journal for the Study of the Old Testament* 38, no. 4 (2014): 487–500.

Hill, Andrew, and John J. Walton, "Hebrew Poetic and Wisdom Literature." *A Survey of the Old Testament*, 375–99. Grand Rapids: Zondervan, 2009.

Longman, Tremper. *Proverbs*. In *Baker Commentary on the Old Testament Wisdom and Psalms*, ed. Tremper Longman III. Grand Rapids: Baker Academic, 2006.

Master, Daniel. "Economy and Exchange in the Iron Age Kingdoms of the Southern Levant," *American Schools of Oriental Research BASOR* 372 (2014): 81–97.

Meyers, Carol. "The Family in Early Israel." In *Families in Ancient Israel*. Edited by Leo G. Perdue. Louisville: Westminster John Knox, 1997: 1–47.

Nam, Roger S. *Portrayals of Economic Exchange in the Book of Kings*. Boston: Brill Academic, 2012.

Nussbaum, Martha C. *Upheavals of Thought: The Intelligence of Emotions*. Cambridge: Cambridge University Press, 2001.

Richter, Sandra. "The Questions of Provenance and the Economics of Deuteronomy." *Journal for the Study of the Old Testament* (2017): 1–54.

———. "Environmental Law in Deuteronomy: One Lens on a Biblical Theology of Creation Care." *Bulletin for Biblical Research* 20, no. 3 (2010): 355–76.

Schultz, Richard L. "Proverbs." In *The Baker Illustrated Bible Commentary*, edited by Gary M. Burge and Andrew E. Hill. Grand Rapids: Barker, 2016.

Simpson, William Kelly, ed. "Instructions, Lamentations, Dialogues." In *The Literature of Ancient Egypt: An Anthology of Stories, Instructions, Stelae, Autobiographies, and Poetry*. New Haven, CT: Yale University Press, 2003: 223–43.

Snell, Daniel C. *Twice Told Proverbs and the Composition of the Book of Proverbs*. Winona Lake, IN: Eisenbaums, 1993.

Wolters, A. "Proverbs xxxi 10–31 as Heroic Hymn: A Form Critical Analysis." *Vetus Testamentum* 38 (1988): 446–57.

Yoder, Christine Roy. "The Woman of Substance (*ēšet ḥayil*): A Socioeconomic Reading of Proverbs 31:10–31." *Journal of Biblical Literature* 122, no. 3 (2003): 426–532.

Yoder, Christine Roy. *Wisdom as a Woman of Substance*. Berlin: Walter De Gruyter, 2001.

BIBLIOGRAPHY

Abrami, Regina M., William C. Kirby, F. Warren McFarlan, and Tracy Yuen Manty. "Inner Mongolia Yili Group: China's Pioneering Dairy Brand." *Harvard Business School Case* 308–052, January 2008. Revised December 2011.

Ackoff, R. L. *Ackoff's Best*. New York: Wiley, 1999.

Adams, R., S. Jeanrenaud, J. Bessant, P. Overy, and D. Denyer. "Innovating for Sustainability: A Systematic Review of Body of Knowledge." Network for Sustainability. nbs.net/knowledge.

Adbi, Arzi, Ajay Bhaskarabhatla, and Chirantan Chatterjee. "Stakeholder Orientation and Market Impact: Evidence from India." *Journal of Business Ethics* 161, no. 2 (2020): 479–96.

Ager, D. L., and M. A. Roberto. "Trader Joe's." *Harvard Business School Case* 714–419, September 2013. Revised April 2014.

Alderson, Wroe. "Factors Governing the Development of Marketing Channels." *Marketing Channels for Manufactured Products*. Edited by Richard M. Clewett. Homewood, IL: Irwin, 1954. 5–34.

Ansoff, H. I. "Managing Strategic Surprise by Response to Weak Signals." *California Management Review* 18, no. 2 (1975): 21–37.

Aristotle. *Nicomachean Ethics: On Practical Wisdom*, Book VI.5, 1140a-b.

The Arthur W. Page Center/Public Relationship Ethics, Penn State University, "Conscious Capitalism: A Definition," https://pagecentertraining.psu.edu /public-relations-ethics/corporate-social-responsibility/lesson-2-introduction -to-conscious-capitalism/conscious-capitalism-a-definition/.

Aßländer, Michael S., Julia Roloff, and Dilek Zamantili Nayir. "Suppliers as Stewards? Managing Social Standards in First-and Second-Tier Suppliers." *Journal of Business Ethics* 139, no. 4 (2016): 661–83.

Austin, James E., and Herman B. "Dutch" Leonard. "Can the Virtuous Mouse and the Wealthy Elephant Live Happily Ever After?" *California Management Review* 51, no. 1 (2008): 77–102.

Avolio, B. J., and W. L. Gardner. "Authentic Leadership Development: Getting to the Root of Positive Forms of Leadership." *The Leadership Quarterly* 16, no. 3 (2005): 315–38.

Bachmann, Claudius, André Habisch, and Claus Dierksmeier. "Practical Wisdom: Management's No Longer Forgotten Virtue." *Journal of Business Ethics* 153, no. 1 (2018): 147–65.

Barasch, Doug S. "God and Toothpaste." *The New York Times Magazine*, December 22, 1996. https://www.nytimes.com/1996/12/22/magazine/god -and-toothpaste.html.

Barlett, Christopher. "Unilever's Lifebuoy in India: Implementing the Sustainability Plan." *Harvard Business School Case Study*, March 8, 2017. https://store.hbr.org/case-studies/.

Barth, Karl, *Church Dogmatics*. Vol. III.1. Edited by G. W. Bromiley and T. F. Torrance. Edinburgh: T&T Clark, 1956–77.

Barton, Dominic, James Manyika, Timothy Koller, Robert Palter, Jonathan Godsall, Joshua Zoffer. "Measuring the Economic Impact of Short-Termism: Discussion Paper." McKinsey Global Institute. 2017. www.mckinsey.com /mgi. https://www.mckinsey.com/~/media/McKinsey/Featured%20Insights /Long%20term%20Capitalism/Where%20companies%20with%20a%20 long%20term%20view%20outperform%20their%20peers/MGI-Measuring -the-economic-impact-of-short-termism.pdf.

Baumhart, R., *An Honest Profit: What Businessmen Say about Ethics in Business*. New York: Holt, Rinehart and Winston, 1968.

Beach, Alison I. *Women as Scribes: Book Production and Monastic Reform in Twelfth Century Bavaria*. Cambridge: Cambridge University Press, 2004.

Bearden, William O., R. Bruce Money, and Jennifer L. Nevins. "A Measure of Long-Term Orientation: Development and Validation." *Journal of the Academy of Marketing* Science 34, no. 3 (2006): 456–67.

Benedict. *The Rule of Our Most Holy Father St. Benedict, Patriarch of Monks*. From the old English edition of 1638. London: R. Washbourne, 1875.

Berman, Shawn L., Andrew C. Wicks, Suresh Kotha, and Thomas M. Jones. "Does Stakeholder Orientation Matter? The Relationship between Stakeholder Management Models and Firm Financial Performance." *Academy of Management Journal* 42, no. 5 (1999): 488–506.

Block, Daniel I. *Deuteronomy*. NIV Application Commentary. Grand Rapids: Zondervan, 2012.

———. *Ruth: A Discourse Analysis of the Hebrew Bible*. Zondervan Exegetical Commentary on the Old Testament. Edited by Daniel I. Block. Grand Rapids: Zondervan Academic, 2015.

Boström, Magnus, Anna Maria Jönsson, Stewart Lockie, Arthur P. J. Mol, and Peter Oosterveer. "Sustainable and Responsible Supply Chain Governance: Challenges and Opportunities." *Journal of Cleaner Production* 107 (2015): 1–7.

Bowersox, Donald J. "Physical Distribution Development, Current Status, and Potential." *Journal of Marketing* 33, no. 1 (1969): 63–70.

Bretsen, Stephen N. "The Creation, the Kingdom of God, and a Theory of the Faithful Corporation." *Christian Scholars Review* 38, no. 1 (2008): 153.

Brews, P., and D. Purohit. "Strategic Planning in Unstable Environments." *Long Range Planning* 40, no. 1 (2007): 64–83.

Brickson, Shelley L. "Organizational Identity Orientation: Genesis of the Role of the Firm and Distinct Forms of Social Value." *Academy of Management Review* 3, no. 3 (2007): 864–88.

Brueggemann, Walter. *Praying the Psalms: Engaging Scripture and the Life of the Spirit.* Eugene, OR: Wipf & Stock, 2007.

Brulhart, Franck, Sandrine Gherra, and Bertrand V. Quelin. "Do Stakeholder Orientation and Environmental Proactivity Impact Firm Profitability?" *Journal of Business Ethics* 158, no. 1 (2019): 25–46.

Cann, Oliver. "Davos 2020: World Economic Forum Announces the Theme." October 17, 2019. https://www.weforum.org/agenda/2019/10/davos-2020 -wef-world-economic-forum-theme/.

Carr, David. "The Cardinal Virtues and Plato's Moral Psychology." *The Philosophical Quarterly* 38, no. 151 (1988): 186–200.

Carter, Craig R., and Dale S. Rogers. "A Framework of Sustainable Supply Chain Management: Moving toward New Theory." *International Journal of Physical Distribution & Logistics Management* (2008).

Castro, Gregorio Martin de, Jose Emilio Navas Lopez, and Pedro Lopez Saez. "Business and Social Reputation: Exploring the Concept and Main Dimensions of Corporate Reputation." *Journal of Business Ethics* 63 (2006): 361–70. doi: 10.1007/s10551-005-3244-z.

Chappell, T. *Managing Upside Down.* New York: William Marrow and Company, 1999.

———. *The Soul of a Business: Managing for Profit and the Consumer Good.* New York: Bantam, 1994.

Cheng, Colin C. J. "Sustainability Orientation, Green Supplier Involvement, and Green Innovation Performance: Evidence from Diversifying Green Entrants." *Journal of Business Ethics* 161, no. 2 (2020): 393–414.

Christopher, Martin. *Logistics and Supply Chain Management.* 5th ed. London: Pearson, 2011.

Ciment, Shoshy. "We Shopped at Both Whole Foods and Trader Joe's, and the Amazon-Owned Chain Was Disappointing in Comparison." *Business Insider.* August 2019. https://www.businessinsider.com/whole-foods-or-trader -joes-best-healthy-grocery-store-2019–8.

Closs, David J., Cheri Speier, and Nathan Meacham. "Sustainability to Support End-To-End Value Chains: The Role of Supply Chain Management." *Journal of the Academy of Marketing Science* 39, no. 1 (2011): 101–16.

Colicchia, Claudia, Gino Marchet, Marco Melacini, and Sara Perotti. "Building Environmental Sustainability: Empirical Evidence from Logistics Service Providers." *Journal of Cleaner Production* 59 (2013): 197–209.

Confucius. *The Analects: Sayings of Confucius.* Translated by D. C. Lau. New York: Penguin Classics, 1998.

Conscious Capitalism. "Melissa Reiff, The Container Store: Hero of Conscious Capitalism." n.d. https://www.consciouscapitalism.org/heroes/melissa-reiff.

Crenshaw, James L. *Old Testament Wisdom: An Introduction.* Louisville: Westminster John Knox, 2010.

Crittenden, V., William F. Crittenden, Linda K. Ferrell, O. C. Ferrell, and Christopher C. Pinney. "Market-Oriented Sustainability: A Conceptual Framework and Propositions." *Journal of the Academy of Marketing Science* 39, no. 1 (2011): 71–85.

Davis, Donna F., and Susan L. Golicic. "Gaining Comparative Advantage in Supply Chain Relationships: The Mediating Role of Market-Oriented IT Competence." *Journal of the Academy of Marketing Science* 38, no. 1 (2010): 56–70.

Davis, J. J. "Ethics and Environmental Marketing." *Journal of Business Ethics* 11, no. 2 (1992): 81–87.

Defee, Cliff C., Theodore P. Stank, Terry L. Esper, and John T. Mentzer. "The Role of Followers in Supply Chains." *Journal of Business Logistics* 30, no. 2 (2009): 65–84.

Dell, Katharine J., and Paul M. Joyce, eds. *Biblical Interpretation and Method: Essays in Honour of John Barton.* Oxford: Oxford University Press, 2013.

Diddams, Margaret, and Denise Daniels. "Good Work with Toil: A Paradigm for Redeemed Work," *Christian Scholars Review* 38, no. 1 (2008): 62.

Dooley, Louis, and Heidi Gruber O'Very. *Prison Saved My Life.* Dubuque, IA: Emmaus International, 2018.

Drucker, Peter. *Management: Tasks, Responsibilities, Practices.* New York: Harper & Row, 1974.

Drucker, P. F. *The Practice of Management.* New York: Harper, 1954.

Dyck, Bruno, Mitchell J. Neubert, and Kenman Wong. "Unchaining Weber's Iron Cage: A Look at What Managers Can Do." *Christian Scholars Review* 38, no. 1 (2008): 50.

Ehrhart, M. G. "Leadership and Procedural Justice Climate as Antecedents of Unit-Level Organizational Citizenship Behavior." *Personnel Psychology* 57, no. 1 (2004): 61–94.

Ellinger, Alexander, Hyunju Shin, William Magnus Northington, Frank G. Adams, Debra Hofman, and Kevin O'Marah. "The Influence of Supply Chain Management Competency on Customer Satisfaction and Shareholder Value." *Supply Chain Management: An International Journal* 17, no. 3 (2012), 249–62. https://doi.org/10.1108/13598541211227090.

Elkington, John. "25 Years Ago I Coined the Phrase 'Triple Bottom Line.' Here's Why It's Time to Rethink It." *Harvard Business Review* 25 (2018). https://hbr.org/2018/06/25-years-ago-i-coined-the-phrase-triple-bottom-line-heres -why-im-giving-up-on-it.

Eriksson, David, and Göran Svensson. "The Process of Responsibility, Decoupling Point, and Disengagement of Moral and Social Responsibility in Supply Chains: Empirical Findings and Prescriptive Thoughts." *Journal of Business Ethics* 134, no. 2 (2016): 281–98.

Erisman, Albert M. *The ServiceMaster Story.* Peabody, MA: Hendrickson Publishers, 2020.

Esper, Terry L., Alexander E. Ellinger, Theodore P. Stank, Daniel J. Flint, and Mark Moon. "Demand and Supply Integration: A Conceptual Framework of Value Creation through Knowledge Management." *Journal of the Academy of Marketing Science* 38, no. 1 (2010): 5–18.

Eva, Nathan, Mulyadi Robin, Sen Sendjaya, Dirk van Dierendonck, and Robert C. Liden. "Servant Leadership: A Systematic Review and Call for Future Research." *The Leadership Quarterly* 30, no. 1 (2019): 114.

Fee, Gordon, and Douglas Stuart. *How to Read the Bible for All It's Worth.* Grand Rapids: Zondervan, 2014.

Felker Jones, Beth. *Practicing Christian Doctrine: An Introduction to Thinking and Living Theologically.* Grand Rapids: Baker Academic, 2014.

Ferman, Roberto A. "The Chipotle Effect: Why America Is Obsessed with Fast Casual Food." *Washington Post,* February 2, 2015. https://www.washington post.com/news/wonk/wp/2015/the-chipotle-effect-why-america-is-obsessed -with-fast-casual-food.

Ferrell, O. C., T. L. Gonzalez-Padron, G. T. M. Hult, and I. Maignan. "From Market Orientation to Stakeholder Orientation." *Journal of Public Policy & Marketing* 29, no. 1 (2010): 93–96.

Fishman, Charles. "The Wal-Mart You Don't Know," *Fast Company*, December 1, 2003, https://www.fastcompany.com/47593/wal-mart-you-dont-know.

Flint, D. J., R. B. Woodruff, and S. F. Gardial. "Customer Value Change in Industrial Marketing Relationships." *Industrial Marketing Management* 26, no. 2 (1997): 163–75.

Flitter, Emily. "The Price of Wells Fargo's Fake Accounts Scandal Grows by $3 Billion." *New York Times* February 21, 2020. https://www.nytimes.com/2020/02/21/business/wells-fargo-settlement.html.

Fombrun, C., and M. Shanley. "What's in a Name? Reputation Building and Corporate Strategy." *Academy of Management Journal* 33 (1990): 233–58.

Fortune. "No Layoffs—Ever! The Container Store; Best Company Rank 21." January 24, 2011. https://archive.fortune.com/galleries/2011/pf/jobs/1101/gallery.no_layoffs.fortune/6.html.

Freeman, M., and D. R. Gilbert. *Corporate Strategy and the Search for Ethics*. Englewood Cliffs, NJ: Prentice Hall, 1988.

Freeman, R. E. *Strategic Management: A Stakeholder Approach*. Boston: Pitman, 1984.

Freeman, R. E., Jeffery S. Harrison, Andrew C. Wicks, L. Bidhan, Simone De Colle Parmar. *Stakeholder Theory: The State of the Art*. Cambridge: Cambridge University Press, 2010.

Friedman, Milton. *Capitalism and Freedom*. Chicago: University of Chicago Press, 1962.

Galvas, A, and J. Mish. "Resources and Capabilities of Triple Bottom Line Firms: Going Over Old or Breaking New Ground?" *Journal of Business Ethics* 127, no. 3 (2015): 623–42.

Gatignon, Hubert, and Jean-Marc Xuereb. "Strategic Orientation." *Journal of Marketing Research* (February 1997): 77–90.

Ghoshal, S. "Bad Management Theories Are Destroying Good Management Practices." *Academy of Management Learning & Education* 4 (2005): 75–91.

Giminez, C., V. Sierra, and J. Rodon. "Sustainable Operations: Their Impact on the Triple Bottom Line." *International Journal Production Economics* 140 (2012): 149–59.

Gold, Betty. "18 Trader Joe's Stores Are Closing Temporarily Due to Possible COVID-19 Contamination." *Real Simple*. April 15, 2020. https://www.realsimple.com/food-recipes/shopping-storing/food/trader-joes-covid-closings.

Golicic, Susan, Courtney Boerstler, and Lisa Ellram. "'Greening' the Transportation in Your Supply Chain." *MIT Sloan Management Review* 51, no. 2 (2010): 47.

Goudreau, Jenna, and Kip Tindell. "The Container Store Ceo Says Women Make Better Executives than Men." *Business Insider.* https://www.businessinsider. com/container-store-ceo-kip-tindell-leadership-women-success-2014-10.

Green, Gene L. *Jude & 2 Peter.* Baker Exegetical Commentary on the New Testament. Grand Rapids: Baker Academic, 2008.

Greenleaf, Robert K. *The Servant as Leader.* Westfield, IN: Greenleaf Center for Servant Leadership, 1970.

———. *Servant Leadership: A Journey into the Nature of Legitimate Power and Leadership.* New York: Paulist, 1977.

Greenleaf, Robert K., and Larry C. Spears. *Servant Leadership: A Journey Into the Nature of Legitimate Power and Greatness.* New York: Paulist, 2002.

Griggs, D., M. Stafford-Smith, O. Gaffney, J. Rockström, M. C. Öhman, P. Shyamsundar, I. Noble. "Policy: Sustainable Development Goals for People and Planet." *Nature* 495, no. 7441 (2013): 305–7. http://doi.org/10.1038/495305a.

Gullapalli, Kal. "How Chipotle became the Gold Standard of Mexican Fast-Food." *Business Insider.* January 21, 2011. http://www.businessinsider.com /chipotle-the-new-gold-standard-2011-1.

Gutman, Jonathon. "A Means-End Chain Model Based on the Customer Categorization Process." *Journal of Marketing* 46, no. 2 (1982): 60–72.

Hamel, G., C. K. Prahalad. *Competing for the Future.* Boston: Harvard Business School Press, 1994.

Handscomb, Christopher, and Shail Thaker. "Activate Agility: The Five Avenues to Success," McKinsey & Company Organization Blog. https://www. mckinsey.com/business-functions/organization/our-insights/the-organization -blog/activate-agility-get-these-five-things-right.

He, Gang, Zhenling Cui, Hao Ying, Huifang Zheng, Zhaohui Wang, and Fusuo Zhang. "Managing the Trade-Offs Among Yield Increase, Water Resources Inputs and Greenhouse Gas Emissions in Irrigated Wheat Production Systems." *Journal of Cleaner Production* 164 (2017): 567–74.

Hofstede, Geert, and Michael Harris Bond. "The Confucius Connection: From Cultural Roots to Economic Growth." *Organizational Dynamics* 16, no. 4 (1988): 5–21.

Hill, Andrew E., and John H. Walton. *A Survey of the Old Testament.* Grand Rapids: Zondervan, 2000.

Hua, Guowei, T. C. E. Cheng, and Shouyang Wang. "Managing Carbon Footprints in Inventory Management." *International Journal of Production Economics* 132, no. 2 (2011): 178–85.

Hult, G. T. M., D. J. Ketchen Jr., G. L. Adams, and J. A. Mena. "Supply Chain Orientation and Balance Scorecard Performance." *Journal of Managerial Issues* 20, no. 4 (2008): 526–44.

Hunt, Shelby, and Donna F. Davis. "Grounding Supply Chain Management in Resource-Advantage Theory: In Defense of a Resource-Based View of the Firm." *Journal of Supply Chain Management* 48, no. 2 (2012): 15–20.

Hunt, Shelby, and Robert M. Morgan. "The Comparative Advantage Theory of Competition." *Journal of Marketing* 59, no. 2 (1995): 1–15.

Hursthouse, Rosalind, and Glen Pettigrove. "Virtue Ethics." *The Stanford Encyclopedia of Philosophy*. Winter 2018. Edited by Edward N. Zalta. https://plato.stanford.edu/archives/win2018/entries/ethics-virtue/.

Isaacson, Andy. "Why the Tom's of Maine Founder Thinks He Can Create the Next Patagonia." *Inc. Magazine*. April 2017. https://www.inc.com/magazine/201704/andy-isaacson/the-very-long-road.html.

Isadore, Chris. "Whole Foods Accused of Massive Overcharging." CNN, June 25, 2015. https://money.cnn.com/2015/06/25/news/companies/whole-foods-overcharging/.

Jadhav, Akshay, Stuart Orr, and Mohsin Malik. "The Role of Supply Chain Orientation in Achieving Supply Chain Sustainability." *International Journal of Production Economics* 217 (2019): 112–25.

Jones, D. "Servant Leadership's Impact on Profit, Employee Satisfaction, and Empowerment Within the Framework of a Participative Culture of Business." *Academy for Studies in Business* 3, no. 2 (2011): 35–49.

Juran, Joseph M. and A. Blanton Godfrey. *Juran's Quality Handbook*. New York: McGraw-Hill, 1998.

Kant, Immanuel. *Groundwork of the Metaphysic of Morals*. Translated by H. J. Paton. New York: Harper and Row, 1964.

Kern, Edmund. "Counter-Reformation Sanctity: The Bollandists' Vita of Blessed Hemma of Gurk." *Journal of Ecclesiastical History* 45, no. 3 (July 1994): 412.

Klassen, Robert D., and Ann Vereecke. "Social Issues in Supply Chains: Capabilities Link Responsibility, Risk (Opportunity), and Performance." *International Journal of Production Economics* 140, no. 1 (2012): 103–15.

Kirchoff, Jon F., Wendy L. Tate, and Diane A. Mollenkopf. "The Impact of Strategic Organizational Orientations on Green Supply Chain Management and Firm Performance." *International Journal of Physical Distribution & Logistics Management* 46, no. 3 (2016): 269–92. https://doi.org/10.1108/IJPDLM-03-2015-0055.

Kuckertz, A., and M. Wagner. "The Influence of Sustainability Orientation on Entrepreneurial Intentions—Investigating the Role of Business Experience." *Journal of Business Venturing* 25, no. 5 (2010): 524–39.

Kull, Alexander J., Jeannette A. Mena, and Daniel Korschun. "A Resource-Based View of Stakeholder Marketing." *Journal of Business Research* 69, no. 12 (2016): 5553–60.

Lever, William Hesketh. "Addressed at: 'The Messel Memorial Lecture', before the Society of Chemical Industry at the Annual Conference at Liverpool University, Liverpool." July 10, 1924. http://unilever-archives.com/Record .aspx?src=CalmView.Catalog&id=GB1752.UNI%2fBD%2f2%2f1%2f1%2f19.

Levy, Max. "From Torah im Derekh Eretz to Torah U-Madda:the Legacy of Samson Raphael Hirsch." *Penn History Review*, 20, no. 1 (2013), 72–93.

Liden, Robert C., Tayla N. Bauer, and Berrin Erdogan. "The Role of Leader-Member Exchange in the Dynamic Relationship Between Employer and Employee: Implications for Employee Socialization, Leaders, and Organization." *The Employment Relationship, Examining Psychological and Contextual Perspectives.* Edited by J. A.-M. Coyle-Shapiro, L. M. Shore, S. M. Taylor, and L. E. Tetrick. Oxford: Oxford University Press: 2004, 226–50.

Liden, R. C., S. J. Wayne, J. D. Meuser, J. Hu, J. Wu, and C. Liao. "Servant Leadership: Validation of a Short Form of the SL-28." *The Leadership Quarterly* 26 (2015): 254–69.

Logsdon, Jeanne M., and Kristi Yuthas. "Corporate Social Performance, Stakeholder Orientation, and Organizational Moral Development." *Journal of Business Ethics* 16 (1997): 1213–26.

Maignan, Isabelle. "Consumers' Perceptions of Corporate Social Responsibilities: A Cross-Cultural Comparison." *Journal of Business Ethics* 30, no. 1 (2001): 57–72.

Maignan, Isabelle, Tracy L. Gonzalez-Padron, G. Thomas Hult, and O. C. Ferrell. "Stakeholder Orientation: Development and Testing of a Framework for Socially Responsible Marketing." *Journal of Strategic Marketing* 19, no. 4 (2011): 313–38.

Manwani, Harish. "Profit's Not Always the Point." TED Talk. https://www .ted.com/talks/harish_manwani_profit_s_not_always_the_point?utm _campaign=tedspread&utm_medium=referral&utm_source=tedcomshare.

Marinova, D., J. Ye, and J. Singh. "Do Frontline Mechanisms Matter? Impact of Quality and Productivity Orientations on Unit Revenue, Efficiency, and Customer Satisfaction." *Journal of Marketing* 72, no, 2 (2008): 28–45.

Maxwell, N. *From Knowledge to Wisdom: A Revolution in the Aims and Methods of Science.* Oxford, England: Basil Blackwell, 1984.

———. "Is Science Neurotic?" *Metaphilosophy* 33, no. 3 (2002): 1036–68.

McCarthy, Niall. "America's Best Large Employers in 2019." Digital image. April 18, 2019. https://www-statista-com.ezproxy.wheaton.edu/chart/17726/top-10 -us-employers-as-rated-by-employees-in-2019/.

McConville, J. G. *A Guide the Prophets.* Downers Grover, IL: InterVarsity Press, 2008.

Mentzer, J. T., W. DeWitt, S. Min, N. W. Nix, C. D. Smith, and Z. G. Zacharia. "Defining Supply Chain Management." *Journal of Business Logistics* 22, no. 2 (2001): 1–25.

Mercier, Guillaume, and Ghislain Deslandes. "There Are No Codes, Only Interpretations: Practical Wisdom and Hermeneutics in Monastic Organizations." *Journal of Business Ethics* 145, no. 4 (2017): 781–94.

Meuser, J. D., W. L. Gardner, J. E. Dinh, J. Hu, R. C. Liden, and R. G.Lord. "A Network Analysis of Leadership Theory: The Infancy of Integration." *Journal of Management* 42, no. 5 (2016): 1374–1403.

Mick, David Glen. "Meaning and Mattering Through Transformative Consumer Research." *Advances in Consumer Research* 33 (2006): 1–4. http://www7511 .ssldomain.com/acrwebsite/assets/PDFs/2005%20ACR%20Presidential%20 Address%20on%20TCR.pdf.

Mick, David Glen, Simone Pettigrew, Cornelia Pechmann, and Julie L. Ozanne, eds. *Transformative Consumer Research for Personal and Collective Well-Being*. New York: Routledge, 2012.

Miles, Morgan P., Gregory Russel, and Danny R. Arnold. "The Quality Orientation: An Emerging Business Philosophy?" *Review of Business* 17, no. 1 (1975): 7–15.

Mill, John Stuart. *The Collected Works of John Stuart Mill*. Edited by John M. Robson. Toronto: University of Toronto Press; London: Routledge and Kegan Paul, 1963, 91.

Miller, David. *God at Work: The History and Promise of the Faith at Work Movement*. New York: Oxford University Press, 2007.

Miller, D., and P. H. Friesen. "Innovation in Conservative and Entrepreneurial Firms: Two Models of Strategic Momentum. *Strategic Management Journal* 3, no. 1 (1982): 1–25.

———. "A Longitudinal Study of the Corporate Life Cycle." *Management Science* 30, no. 10 (1984): 1161–83.

Min, S., J. T. Mentzer, and R.T. Ladd. "Market Orientation in Supply Chain Management." *Journal of the Academy of Marketing Science* 35, no. 4 (2007): 507–22.

Mohr-Jackson, I. "Conceptualizing Total Quality Orientation." *European Journal of Marketing* 31, no. 1/2 (1998): 13–22.

———. "Managing a Total Quality Orientation: Factors Affecting Customer Satisfaction. *Industrial Marketing Management* 27, no. 2 (1998): 109–25.

Mollenkopf, D. A., H. J. Stolze, W. Tate, and M. Ueltschy. "Green, Lean, and Global Supply Chains." *International Journal of Physical Distribution and Logistics Management* 40, no. 1/2 (2010), 14–41.

Mollenkopf, Diane A., Lucie K. Ozanne, and Hannah J. Stolze. "A Transformative Supply Chain Response to COVID-19." *Journal of Services Management* (August 24, 2020). https://doi.org/10.1108/JOSM-05–2020–0143.

Montabon, Frank, Mark Pagell, and Zhaohui Wu. "Making Sustainability Sustainable." *Journal of Supply Chain Management* 52, no. 2 (2016): 11–27.

Morrison, Patt. "Joe's Joe: Joe Coulombe." *Los Angeles Times.* May 7, 2011. https://www.latimes.com/opinion/la-xpm-2011-may-07-la-oe-morrison-joe -coulombe-043011-story.html.

Narver, J. C., S. F. Slater, D. L. MacLachlan. "Responsive and Proactive Market Orientation and New-Product Success." *Journal of Product Innovation Management* 21, no. 5 (2004): 334–47.

Nevins, Jennifer, William O. Bearden, Bruce Money. "Ethical Values and Long-Term Orientation." *Journal of Business Ethics* 71, no. 3 (2007): 261–74.

Newman, A., G. Schwarz, B. Cooper, S. Sendjaya. "How Servant Leadership Influences Organizational Citizenship Behavior: The Roles of lmx, Empowerment, and Proactive Personality." *Journal of Business Ethics* 145 (2017): 49–62.

Omar, Ayman, Beth Davis-Sramek, Brian S. Fugate, and John T. Mentzer. "Exploring the Complex Social Processes of Organizational Change: Supply Chain Orientation from a Manager's Perspective." *Journal of Business Logistics* 33, no. 1 (2012): 4–19.

Organ, D. W. *Organizational Citizenship Behavior: The Good Soldier Syndrome.* Lexington, MA: Lexington, 1988.

Overstreet, Robert E., B. T. Hazen, J. B. Skipper, and J. B. Hanna. "Bridging the Gap Between Strategy and Performance: Using Leadership Style to Enable Structural Elements." *Journal of Business Logistics* 35, no. 2 (2014): 136–49.

Perry, Mark J. "Only 52 US Companies Have Been on the Fortune 500 Since 1955, Thanks to the Creative Destruction that Fuels Economic Prosperity." AEIdeas Blog. May 22, 2019. https://www.aei.org/carpe-diem/only-52-us -companies-have-been-on-the-fortune-500-since-1955-thanks-to-the-creative -destruction-that-fuels-economic-prosperity/.

Peterson, R. S., D. B. Smith, P. V. Martorana, and P. D. Owens. "The Impact of Chief Executive Officer Personality on Top Management Team Dynamics: One Mechanism by Which Leadership Affects Organizational Performance." *Journal of Applied Psychology* 88, no. 5 (2003): 795–808.

Pew Research Center. 2018. https://www.pewinternet.org/fact-sheet/social -media/.

Phills, James A., Kriss Deiglmeier, and Dale T. Miller. "Rediscovering Social Innovation." *Stanford Social Innovation Review* 6, no. 4 (2008): 34–43.

Pinheiro, J. Q. "Comprometimento Ambiental: Perspectiva Temporal e Sustentabilidade [Environmental Commitment: Time Perspective and Sustainability]" in *Temas Selectos de Psicologia Ambiental. [Selected Themes of Environmental Psychology]*. Edited by J. Guevara and S. Mercado. Mexico City: UNAM, GRECO & Fundacio'n Unilibre, (2006): 463–81.

Pollard, C. William. "Speech at Drucker Education Seminar" (1991). *C. William Pollard Papers* 18. https://digitalcommons.spu.edu/pollard_papers/18.

———. *The Soul of the Firm*. Grand Rapids: Zondervan, 1996.

———. "The Soul of the Firm (Phoenix)" (1995). *C. William Pollard Papers* 78. https://digitalcommons.spu.edu/pollard_papers/78.

———. "The Soul of the Firm (Nairobi, Kenya)" (1996). *C. William Pollard Papers* 49. https://digitalcommons.spu.edu/pollard_papers/49.

———. "Mission as an Organizing Principle" (1999). *C. William Pollard Papers* 65, 7. https://digitalcommons.spu.edu/pollard_papers/65.

———. *Serving Two Masters*. New York: Harper Collins, 2006.

———. "Faith in the Workplace" (2008). *C. William Pollard Papers* 73. https://digitalcommons.spu.edu/pollard_papers/73.

———. "Reflections for the Herman Miller Board" (2008). *C. William Pollard Papers* 72, 6. https://digitalcommons.spu.edu/pollard_papers/72.

———. "The Virtue of Profit (Wheaton College)" (2009). *C. William Pollard Papers* 243:4. https://digitalcommons.spu.edu/pollard_papers/243

———. *The Soul of a Firm*. Lee Summit, MO: Delta One Leadership Institute, 2009.

———. "The Virtue of Profit." Delta One Leadership Institute. 2012. *C. William Pollard Papers* 93. https://digitalcommons.spu.edu/pollard_papers/93.

———. *The Tides of Life*. Wheaton, IL: Crossway: 2014.

Ponzi, L. J., C. J. Fombrun, and N. A. Gardberg. "RepTrak™ Pulse: Conceptualizing and Validating a Short-Form Measure of Corporate Reputation." *Corporate Reputation Review* 14 (2011): 15–35.

Porter, Michael E. "America's Green Strategy." *Scientific American* 264, no. 4 (1991): 168.

———. "The Case for Letting Business Solve Social Problems." TED Talk. 2013. https://www.ted.com/talks/michael_porter_the_case_for_letting _business_solve_social_problems?utm_campaign=tedspread&utm _medium=referral&utm_source=tedcomshare.

———. "Why Business Can Be Good at Solving Social Problems." TED Talk. 2013. https://youtu.be/0iIh5YYDR2o.

———. "The Competitive Advantage of Nations." *Harvard Business Review* 68, no. 2 (1990): 73–93.

Porter, Michael E., and Competitive Advantage. "Creating and Sustaining Superior Performance." *Competitive Advantage* 167 (1985): 167–206.

Porter, Michael E., and C. van der Linde. "Green and Competitive: Ending the Stalemate." *Harvard Business Review* 73(5) (1995): 120–34.

Powell, T. C. "Total Quality Management as Competitive Advantage: A Review and Empirical Study." *Strategic Management Journal* 16 (1995): 15–37.

Prahalad, Coimbatore K. and Venkat Ramaswamy, "Co-Creation Experiences: The Next Practice in Value Creation," *Journal of Interactive Marketing* 18, no. 3 (2004): 5–14.

Putnam, Robert D. *Bowling Alone: The Collapse and Revival of American Community.* New York: Simon and Schuster, 2000.

Putnam, Robert D., and David E. Campbell. *American Grace: How Religion Divides and Unites Us.* New York: Simon and Schuster, 2012.

Reeves, Martin, Knut Haanaes, and Janmejaya Sinha. "Navigating the Dozens of Different Strategy Options." *Harvard Business Review* (June 24, 2015). https://hbr.org/2015/06/navigating-the-dozens-of-different-strategy-options.

Ricardo, David. *On the Principles of Political Economy and Taxation.* London: John Murray, 1817.

Richter, Sandra. "Environmental Law in Deuteronomy: One Lens on a Biblical Theology of Creation Care." *Bulletin for Biblical Research* 20, no. 3 (2010): 355–76.

Roberts, P. W., and G. R. Dowling. "Corporate Reputation and Sustained Superior Financial Performance" *Strategic Management Journal* 23 (2002): 1077–93.

Rokeach, M. J. *Beliefs, Attitudes and Values.* San Francisco: Jossey Bass, 1968.

———. *The Nature of Human Values.* New York: The Free Press, 1973.

Rosenbaum, M., C. Corus, A. Ostrom, L. Anderson, R. Fisk, A. Gallan, M. Giraldo, M. Mende, M. Mulder, S. Rayburn, KShirahada, and J. Williams. "Conceptualisation and Aspirations of Transformative Service Research." *Journal of Research for Consumers* 19 (2011): 1–6.

Roxas, B., and A. Coetzer. "Institutional Environment, Managerial Attitudes and Environmental Sustainability Orientation of Small Firms." *Journal of Business Ethics* 111, no. 4 (2012): 461–76.

Rust, Roland T., Anthony J. Zahorik, Timothy Keiningham. "Return on Quality (ROQ): Making Service Quality Financially Accountable." *Journal of Marketing* 59, no. 2 (1995): 58–70.

Ryan, Camille. "Computer and Internet Use in the United States: 2016." US Census Bureau, August 8, 2018. https://www.census.gov/library/publications/2018/acs/acs-39.html.

"Sales of the Leading Fast-Casual Restaurant Chains in the United States in 2019 (in Million U.S. Dollars)." Statista. Chart. April 21, 2020. https://www.statista.com/statistics/299350/leading-fast-casual-restaurant-segments-by-their-largest-selling-chains-us/.

Sandino, Tatiana, Zeynep Ton, and Aldo Sesia. "The Container Store." *Harvard Business School Case* 116–120 (April 2016). Revised December 2016.

Satinover Nichols, Bridget, Hannah Stolze, and Jon F. Kirchoff. "Spillover Effects of Supply Chain News on Consumers' Perceptions of Product Quality: An Examination within the Triple Bottom Line." *Journal of Operations Management* 65, no. 6 (2019): 536–59.

Schultz, Richard L. "Proverbs." *The Baker Illustrated Bible Commentary*, edited by Gary M. Burge and Andrew E. Hill. Grand Rapids: Baker, 2016.

Schwantes, Marcel. "The World's Top 10 CEOs (They Lead in a Totally Unique Way)." *Inc.com.* March 29, 2017. https://www.inc.com/marcel-schwantes/heres-a-top-10-list-of-the-worlds-best-ceos-but-they-lead-in-a-totally-unique-wa.html.

Schwartz, Mark. "The Nature of the Relationship between Corporate Codes of Ethics and Behaviour." *Journal of Business Ethics* 32, no. 3 (2001): 247–62.

Sendjaya, S. *Personal and Organizational Excellence through Servant Leadership: Learning to Serve, Serving to Lead, Leading to Transform.* Switzerland: Springer, 2015.

Seuring, Stefan, and Martin Müller. "From a Literature Review to a Conceptual Framework for Sustainable Supply Chain Management." *Journal of Cleaner Production* 16, no. 15 (2008): 1699–1710.

Simpson, William Kelly, ed. *The Literature of Ancient Egypt: An Anthology of Stories, Instructions, Stelae, Autobiographies, and Poetry.* New Haven, CT: Yale University Press, 2003.

Sisodia, Raj, and John Mackey. *Conscious Capitalism.* Boston: Harvard Business School Publishing Corporation, 2014.

Sittimalakron, Wuthichai, and Susan Hart. "Market Orientation Versus Quality Orientation: Sources of Superior Business Performance." *Journal of Strategic Marketing* 12, no. (2004): 243–53.

Slater, Stanley F., and John C. Narver. "Market Orientation and the Learning Organization." *Journal of Marketing* 59, no. 3 (1995): 63–74.

Smith, H. Jeff. "The Shareholders vs. Stakeholders Debate." *MIT Sloan Management Review* 44, no. 4 (2003): 85.

Spears, Larry C. "Character and Servant Leadership: Ten Characteristics of Effective, Caring Leaders." *The Journal of Virtues & Leadership* 1, no. 1 (2010): 25–30.

Sprecher, S., and B. Fehr. "Compassionate Love for Close Others and Humanity." *Journal of Social and Personal Relationships* 22, no.5 (2005): 629–51. doi: 10.1177/0265407505056.

Srivastava, Samir K. "Green Supply-Chain Management: A State-Of-The-Art Literature Review." *International Journal of Management Reviews* 9, no. 1 (2007): 53–80.

Soundararajan, V., J. A. Brown, and A. C. Wicks, "Can Multi-Stakeholder Initiatives Improve Global Supply Chains? Improving Deliberative Capacity with a Stakeholder Orientation." *Business Ethics Quarterly* 29, no. 3 (2019): 385–412.

Stank, Theodore P., Terry L. Esper, T. Russell Crook, and Chad W. Autry. "Creating Relevant Value through Demand and Supply Integration." *Journal of Business Logistics* 33, no. 2 (2012): 167–72.

Steinmetz, Katy. "Chipotle's Second Act." *TIME* 193, no. 4/5 (2019): 88–91, https://time.com/longform/chipotle-plan-to-make-you-love-it-again/.

Sternard, Dietmar. "Long-term Orientation in the Benedictine Monastery of Admont." *Harvard Business Case Study*. March 21, 2016. https://store.hbr .org/product/long-term-orientation-in-the-benedictine-monastery-of-admont /W16144.

Stolze, Hannah, Diane Mollenkopf, and Dan Flint. "What is the Right Supply Chain for Your Shopper: Exploring a Shopper Service Ecosystem." *Journal of Business Logistics* 37, no. 2 (2015): 185–197.

"Supply Chain Logistics Is the Name of the Game." *Materials Handling & Logistics*, October 14, 2009. https://www.mhlnews.com/transportation -distribution/article/22041842/supply-chain-logistics-is-the-name-of-the -game.

Tate, Wendy L., Lisa M. Ellram, and Jon F. Kirchoff. "Corporate Social Responsibility Reports: A Thematic Analysis Related to Supply Chain Management." *Journal of Supply Chain Management* 46, no. 1 (2010): 19–44.

Theology of Work Project, Inc. *Theology of Work Bible Commentary*. 1 vol. ed. Peabody, MA: Hendrickson, 2015–2016.

Tiayuan, Wang, and Pratima Bansal. "Social Responsibility in New Ventures: Profiting from a Long-Term Orientation." *Strategic Management Journal* 33 (2012): 1135–53.

Tindell, Kip. "The Container Store's CEO on Finding and Keeping Front-Line Talent." *Harvard Business Review* (2014): https://hbr.org/2014/11/the -container-stores-ceo-on-finding-and-keeping-front-line-talent.

———. *Uncontained*. New York: Grand Central, 2014.

Tom's of Maine. "The Backstory." https://www.tomsofmaine.com/the-backstory.

Tom's of Maine. "Our Stewardship Model." https://www.tomsofmaine.com/our -promise/stewardship-model.

Ton, Zeynep. "Why 'Good Jobs' Are Good for Retailers." *Harvard Business Review*, January-February, 2012. https://hbr.org/2012/01/why-good-jobs-are -good-for-retailers.

"Trader Joe's Bans GMOs from Private-label Products." *Progressive Grocer*. November 15, 2001. https://progressivegrocer.com/trader-joes-bans-gmos -private-label-products.

Tunehag, Mats, Wayne McGee, and Josie Plummer. "Business as Mission." *Lausanne Occasional Paper*, no. 59. South Hamilton, MA: Lausanne Committee for World Evangelism, 2005.

Turner, Matt. "Here is the Letter the World's Largest Investor, BlackRock CEO Larry Fink, Just Sent to CEOs Everywhere." Business Insider. https://www .businessinsider.com/blackrock-ceo-larry-fink-letter-to-sp-500-ceos-2016-2.

Tuttle, Brad. "How Two German-Owned Sister Supermarket Brands Became Hot Trendsetters in the U.S." *Time*. July 29, 2013. https://business.time .com/2013/07/29/how-two-german-owned-sister-supermarket-brands -became-hot-trendsetters-in-the-u-s/.

van Dierendonck, D. "Servant Leadership: A Review and Synthesis." *Journal of Management* 37 (2011): 1228–61.

van Dierendonck, D., and Kathleen Patterson. "Compassionate Love as Cornerstone of Servant Leadership: An Integration of Previous Theorizing and Research." *Journal of Business Ethics* 128 (2015): 119–31.

Vasel, Kathryn. "JCPenney, Kohl's, Macy's and Sears Sued over Misleading Prices." CNN, December 9, 2016. https://money.cnn.com/2016/12/09/pf /price-scheme-jcpenney-kohls-sears-macys/.

Venkatraman, N. "Strategic Orientation of Business Enterprises: The Construct, Dimensionality, and Measurement." *Management Science* 35, 8 (1989): 942–62.

Vlaskovits, Patrick. "Henry Ford, Innovation, and That 'Faster Horse' Quote." *Harvard Business Review*, August, 29, 2011. https://hbr.org/2011/08 /henry-ford-never-said-the-fast.

Waalkes, Scott. "Money or Business? A Case Study of Christian Virtue Ethics in Corporate Work." *Christian Scholars Review* 38, no. 1 (2008): 15.

Wade, Marion E. *The Lord Is My Counsel*. Englewood Cliffs, NJ: Prentice Hall, 1966.

Wagner, Rodd, and Jim Harter. "The Fifth Element of Great Managing." *Gallup Business Journal*. September 13, 2007. https://news.gallup.com /businessjournal/28561/fifth-element-great-managing.aspx.

Waltke, Bruce. *The Book of Proverbs, Chapters 1–15*. The New International Commentary on the Old Testament. Grand Rapids: Eerdmans, 2004.

———. "The Book of Proverbs and Ancient Wisdom Literature." *Bibliotheca Sacra* 136, no. 543 (1979): 221–38.

Walumbwa, F. O., C. A. Hartnell, and A. Oke. "Servant Leadership, Procedural Justice Climate, Service Climate, Employee Attitudes, and Organizational Citizenship Behavior: A Cross-Level Investigation." *Journal of Applied Psychology* 95 (2010): 517–29.

Wang, Taiyuan, and Pratima Bansal. "Social Responsibility in New Ventures: Profiting from a Long-Term Orientation." *Strategic Management Journal* 33, no. 10 (2012): 1135–53.

Wang, Yijing, and Guido Berens. "The Impact of Four Types of Corporate Social Performance on Reputation and Financial Performance." *Journal of Business Ethics* 131, no. 2 (2015): 337–59.

Warne, John L. "Developing a Quality Orientation" *Target*. Summer 1987. https://www.ame.org/sites/default/files/target_articles/87Q2A2.pdf.

Wolters, Al. "Proverbs xxxi 10–31 as Heroic Hymn: A Form Critical Analysis." *Vetus Testamentum* 38 (1988): 446–57.

Womack, James P., Daniel T. Jones, and Daniel Roos. *The Machine That Changed the World*. New York: Free Press, 1990.

Wong, Kenman, and R. Martinez. "Introduction to the Theme Issue: The Iron Cage Unchained: Christian Perspectives on Business in the Post-Modern Age." *Christian Scholar's Review* 38, no. 1 (2008): 11.

Wright, N. T. *How God Became King: The Forgotten Story of the Gospels*. San Francisco: HarperOne, 2012.

Kirby, William C., and Nancy Hua Dai. "Yili Group: Building a Global Dairy Company." *Harvard Business Review*, October 25, 2016.

Yoshida, D. T., S. Sendjaya, G. Hirst, and B. Cooper. "Does Servant Leadership Foster Creativity and Innovation? A Multi-Level Mediation Study of Identification and Prototypicality." *Journal of Business Research* 67 (2014): 1395–1404.

Zhu, Zhe. "Melamine Found in More Milk." *China Daily*, September 9, 2008.

INDEX

and servant leadership, 44–45
and stewardship, 8
and sustainability, 161
and understanding, 9
and the way, 66, 67–68
and wisdom, 9, 14, 75, 101, 216
World Vision, 214
worldly mindset, vs. kingdom mindset,
 168
Yili Group, the
 and brand differentiation, 58

and comparative advantage, 57, 60
growth of, 58–59
and innovation, 59, 60
needs met by, 209
orientations of, 60–62, 63, 64, 75
and research and development, 59, 60
stakeholder orientation of, 59, 60–61
supply chain of, 58–59, 60
and sustainability, 59–61, 168
and worldly mindset, 168
Zacchaeus, 180–81, 182, 183